TEST EVERYTHING

GEORGE CARDINAL PELL

TEST EVERYTHING
Hold Fast to What Is Good

~

Edited by
TESS LIVINGSTONE

IGNATIUS PRESS   SAN FRANCISCO

First edition was published by
Connor Court Publishing Pty Ltd.,
Ballarat, Victoria, Australia 2010
© 2010 by George Pell and Tess Livingstone

Cover art:
Christ the Savior (Pantocrator)
Sixth century icon
Saint Catherine's Monastery, Mount Sinai
Wikimedia Commons

Cover design by
Enrique Javier Aguilar Pinto

© 2015 by Ignatius Press, San Francisco
All rights reserved
ISBN 978-1-58617-992-2
Library of Congress Control Number 2014949944
Printed in the United States of America ∞

To my sister Margaret, much loved, true friend

CONTENTS

EDITOR'S FOREWORD
TO THE SECOND EDITION

Two thousand years after he wrote it, Saint Paul's advice to the Thessalonians, "Test everything. Hold fast to what is good" is as pertinent as ever. Halfway through the second decade of the twenty-first century, the civilized world is being severely tested, especially by the barbarism of ISIS, the self-styled "Islamic State". Amid reports of its almost unimaginable atrocities, the death cult's propaganda magazine has boasted of its ambition to hoist its sinister banner atop St Peter's Square. For faithful Catholics, the situation is surely another reason to "hold fast to what is good" by turning to Our Lord, and to His Blessed Mother and the saints in prayer.

These are also tumultuous times within Christ's Church. In February 2014, a year after the resignation of Pope Benedict XVI, the enigmatic Pope Francis shrewdly promoted Australian Cardinal George Pell to the senior Vatican position of Prefect of the Secretariat for the Economy. After decades of criminal corruption and scandals involving millions of euros, the reform and modernization of Vatican finances were desperately overdue. Within three months, the Pope indicated the unholy mess was beginning to be turned around, lauding Cardinal Pell's tenacity as "the Vatican's resident rugby player". Right sentiment, wrong football code, however. Before entering the Seminary in 1960, the young George Pell had a professional contract to play Australian Rules football. Later in 2014, with characteristic forthrightness and insight, the cardinal Prefect spoke out amid the confusion over divorce, remarriage and the reception of Holy Communion surrounding the controversial Synod on the Family. In the foreword to *The Gospel of the Family*[1] he reasserted that "indissolubility of marriage is one of the rich truths of divine revelation."

---

[1] Juan José Pérez-Soba and Stephan Kampowski, *The Gospel of the Family: Going Beyond Cardinal Kasper's Proposal in the Debate on Marriage, Civil Re-Marriage, and Communion in the Church* (San Francisco: Ignatius Press, 2014), p. 8.

Internal conflict and intrigue, of course, are nothing new to the Church. Cardinal Pell's office in the Apostolic Palace overlooks the ancient stairway that was Pope Pius IX's escape route when he fled the Vatican, dressed as an ordinary priest, during the European upheavals of 1848.

Cardinal Pell's current focus is Vatican finances. But this collection is a snapshot of how he has taught the faith, in all its richness, for decades. As he writes, human beings, especially the young,

> need a person to follow, a cause to embrace, reasons to believe. Most importantly, they need to find among those of us who are older credible signs of faith and goodness and caring communities of service.
>
> The best the Catholic Church has to offer is the gift of faith. To know the love and forgiveness of the one true God offered to us by His Son Jesus Christ provides an unparalleled sense of security and makes a world of difference in everyday living and in eternity. God is invisible, but God is real.

From the Old Testament prophets, the collection proceeds to examine the "God question" and to explore the historical figure of Christ and His teachings. It delves into some of the extraordinary characters the Church has produced through the centuries, including Saint Paul the missionary trailblazer, Australia's Saint Mary of the Cross MacKillop, the heroic Japanese Martyrs of Nagasaki and England's Thomas More and John Fisher, among others. Other pieces focus on prayer, love, leadership and the contribution of military chaplains.

The 80 pieces, delivered originally as far afield as Front Royal Virginia, Oxford, Malta, California, Ireland, Rome, the Isle of Wight, Germany, and of course Australia, are incisive, often unpredictable, sometimes sensitive, occasionally hard-hitting and always engaging. None are dull. While Australian in flavor, they will resonate in all corners of the universal Church. They reflect the cardinal's wealth of experience as Archbishop of Sydney for thirteen years; Archbishop of Melbourne for five years; fostering of a new generation of young priests; leading World Youth Day in Sydney in 2008; reforming school catechetics; founding Catholic universities and establishing Domus Australia in Rome.

Many readers will be delighted, a few will be outraged and some will be stunned by the frank expose of a few modernist theologians' efforts to trivialize Jesus Christ and His sufferings on the Cross. Like many good books, this one poses a raft of new questions to be explored. The cardinal's contention that "Children who are not loved by their parents or other significant figures find it hard to understand God's love", for instance, could prompt an altogether different book or psychological treatise.

The collection challenges readers, whatever their beliefs or understandings, to consider some of the "ultimate" questions that confront us all, sooner or later: "Why are we here on earth? What is the point of it all, given suffering and death? What is the good life?"

After more than forty-eight years service as a priest, an Oxford doctorate in history and years of studying philosophy and theology, Cardinal Pell is convinced: "It is more reasonable to believe in God than to reject the hypothesis of God by appealing to chance. . . . Goodness, truth, and beauty call for an explanation as do the principles of mathematics, physics, and the purpose-driven miracles of biology which run through our universe. The human capacities to recognize these qualities of truth, goodness, and beauty, to invent and construct, also call for an explanation."

From the United States to Ireland, Canada to New Zealand, English-speaking Catholics are reaping the benefits of a more reverent and up-lifting Mass as a result of Cardinal Pell overseeing the English translation of the Roman Missal, under the Pontificates of Saint John Paul II and Benedict XVI. Those yet to discover the cardinal's writings have a treat in store. In what is unfortunately turning into a fairly bleak and barren landscape, this collection will serve readers outside Australia as an introduction to one of the twenty-first century Church's more interesting leaders.

In carrying out Christ's instruction to Saint Peter "Go teach all nations", the Church's task is harder these days than it was for centuries. The public square is no longer a community hub outside the local parish. It is a worldwide marketplace of often conflicting ideas and philosophies, accessible anywhere, by anyone, at any hour of the day or night, at the touch of a button. This is no time for Catholic leaders to be shrinking violets. *Test Everything. Hold fast to what is Good* has the gravitas and style to thrive in the global public square.

TESS LIVINGSTONE
Ash Wednesday, 2015

INTRODUCTION

T HIS PUBLICATION collects eighty homilies, discourses, and pastoral letters of a great, contemporary man of the Church, George Cardinal Pell, the archbishop of Sydney. The earliest was written in 1984, the last in 2009. In 1984, Doctor Pell was the relatively youthful rector of Corpus Christi, the regional seminary located in the archdiocese of Melbourne. He had not yet been consecrated a bishop. That event would take place in 1987, when, at the age of forty-five, he was consecrated to assist the archbishop of Melbourne, Frank Little, as auxiliary. So the writings in this collection span nearly a generation. During that time, Australians have become more and more alert to the dramatic fact that "the truth cannot happen without suffering." Cardinal Pell has become a central protagonist in the drama.

What is the view from the cardinal's heights? He is a leader who knows his people well and writes with clarity and insight. His critical choices regarding "the cultural wars" are on target. With irony, humor, and easily worn scholarship, he counsels and cajoles the reader, always using the Cross of Christ as the unique and final measure of what it means to be human and thus holy.

His writings reveal a strong, gentle, and all-embracing heart. The style is fluent and fresh. Mulling over them is a source of joy, wisdom, and wonder. Besides the cathedrals of Melbourne and Sydney, their settings include Rome, Dusseldorf, the Isle of Wight, Oxford, and others. The topics unfold a splendid panoply of Christian thought. All are peppered with calls to conversion; some are very urgent. But he is consistently beyond moralism. Without laboring to do so, he penetrates to the depths of the Paschal Triduum. The reader is faced with the mystery of God's absolute love. Without doubt, the cardinal's writings make easy and delightful reading, but they are anything but easy-going in doctrine or moral application. He emphasizes the "real"

in Christianity. The homilies are inescapably personal. In one of his
most powerful homilies, "Redemption and Suffering", he speaks to
young people about "crucifixion Christianity". "Many Christians today pass over Jesus' violent death quickly. In Australia we have more at
our Christmas Masses than at Easter. So too outsiders and even Catholics who believe in a one-dimensional, kind, and tolerant Jesus are
disconcerted when reminded that Jesus was killed for His teaching and
activities. They are uneasy about crucifixion Christianity."

The eight general topics—Test Everything, Forerunners, The One
True God, Jesus Christ our Redeemer, The Body of Christ, Jesus' Call
to Follow (with subsections on Christians in Public Life and in Universities, Hospitals, and Schools), Saint Paul, Hold Fast to What Is Good
—highlight what have become his watermark throughout the world:
the cardinal's courageous and prophetic voice. He does not pull his
punches. By addressing ecclesial dissent head-on, he discloses a deep-
seated conviction that Catholics have the right to hear the Church's
teachings in their full integrity. His episcopal ministry is a model for
those exercising the task of mystagogy, that is, of postbaptismal cate-
chesis.

His description of the Catholic reality is memorable, "Catholicism
is a ferment of love." Those who have experienced Christ's forgiveness would second the choice of "ferment". It means a state of unrest,
agitation, excitement, tumult. The Catholic state of life is anything but
sleepy. He writes to young people, "The Eucharist in particular should
give us the strength and energy to take God's love into the world. But
for this to be effective, every lover must be a fighter."

Time and again he insists that Catholicism is informed with the logic
of divine love. Such love is totally, wholly other. God's forgiveness is
its heartbeat. It points to the community of disciples as His chief instrument. Throughout his writings, we find that forgiveness must fully
engage every person in a parish and diocese. It is one thing to admit the
calamitous decline of ecclesial forgiveness; it is another to implement
the praxis of the early Church, which saw the necessary connection between the Body of Christ and the Passion. Both forgiving and forgiven
Christians must relearn the radical expression of discipleship through
forbearance, fraternal correction, tears, and intercessory prayer. Practice requires "tough" love. His vision of the human person rejects the
"coasting sightseer" view of life. On the contrary, his style and content
portray the sternness of discipleship. To act on behalf of Christ is to

become acquainted with the pains of childbirth and of death. Typical of his call to action is the following, "It is not good enough to be only a passenger, to try to live in 'no man's land' between the warring parties. Life forces us to choose, eventually destroys any possibility of neutrality."

Cardinal Pell's writings share with John Henry Newman's sermons a profound distaste for those views that advocate cheap grace. Newman wrote:

> Such men have certain benevolent *feelings* toward the world,—feelings and nothing more;—nothing more than unstable feelings, the mere offspring of an indulged imagination, which exist only when their minds are wrought upon, and are sure to fail them in the hour of need. This is not to love men, it is but to talk about love.—The real love of man *must* depend upon practice, and therefore, must begin by exercising itself on our friends around us, otherwise it will have no existence.[1]

This collection also reinforces the cardinal's image as a genuine Australian patriot. Respect and love for his native country shine throughout the collection. There are frequent, sometimes humorous, references to Australian life and customs. Yet, even though the message and audience are necessarily specific, his insights will resonate sympathetically among various cultures and peoples. For he has the heart and mind of a shepherd of souls; his judgments are clear, firm, and balanced. He is acute in discerning what is human and what is not.

Drama has a universal audience. The cardinal believes that every human biography must be received as dramatic art with both lyric and tragic passages. Through his eyes, human life has a determined form. A virtuous decision is a genuine movement of freedom and requires an openness to the beyond. At the same time, it sets limits and requires exclusions. A virtuous act is the only expression of true freedom.

In his 2007 Apostolic Exhortation *Sacramentum Caritatis*, Pope Benedict XVI offered practical directives for homilies. "In particular, I ask [ordained ministers] to preach in such a way that the homily closely relates the proclamation of the word of God to the sacramental celebration and the life of the community, so that the word of God truly becomes the Church's vital nourishment and support" (46).

---

[1] *Parochial and Plain Sermons* (San Francisco: Ignatius Press, 1997), 261.

It is clear that Cardinal Pell has been acquainted with the substance of the Holy Father's advice. These eighty homilies and talks are extended commentaries on the word of God. The title itself, *Test Everything*, is taken from Saint Paul and is the leitmotif of the book. He exhorts Christians, especially the young: "Look before you leap. Search out genuine love and service. Reject evil. Test the claims of the advertisers as carefully as you examine Christian claims. Choosing the good life is not just an optional extra."

Readers will not be held in suspense about the relevance of Catholic faith to everyday life. The cardinal gives practical moral applications, always adapted to the audience being addressed. The golden thread uniting the writings of this impressive collection is similar to that which guided the great nineteenth-century Cardinal Newman: "We must become what we are not; we must learn to love what we do not love, and practise ourselves in what is difficult" (*Parochial and Plain Sermons*, p. 742).

JAMES FRANCIS CARDINAL STAFFORD
Major Penitentiary Emeritus
Feast of the Conversion of Saint Paul, 2010

I

Test Everything

TEST EVERYTHING

"Test everything; hold fast to what is good; abstain from evil."

1 Thessalonians 5:21

I N THE EARLIEST LETTER of the New Testament, Saint Paul gave this advice to the people of Thessalonica. It remains sound teaching for us all.

I want to speak to young people about the challenges before them and to the whole Catholic community about our obligations to the young. No generation in Australian history has been offered richer prizes for success or been forced to pay more for failure. No other generation has been so flattered or exploited. Greater physical comforts, more years of education, the marvels of modern health care, overseas travel for many, and fabulous salaries for a few. These are real prizes, but not the whole picture.

Increasing family breakdown, homelessness, and abortion; youth suicide, growing environmental damage, and easy access to soft and hard drugs are also grim realities for many. Employment is also a challenge, especially in economic downturns.

Conflicting Pressures

To young people battling with conflicting pressures, I repeat Saint Paul's urgings as you search for the truth. Look before you leap. Search out genuine love and service. Reject evil. Test the claims of the advertisers as carefully as you examine Christian claims. Choosing the good life is not just an optional extra.

Young people I talk to stress the importance of a sense of purpose and direction. Young people, like their elders, need a goal, to know where they are heading. They need a person to follow, a cause to embrace, reasons to believe. Most importantly, they need to find among those of us who are older credible signs of faith and goodness and caring communities of service.

The best the Catholic Church has to offer is the gift of faith. To know the love and forgiveness of the one true God offered to us by His Son Jesus Christ provides an unparalleled sense of security and makes a world of difference in everyday living and in eternity. God is invisible, but God is real.

The one true God is worshipped not just by Christians, but by Muslims and Jews as well. A pagan is someone unable or unwilling to believe in the one true God. The new pagans believe that the universe is a fluke, the product of blind chance, without purpose or meaning. Young people continue to reject this bleak absence of explanation.

Young Catholics deserve clear and positive explanations of why the Church holds her particular doctrines about goodness and faith. We have to be able to back up our claims, present reasons for our hope. Just as importantly, the young need to see that we practice what we preach. Many young Catholics, even those who are not regular Mass-goers, pray regularly. Families, schools, and parishes must recognize this and encourage all these signs of young people's openness and willingness to serve, rather than fastening only onto negative stereotypes. Young people ask to be heard, respected, and helped. This is their right.

Some young people argue passionately that the way forward for the Church is to soften her demands, especially in the areas of life, family, and sexuality. They argue that times have changed enormously since Christ lived two thousand years ago, that the Church needs to be more accommodating and inclusive, not so strict and old-fashioned.

In one sense, the Church has always been inclusive. We have always been a Church of sinners. However, true Christians recognize their sins and confidently ask God's forgiveness. They do not try to define sin out of existence.

All Christians believe that our basic teachings come from God. They have been understood and explained in different ways, sometimes better, sometimes less well. But the Church cannot compromise her basic beliefs, especially Christ's hard teachings. The Cross is always one part of the story, necessary for growth and resurrection. Saying otherwise would betray our tradition.

There is another reason why the Church cannot soften some of her teachings to seem to be more accommodating. It is not just that true love can be fierce and demanding, that young people are capable of answering a challenge. Experience also shows that some of the alternative life-styles foisted on young people hurt rather than help, lead to despair rather than hope.

Illusions

For example, young people are often encouraged to believe that sex is just for fun, that love and commitment depend on sexual performance, that "the problem" of pregnancy is solved by contraception and even abortion, both of which are presented as good or at least physically trouble free, and that if they do not feel this way about these things then something is wrong with them. Such illusions are presented as normal and common in such a way that disagreement provokes isolation and rejection.

These mistakes are endlessly repeated online, through television, movies, and magazines and through advertising, which targets the pockets of the young with little or no concern for their well-being. The natural feelings of most young people are quite different, but they are eroded by constant propaganda and the fear of not belonging. Many young people have been harmed by these messages and made bitter in their hurt.

To every one of you who has heard these pagan voices, and especially to those who wonder whether happiness lies in that direction, I say again: "Test everything; hold fast to what is good; abstain from every form of evil." Listen to the promptings in your heart, for they come from God. You are right to suspect that these messages are lies that cannot bring happiness. They are certainly a poor preparation for a good marriage and for bringing up good children. Do not be afraid to reject these lies, because you are not alone in doing so. Many others believe as you do, and the demanding Christian alternatives have stood the test of time. In the long run they bring peace and healing.

Consider carefully the evidence for good and evil, for happiness and misery in the society that surrounds you. The terrible problem of youth suicide is the tip of an iceberg hiding a mass of society's sins, lies, sickness, and suffering.

Truth

Jesus Christ offers you the truth about this life and the next; His yoke is easy, and His burden light (Mt 11:28). No matter how much you have been hurt, no matter how deep your doubts and confusion, He asks you to pray to Him, the Son of the one true God, with your hopes and ambitions, your sorrows and fears. Jesus offers you the truth. He does not lie. He is the way, the truth, and the life (Jn 14:6).

To those of you who know Christ and have accepted His Cross, I ask you to join the struggle for good against evil; for service against selfishness; for faith and hope, rather than despair. You are not alone. Search out those of like mind and heart. Work together.

Do not underestimate the Catholic capacity to influence our fellow Australians. We are blessed by living in a democracy where everyone can work for majority acceptance. With the decline of religious prejudice, many outside are prepared to listen and to judge our words and deeds.

I know that some young Catholics, and many other young people, will not be able to accept all Christ's teachings and all that the Catholic Church offers. To you I repeat Saint Paul's message. Do not simply follow the crowd. Do not blindly accept the propaganda that rains down on you. Ask Mary, the Mother of God, to help you. "Test everything; hold fast to what is good." If you do this, Christ will do the rest.

Melbourne, 1997
Pentecost Pastoral Letter to Young People

THE BIG QUESTIONS

Micah 6:6–8; 1 Peter 4:7–11; Matthew 16:24–27

Then Yahweh answered and said: "write the vision down, inscribe it on tablets to be easily read . . . eager for its own fulfilment, it does not deceive; if it comes slowly, wait, for come it will, without fail."

Habakkuk 2:2–4

T HESE WORDS of God our Father, the one great God, to the prophet Habakkuk in Old Testament times are part of a beautiful dialogue between God and the prophet, probably written in the seventh century before Christ, when the Babylonians were oppressing the Jews. We belong to a long tradition, the Judaeo-Christian tradition, which predates Our Lord's birth by nearly two thousand years. As Catholics, we see ourselves as the fullest embodiment of that tradition today— certainly a privileged position, sometimes mistaken for arrogance by outsiders, but a privileged position that places responsibilities on us, which the irreligious do not have to carry. We are called to act justly, to love tenderly, to walk humbly with our God. These things are easily said, but to do so regularly is often hard work. It means renouncing ourselves, curbing our "fat relentless egos", as the English writer Iris Murdoch wrote, which is the taking up of our cross, in Our Lord's terminology.

These words from Habakkuk, more than twenty-five hundred years ago, also remind us that we are a people dedicated to searching for the truth about life and a people who believe we know a lot about life's secrets, because God has told us. Christians do not believe they are condemned to searching and never finding, traveling and not arriving.

Today we celebrate Founder's Day, when we remember the vision and achievement of Edmund Ignatius Rice and his teaching brothers.

25

The *Weekend Australian* recently carried a long, controversial article on American education; a review article prompted by the success of a book called *The Closing of the American Mind*, by Allan Bloom. The book sold more than a quarter of a million copies in the United States and is a biting indictment of American education.

Bloom claims that American students have "powerful images of what a perfect body is and pursue it incessantly. But . . . they no longer have any image of a perfect soul and hence do not long to have one." Could this be honestly written about many students in Catholic schools, many students in Saint Kevin's?

Bloom states that Western countries are producing a race of moral illiterates, who have never asked the great questions of good and evil, or truth and beauty. Encouraged by their elders, many Australians grow up dodging the great questions, ignoring them as not worth asking and too "airy-fairy" for a practical world. Is there a God? Is there freedom? Is there punishment, in this life and the next, for evil deeds? What is a good life, a good society? Is there certain knowledge?

No Catholic school or parents can coerce young adults into giving a particular type of answer. You will decide for yourselves, as we did. But you are not free to choose untruths. That would be a contradiction in terms for an educated man or woman. However, a Catholic school should ensure that all its senior students cannot avoid confronting the great questions, that they cannot avoid the uncompromising Catholic claim to truth in these areas.

I am speaking mainly to the year nine, ten, eleven, and twelve students, who are starting to make up your minds on these issues. You are the most powerful source of influence on public opinion in the college; real public opinion, not the public face presented to parents, teachers, priests, or visiting bishops. What kind of public opinion do you want in the school on the great questions? What kind of attitudes do you want your young brothers to pick up?

You might not like general questions about freedom, the good life, knowledge; even if you are more interested in God and punishment. Let me ask the questions another way. Who are your heroes? What books do you really admire? These are good questions for internal assessment, in your heart of hearts, where you do not have to offer any image to inquisitive adults.

Would Christ approve of your choices? Could you describe your private answers as Catholic answers? Would your answers be closer to what Bloom claims are the three great themes of rock music: "sex, hate and a smarmy, hypocritical version of brotherly love"?

In the Gospel, Our Lord takes a very different tack. Anyone who wants to save his life will lose it; but "anyone who loses his life for My sake will find it." In every age and culture, Our Lord's words have provoked and inspired the idealism of young people. "What then", He asked, "will a man gain if he wins the whole world and ruins his life? Or what has a man to offer in exchange for his life, for his soul?"

These are good questions, and in the Catholic tradition lived by the great majority of Christian Brothers you will find answers to all the great questions. A belief in God as a loving Father, who sent His Son to teach us and save us; a God who is among us today, with a special love for the spiritually and materially poor; a God who has a special love for those who do not love themselves, especially those young people who cannot see how lovable they are and how valuable they are. Saint Paul tells us that each one of us has a special grace.

This is a community that believes in right and wrong. This is not a community that says everything is grey; nor is it a community that says you can paint your world picture in any colors you choose. Saint Kevin's believes in community, where people respect and care for one another; it believes in the dignity and freedom of the individual, in justice for the poor. Saint Kevin's supports the vital and difficult work of parents and urges Christian patterns of sexuality and family living.

At another level, though, questions remain. How do you make that policy part of your lives? How do we effectively help you to choose Christ's answers as your own? How do we help you to break away from the prevailing Australian viewpoint that most religions are mildly useful as long as they are not taken too seriously and confined largely to formal and public occasions like weddings and funerals?

Important changes rarely happen quickly. To those of you who accept most of the Catholic package, I urge you to deepen your understanding, to try to live it out more perfectly.

To those of you who are still looking for God, to those who have difficulty with particular points, to those who are bored by the whole exercise, I must say different things. Those of you who are honest with yourselves, those who want to find the truth (and truth can take us to unwelcome places) will be helped enormously by the Saint Kevin's community and the vision that inspires it.

Those who refuse to consider the great questions, those who knock and oppose the Christian viewpoint and honest searchers are missing a great opportunity. They also risk damaging themselves. I hope those in this situation are a small and diminishing number.

My hope and prayer for all of you is in the prophecy to Habakkuk where I began. The Christian vision is "eager for its own fulfilment, it does not deceive; if it comes slowly, wait, for come it will without fail."

July 31, 1987
Saint Kevin's College, Toorak, Melbourne

SEARCHING FOR TRUTH

Galatians 5:16–17, 22–23a, 24–25;
Psalm 23; John 16:12–15

I N THE READINGS TODAY, John has Jesus promising that when He comes, the Spirit of Truth will bring us into the complete truth. There are many things to say, and sometimes too much to bear, but we should continue under the inspiration of the Holy Spirit to spell out what we might find in our searching for truth.

Paul writing to the Galatians spoke of the necessity of struggle for self-mastery, the necessity to crucify our unruly passions and desires. Christ said, "If you love me, keep the commandments", and Paul spells out further the consequences of being guided by the Spirit, rather than by self-indulgence. Some sections are omitted in this reading—the full Pauline listing of the fruits of self-indulgence, which include squabbling factions, exhibitions of malice, drunkenness, orgies, as well as the more mundane provocations and envy.

The Holy Spirit teaches us that the wages of sin are real. The wounds of the permissive society are bleeding. We see around us, to a greater or lesser extent, the culture of death.

Certainly the culture of death was worse in Roman times (outside Jewish life): human life counted for little. Gladiators fought one another to death; infanticide and abortion were common; every type of sexual abuse was permitted, and sexual relations were dominated by the exercise of power.

The slaughter of the innocents by King Herod is a brutal reminder of the terrible evil that can accompany God's important work. The infant king (Christ) was in danger from the moment of His birth. The struggle with evil, the temptations to turn from the narrow way that leads to salvation, will always be with us.

29

It is particularly significant for young adults, as you achieve independence from your parents and family and set your own direction, that you establish the values or truths central to your life project or journey. So the Christian message of peace throws down a challenge to the powers of evil, thereby ensuring that there will be struggle and problems internally; Christ's power as future Judge is foreshadowed.

The Holy Innocents bore witness to Christ, not by speaking but by dying. This was no adult decision, no act of commitment after a dawning realization of truth and beauty. A modern equivalent would be the one Australian aborted for every three live births. While politically inspired slaughter of young babies is light years away from us, a cheap private abortion is an everyday possibility; a murderous way out, an alternative to years of self-sacrifice, but also the destruction of a wonderful, rewarding love that the parents, through their selfishness, will never know.

Serious evil, death-bearing sin, is not always committed by other people; or only by those who are regularly moral monsters. We, too, can fall and fall badly. We begin slowly, hesitantly; then regularly; worse and worse follows until we are trapped.

Identify your weaknesses, and stay away from trouble. For example, when lonely or depressed, it might be necessary to stay away from alcohol (or drinking alone) or the porn-laden Internet. An alcoholic has to swear off all alcohol (usually). Mary and Joseph fled from Herod into Egypt. More mundanely, Saint Bernardine of Siena, a fifteenth-century preacher to university students, was asked what to do about a donkey that kept kicking people. He suggested the villagers measure out a length of string to a point where the donkey's kick could not reach them and stay that far away from him.

Searching for God, for goodness, for deeper appreciation of the Truth under the guidance of the Holy Spirit always requires forgiveness from God, from others, and forgiving others ourselves. To forgive can be the hardest Christian teaching! Many years ago I saw a poster of a handsome couple with the caption "Love means never having to say you are sorry." The couple in the picture are now divorced, and the message was dramatically false, because true love means being able to say "sorry" and accept the "sorry" of others.

Finally, too, we should realize that there is no balm like God's healing forgiveness: our spirit is restored; we receive saving justice; we are anointed. The Good Shepherd does lift us up, too, and carry us.

August 1, 2005
Mass of the Holy Spirit, World Youth Day Cologne
Saint Matthias Church, Lever Kusen, Germany

LEADERSHIP

Jesus christ is a great leader. More people have chosen to follow Him than any other person in history. Nearly two thousand years after His death, we Australian Catholics are His followers, in a continent on the other side of the world from His homeland. Why is the number of Catholics still increasing in Australia and throughout many countries? What teachings of Jesus must His followers accept to be called Christian?

Jesus the Good Shepherd

Jesus' teachings on leadership are unusual. He preached more on the importance of service than on the exercise of authority (Mt 20). He left us nothing on the duties of kings or princes, much on the danger of riches (Mt 19).

At the Last Supper, the day before He was crucified, Jesus gave us an example to be followed when He washed the feet of His disciples with a basin and towel. "You call me Master and Lord, and rightly: so I am. If I, then, the Lord and Master, have washed your feet, you must wash each other's feet" (Jn 13).

Jesus often described Himself as the Good Shepherd. His leadership is an exercise of love; often strong love, even tough love, as He confronts evildoers. Jesus drove the money changers out of the Temple (Mt 21). But Jesus was not a careerist. He came to do the will of God His Father (Jn 5). In no way was He a "powerhead". He was the ultimate example of servant leadership.

Jesus was not a smooth-talking leader who only told His listeners what they wanted to hear. When He explained that He was proposing to leave His Body to eat and Blood to drink, many left Him (Jn 6). His followers were told that following Christ only comes at some personal cost; that they had to take up their own cross (Mt 16). This burden was not too heavy, and Christians have the promise of eternal life after death (Jn 6).

Jesus led by example, but His message then, as now in Australia, had a mixed reception. Some teachings were popular; some were unpopular; other teachings were thought to be farfetched, impossibly difficult, over the top. Jesus usually did not teach in a lecture hall or in a synagogue where the audience would not interrupt. He taught the crowds in the open, surrounded by friends, enemies trying to trap Him, the curious, and those with nothing better to do. There were often confrontations.

Many joined up, became His followers because they realized that here was a leader who spoke with authority (Mt 7); someone who was sincere, enthusiastic, knew what He was talking about, and practiced what He preached. No one could convict Him of sin (Jn 8). He gained strength and wisdom through His regular prayer (Mk 1).

What Qualities Do Leaders Need?

Many times since I was a boy I have heard it said that unless people stand for something they will fall for anything. This is almost completely true.

If Christian belief and practice declined radically in Australia (there is some evidence the rise in unbelief has leveled off), most people would not turn to science and reason. They would be superstitious, choosing bits and pieces from a mishmash of the great religious traditions and New Age recipes. Think of the tens of thousands of Australians who look at their horoscopes each day to read their future in the stars. Some of them are even serious about this neopagan nonsense. All genuine leaders must have clear, sound principles, personally chosen.

Such principles will not be self-centered, but directed outward from the heart, based on an understanding of what is good for society; for their Church or school, business or sport, for their work or profession. Such principles will enable leaders to set clear goals for themselves, to have clear ambitions for their groups, and so help others to plot their course, discover the direction in which they should be traveling.

Naturally, leaders must like and respect their peers and those they

serve and lead. This means being able to listen, to understand problems so that there is effective two-way communication. All good leaders strive to enhance a genuine sense of community. Good leaders are
enthusiastic, not necessarily demonstrative, and able to inspire enthusiasm in others. Good leaders say "thanks" regularly and mean it. A
few, very few, seem born to lead, but most leaders are made, formed,
and helped by the leadership of mentors. Sometimes we learn from
experience what leaders should not do. But we should not be envious,
regularly cutting down the "tall poppies".

It is unhealthy for any organization when members are afraid to
criticize and when leaders take policy criticisms as always being personal insults. Composure and courtesy under pressure enhance good
leadership. Panic and pessimism are catching and counterproductive.
Consistency and a regular striving to treat people fairly help produce
stability.

It is often claimed that Edmund Burke, the great Irish statesman of
the eighteenth century, said: "It is necessary only for the good man
to do nothing for evil to triumph." This truth is not found anywhere
in his writings, but he did write, with equal truth: "When bad men
combine, the good must associate; else they will fall, one by one."
Therefore, genuine leadership always involves some sort of struggle
to prevent the advancement of evil; in our families, parishes, schools,
business, politics, even sport and the arts. Good people should work
together. Sometimes this struggle for good is unpopular and misun-
derstood. Often leaders need courage, "grace under pressure", to take
these stands.

The first such occasion when we go against the flow is often the
most difficult. Every time we take a stand, it becomes a little easier next
time. Every time we fail to rise to the challenge, it becomes harder.
When we regularly face the small challenges, we are better able to resist
grave temptations. When I was educated years ago, again and again,
we were urged to stand on our own feet, make up our own mind, not
go with the crowd. This was good, indeed invaluable, advice. Leaders,
too, are called to act against abuses, justly and prudently. Victims and
outsiders of goodwill require this. So does justice. Pope John Paul II,
one of the great leaders of our age, has called on young people to be
the light of the world, the salt of the earth (Mt 5). In his Jubilee 2000
message, he called you to be "saints of the new millennium".

Australians like winners, those who are successful, although most Australians have a genuine sympathy for the underdog, if we meet one of them in real life. But that appreciation gives us an affinity with the old saying "Born in castles or cottages, the greatest was born in a stable."

Pentecost Pastoral Letter for Youth, Sydney 2003

2

Forerunners

ABRAHAM AND THE SACRIFICE OF ISAAC

Genesis 22:1–2, 9–13, 15–18

OVER THE YEARS as a bishop, I have been asked by the press to nominate my favorite music, my favorite books, five or six persons from history I would invite to a dinner party, and of course my favorite Scripture passages. Today's passage from Genesis is not one of my most loved scriptural excerpts, but it is certainly one of the most mysterious and difficult, describing events from the history of the Jewish people that help us understand Jesus' redemptive death on the Cross before His glorious Resurrection. Leon Kass, in *The Beginning of Wisdom*, wrote that "no story in Genesis is as terrible, as powerful, as mysterious, as elusive" as this one. It defies easy and confident interpretations.

As a preliminary consideration, I must confess that I have a philosophical or logical difficulty that colors my whole approach to the passage. I believe there are moral truths and that humans are constrained to search for these truths, to recognize them. Such truths are not relative to their circumstances and not human constructs.

As someone who believes that the one true God is the Creator of the universe and is eminently reasonable, I believe that the moral truths I mentioned, which are expressed incompletely in the Ten Commandments given to Moses, reflect God's reasonableness and not His arbitrary decisions, not some act of divine will that could be cranky or wrongheaded. I do not want to constrain the omnipotent God by the limitations of my personal reasoning, but I find it difficult to understand how God could have commanded or requested Abraham to kill his innocent son, even in a sacrifice to God Himself.

For a parent to be asked to kill a child is terrible enough, but there was another dimension to Abraham's dilemma, who had been promised

by God that through his own flesh and blood he would have innumerable descendants. God had said: "Look up to heaven and count the
stars if you can. Such will be your descendants" (Gen 15:5). Abraham
believed this and "put his faith in Yahweh, who counted this as making him justified". What was to happen to these promises if Isaac was
sacrificed?

For some reason, Abraham did not try to bargain with God, did not
try to find some alternative to Isaac as he had pleaded with God for
the righteous inhabitants of Sodom before its destruction. Apparently,
too, in the Hebrew text, God's words are more properly translated as a
request rather than a command, although most of the English transla-
tions fail to reflect this. Whether Abraham might have felt any greater
freedom to disregard a request, rather than disobey a Godly command,
is a point we cannot answer.

Let me now try to identify a few firm points for consideration, even
as we agree that much of the incident is shrouded in mystery and our
own uncertainties and incomprehension. An easy opting out would
be to claim that the author has simply misreported whatever were the
facts of the original event, but I am unwilling to do this, because we do
not have sufficient grounds within either a Jewish or Christian framework to justify such an escape. We have to wrestle with the facts, and
especially with the overwhelming factor that the one true God, awe
inspiring and all powerful, largely incomprehensible to us despite His
goodness and rationality, is the principal actor. In our age, we are generally not good at feeling awe when confronted by an invisible, spiritual God, as we are more used to reserving our awe for the material
wonders of contemporary science, technology, or medicine.

Abraham had heard God's call on a number of occasions and had
answered these calls. He had ratified the new covenant with the rite
of circumcision, seen God's judgment on Sodom and Gomorrah, been
blessed through the birth of Isaac to his wife Sarah. This incident was a
test for Abraham, who had to decide to place God in front of his own
flesh and blood, his aspirations for his progeny in the years to come,
and even before the promises God had already made to him. God came
first, and He must have been confident of His choice of Abraham as
our father in faith.

One professor of Judaica has raised the fascinating possibility that
Abraham gave the wrong answer and should have pointed out to God

that it was against God's own commands to kill the innocent; that it was only zealots and fanatics who perpetrated child sacrifice. Was Abraham proposing to do the wrong deed (sacrifice his son) for the right reason (accepting the one true God's sovereignty), and were his obedience and generosity to God sufficient to justify God's lavish promises; "Your descendants (will be) as many as the stars in heaven and the grains of sand on the seashore." Such a hypothesis would resolve my logical problem with the usual interpretations of the account of the aborted sacrifice.

We do not have precisely the same problems with Our Lord's sacrificial death because the Father did not kill His Son, and we readily acknowledge the different levels of evildoing for Judas, and the Jewish and Roman authorities, even though they did not fully understand what they were doing. However, it is also clear that good will never triumph and faith will not survive if selfish or overprotective fathers successfully prevent their sons and daughters from entering into the age-old struggle between good and evil because they fear the wounds and hurt their children will suffer.

March 8, 2009
Saint Benet's Hall, Oxford University

NOAH'S COVENANT

Genesis 1:26–31; 1 John 4:11–16; John 14:23–29

A JUST SYSTEM OF LAW, administered by just and competent men and women of the law, is one of the characteristics of societies that endure and that deserve to endure. We all believe that Australia generally, and New South Wales in particular, truly belong in this category as we gather for the annual Red Mass in Saint Mary's Cathedral, celebrated every year since 1931. We thank God for the traditions we have inherited and pray that the Spirit of Truth, which has been promised, will continue to be active in our courts.

The origins of the Red Mass are found in the Middle Ages in both France and England with some linking it with the presence of the papacy in Avignon from 1309–1377. The practice was introduced into the United States in 1928, where the Red Mass has been attended by almost every President since Truman. It will be interesting to learn whether President Obama attends. We are grateful to the Saint Thomas More Society for the continuing sponsorship of the Mass and appreciate the ancient prayers and hymns set to the sixteenth-century music and sung by the Capella Sublima.

By way of a change, I want to reflect on the role of law in society by focusing on the first reading from the Book of Genesis, the first book of the Jewish Scriptures that we know as the Old Testament. There we read of the creation: "God created man in the image of Himself, in the image of God He created him, male and female He created them." God instructs them to increase and multiply and makes them "masters of the fish of the sea, the birds of heaven, the cattle, all the wild animals, and all the creatures that creep along the ground."

In the first chapter of Genesis, man is like God because of his capacity for speech and reason, his freedom in doing and making, and his powers of contemplation, judgment, and care. A second layer of likeness comes from the human capacity to distinguish good and evil. Animals instinctively seek what is good and avoid what is bad, but they have no notions of either.

Both these layers of capacity provide a foundation for the God-like human capacity to set out rules of conduct, generalized and intelligible, with punishments for infractions. Genesis, as Leon R. Kass sets out in his 2003 book *The Beginning of Wisdom*, tells us that the early generations became so wicked and insolent that God regretted having made them. The earth was corrupt, and God decided to destroy them (Gen 6) in the Great Flood, except for Noah, his wife and descendants, and two of every kind of living creature.

It was only after the flood subsided that the Scriptures narrate that the new covenant and the law were established by God Himself. After Noah's sacrifice, God promised never to curse the earth again or strike down every living thing (Gen 8). It was a promise that Christians believe still endures today, without guaranteeing us against awful regional or local catastrophes.

God's covenant with Noah and his descendants, with the rainbow as the sign of this covenant, is essentially connected with the prohibition of murder and its punishment ("he who sheds the blood of man by man shall his blood be shed" [Gen 9:6]) and to the command to increase and multiply and subdue the earth. Communities are created by hope and security.

Here we see an account of civilization emerging from the law of the jungle, where might is right. Now might was to be subject to justice. While still primitive by our standards, it was a decisive development. This universal prototypical law, instituted ten generations before the election of Abraham and what many have seen as the basis for our concept of natural law, is the founding document of the new world order because it provides the conditions for hope in a durable human future. The law is a reaction against general lawlessness, against the pre-legal instinct for excessive vengeance, to a system where we find an impersonal retribution, limited in extent and universal in scope, because all humans bear the image of God.

Genesis has a realistic understanding of human nature, which had been justified by human folly for centuries. It implicitly rejects any notion of a pure and nonviolent humanity and sets out to contain the inevitable human violence through the law. It recognizes that executing justice is necessarily harsh and ugly, because human life cannot be defended without getting one's hands dirty; even today, I might add, when our society generally and properly rejects capital punishment.

God also plays an important part in this ancient Jewish account of the first human legal system. According to this text, it was Noah who turned to God after the liberation from the Ark, built an altar, and presented burnt offerings (Gen 8:20–21), an acknowledgment of Transcendence, of the mysterious Power beyond and behind the cosmos. But it was God who responded with a law and a special pact or covenant for Noah.

An old pagan saying claimed "no gods, no city", and many ancient Greek cities traced their mythic origins to a god. More recently and more than any other century in history, the twentieth century provided evidence for the view of many political philosophers that a belief in interested and judgmental gods (or God) is necessary for every decent human society. The Nazis and the Communists labored mightily to validate Dostoevsky's prophetic claim in the *Brothers Karamazov* that if belief in immortality were destroyed, "nothing would be immoral, everything would be permissible."

At a minimum, beliefs in the justice of law, the necessity for punishment, and a secure future for mankind are reinforced by a belief in divine guarantees. We dispense with the one true God at our peril, no matter where we might be working, but especially when we are developing or administering the law.

The origins of the Book of Genesis and their dates are lost in the mists of antiquity. Traditionally ascribed to the authorship of Moses, the final forms we now have would all be later, but some of the basic traditions could be much earlier. However, these texts can still give us food for thought as we consider the nature of God, man's place in the cosmos, his capacity to be infinitely greater than the animals, the continuing mysteries of evil and human cruelty, and the vital role of the law, not in perfecting humans, but in protecting us from our worst selves.

February 2, 2009
Red Mass (for judges and lawyers)
Saint Mary's Cathedral, Sydney

MOSES

I T CAME AS A SURPRISE to me after forty years of priesthood to realize that I had no record of ever devoting a complete sermon to
Moses, the Lawgiver and Founder of the Jewish nation, although I
had mentioned him many times during Holy Week. His story is, of
course, better known than that of most saints, and his importance for
us is underlined by his appearance with Elijah at the miracle of the
Transfiguration (Mt 17:1–8).

I once saw a poster in Rome on the roadside after the fall of European Communism comparing Pope John Paul II to Moses, obviously
linking the Jewish liberation from Egypt to the religious and political
freedom that followed in 1989. When I recounted this to a friend, he
remarked that only Christ should be described as a second Moses.

Another reference to Moses was quite different and initially disconcerting. Not many Australians realize that the Islamic religion spread
dramatically in the one hundred years after Muhammad's death through
a stunning series of military victories, which saw the Middle East and
Persia conquered and expansion across North Africa into Spain, and
briefly into Southern France, where Muslim troops were repulsed by
Charles Martel in 732 at Poitiers. Muslims regularly see Muhammad
and his successors as following the example of Moses as he battled his
way toward the Promised Land.

Moses also featured indirectly in another unusual pastoral experience
of mine. In Melbourne, I was on parish visitation with the most junior
class in a primary school, when the principal incautiously asked the
youngsters if they had any questions for me. One young lad from the
preparatory class promptly asked me the name of Moses' mother. I was
caught; muttered that I did not think it was in the Scriptures ("yes it
was", insisted my interrogator); that it was not Miriam, Moses' sister,
and I concluded hopefully that it was probably a Hebrew name. "Of

course it is", the youngster explained confidently. I had to confess my ignorance. "Jochebed", he explained triumphantly. I caused mild consternation in the staff room at morning tea by asking for a Bible to check out the truth. He was correct as Jochebed is named (Ex 6:20). She had married Amram, her nephew, the father of Moses and Miriam.

My only consolation on returning to the cathedral presbytery for lunch was to discover that Archbishop Eric D'Arcy, who had lectured at Melbourne University for twenty years (admittedly in philosophy), did not know either, although my Master of Ceremonies, Father Charles Portelli, remembered that he had been told the name by a nun in primary school.

Moses, who was an outstanding servant of God, powerful in speech and action, narrowly escaped death soon after his birth and was educated in the Egyptian royal family. The days when Joseph, Jacob's youngest son, was a powerful Egyptian official, well able to protect his Jewish kin, were long gone, and the Egyptian authorities, probably under Pharaoh Seti I (1315–1290 B.C.), were practicing ethnic cleansing on the Jews, killing all the newborn males at birth.

Moses survived through the cunning and compassion of five women after his mother placed him in a papyrus basket by the river. Pharaoh's daughter had pity on him and unknowingly consigned him to his mother at his sister's suggestion. He was eventually educated in the royal household.

Many of us would be aware of Michelangelo's magnificent marble statue of Moses in the church of Saint Peter in Chains in Rome; an utterly formidable figure spiritually, morally, and physically. This statue captures Moses' personality and dramatic achievements, including the fact that he killed an Egyptian who was mistreating a fellow Jew, and had to flee from the Egyptian authorities into Midianite territory on the Sinai Peninsula.

He settled there, marrying Zipporah, the daughter of Jethro, the Midianite high priest. At Horeb, the mountain of the Lord, Moses had a mysterious encounter with the one true God, who appeared in a burning bush, which continued to burn but was not consumed. This was holy ground, where God confirmed that He was the God of Abraham, Isaac, and Jacob; that His name was "I am", and that Moses was to return to Egypt to free His people and lead them to the Promised Land, rich and broad, flowing with milk and honey. Unlike us, Moses spoke to God face to face, but he still could not see God's face, only his back!

This is the God we worship, because this is the God of Jesus Christ. Recently a Catholic priest on the edge of the Church community rejected any notion of a tribal God who would want or require people to pray to Him and claimed his notion of divinity came from the Upanishads, an important Hindu document reducing God to an impersonal world soul. This is not compatible with Christianity. The one true God was worshipped by Abraham, Isaac, Jacob, and Moses and is the God of Jesus Christ. This is the Trinitarian God we follow.

Knowing something of the struggle that lay before him, Moses was reluctant to take up the call to lead the liberation. He was not a good public speaker, was slow and hesitant of speech. God explained that his brother Aaron, the Levite, would perform that task well.

At every Easter Vigil, we hear of the mighty struggle with the Egyptian rulers, of the ten plagues, of the miraculous crossing of the Sea of Reeds after Moses took up the challenge to lead his people. And under his leadership, the collection of Jewish tribes did become one people. Moses was the initial Jewish nation builder.

It was Moses who received the Ten Commandments, which consolidated the new identity of the twelve loosely linked tribes, and these Ten Commandments remain essential for our Catholic identity today, especially when they are followed as exemplifying the two great Commandments of love; love of God (the first three Commandments) and love of our neighbor (the fourth to the tenth Commandments).

Christians are people who follow Jesus Christ and accept his teachings on faith and morals. They are not admirers who ignore what He said. The Ten Commandments given to Moses are an essential part of this package, especially today when there is so much genuine confusion, caused by the multiplicity of voices calling us in other directions. Catholics should not be pickers and choosers; certainly not from among the Ten Commandments. The Commandments are not like a final examination, where only six of the ten questions need be answered.

When Moses descended from Mount Sinai with the commandments after communing with God in the cloud for forty days, he found his people, led by his brother Aaron, worshipping a golden calf. They had then sat down to eat and drink and risen up to take their pleasures.

Moses was furious, throwing down and shattering the tablets of the Law and then destroying the golden calf and grinding it to dust. We are told God threatened to abandon and destroy his people, but Moses argued successfully that they be spared.

Their infidelity at such a sacred moment is a reminder of our own actual and potential weakness, just as it reminds us that the contemporary flight from God, today's rejection of the one true God, has plenty of unfortunate precedents throughout history. Apostasy and idolatry are old-fashioned. But the Jews did repent and recover to enter the Promised Land, although Moses and Aaron never shared that privilege. Moses experienced rejection, doubt, and revolt, but he managed to ensure that his people arrived at their destination.

Christ is more powerful than Moses ever was and has brought us a liberation that is more than political or territorial. May we continue to follow Christ our Redeemer, the fulfillment of what Moses hoped for imperfectly. And may more and more of our sisters and brothers recognize the truth of Christ's calling and choose to follow.

October 17 and 18, 2009
Student camp, Benedict XVI Retreat Centre,
Grose Vale and Youth Mass,
Saint Mary's Cathedral, Sydney

ELIJAH

1 Kings 19:9a, 11–13a; Romans 9:1–5;
Matthew 14:22–33

I N THE FIRST READING today from the First Book of Kings, we have the
strange figure of Elijah, the greatest of the Old Testament prophets,
who appeared with Moses and Our Lord at the miracle of the Transfiguration. The importance of Elijah derives, not from his writings,
because he wrote nothing that has survived, but from his successful
struggle against idolatry, the worship of false gods. Like Enoch he did
not die but was transported to heaven.

The First Book of Kings is a theological text designed to emphasize
three key points and which uses history for these purposes. Written
during the Jewish exile in Babylon in the sixth century B.C., it draws
on ninth-century B.C. sources for the story of Elijah as it struggles to
see God's hand in defeat and exile.

The three lessons from history are as follows. First of all, catastrophe
has overtaken Israel because her kings have been unfaithful to God's
covenant and the Temple. God himself is not unreliable. Secondly, it
was God speaking through Moses at Sinai who created Israel and the
word of God coming through the prophets that shaped Israel's history.
Thirdly, and despite the destruction of the Northern Kingdom and the
exile of the Southern Kingdom in Babylon, God's promise to David
that his kingdom would last forever was still in force and would be
fulfilled in some way or other.

Elijah the Tishbite of Tishbe in Gilead was a prophet in the ninth
century B.C., active from around 870 B.C. to after 850 B.C., when Ahab
was King of Israel and worse than all his predecessors. The notorious
Jezebel, daughter of Ethbaal the Sidonian King of Tyre and a zealot
for the worship of Baal, was his wife. Elijah is important because he

preserved the worship of the one true God, when this might have dis-appeared under Jezebel's onslaught for paganism.

Today, some people are tempted to believe that it is sufficient to be religious in any one of a variety of ways, although a superstitious rever-ence or awe for nature is now a more likely substitute for monotheism than Baal worship. The Jewish people of nearly three thousand years ago were clearer about the alternatives as Baal was worshipped by the Phoenicians.

The prophets were a recognized group in preexilic Judaism with sig-nificant religious and social functions. They usually were not priests, although their communities were often connected with worship and places of worship. Elijah established an altar to Yahweh on Mount Carmel. Their role had some similarities with that of Islamic dervishes, and they were numerous in Ahab's time, as at one stage he assembled four hundred of them in one place.

They often had a stigma or sign on their foreheads and wore a dis-tinctive dress. Elijah's was a mantle of sheep- or goatskin and a leather loincloth. They would have made a disconcerting sight, and opinion was divided about them because they were loved and revered by some as well as hated and feared by others. They were seen as men of God, who experienced His power and lived in His presence and so were consulted by every type of person from army commanders and offi-cials of Ahab to ordinary people.

Elijah was unpredictable, moving from place to place, delivering God's messages or oracles even when not asked. People realized he could see into their hearts, and Ahab feared him because of his rebukes and the distress he brought on Israel because of Ahab's infidelity.

It was Elijah who brought the terrible drought on the country, with neither dew nor rain for three years. In revenge, Ahab was butchering the prophets of Yahweh, and Elijah had to flee into the desert east of the Jordan. First of all, he was fed by ravens and then by a penniless widow and her son, whose small store of meal and oil was miracu-lously replenished. Disaster then struck, and her son died. Had this God-botherer made her pay for her sins? Elijah interceded with God and with some difficulty, after laying himself on the boy three times, was eventually able to restore his life.

After meeting Obadiah, Ahab's master of the palace but a true be-liever, Elijah obtained Ahab's permission for a mighty contest between

Yahweh and Elijah, the only remaining prophet of the one true God, on the one hand, and the 450 prophets of Baal. Who could call down fire to consume the sacrificial bull? From morning until midday, Baal's prophets danced and cavorted around the altar, wailing and slashing themselves in ineffectual frenzy as Elijah mocked and insulted them and their god. Was he asleep or away on a journey or busy?

In his turn, Elijah built an altar, dismembered the bull, and placed it on the wood, dousing it all with water three times. He prayed aloud, "Yahweh, God of Abraham, Isaac and Israel, let them know today that you are God in Israel and that I am your servant." Then fire came, consuming the offering and the wood. "Yahweh is God", shouted the crowd, who seized the exhausted prophets of Baal and slaughtered them.

The stakes were high in these ancient contests, where pluralism and tolerance were so rare as to be nonexistent. Elijah told Ahab to return to his palace for a meal, because rain was approaching. Waiting on top of Mount Carmel, Elijah had to send his servant seven times before he saw on the horizon a cloud, "small as a man's hand". The drought was over.

Jezebel was made of much sterner pagan stuff than Ahab and was furious with these developments. Refusing to draw the obvious conclusion, she threatened Elijah with death within twenty-four hours. Once again he had to flee, this time to Horeb, God's holy mountain. On that mountain, Elijah, fresh from his triumph and the slaughter of his opponents, once again encountered the God of his forefathers and received an important lesson. God was not in the powerful hurricane that split the rocks, not in the earthquakes, and not in the fire. Elijah heard God's voice in the gentle breeze, a light murmuring sound, commissioning him to anoint the Kings of Aram and Israel and Elisha son of Shaphat as his own successor. What would Elijah, this fugitive aflame with the faith, brimming over with jealous zeal and ready for violence, have made of this lesson?

In the Middle Ages, the Crusaders built a castle on Mount Carmel, which remains a place of pilgrimage. In the year 2000, before the intifada, or uprising, when hopes for peace were high, I led two hundred young Melbourne pilgrims through the Holy Land en route to Rome's World Youth Day. Our first Mass there was celebrated on Mount Carmel in the open on the hillside, and Father Des Byrne preached a remarkable sermon, worthy of the place and almost worthy of Elijah himself. It was a perfect beginning for our pilgrimage. Led by lay leaders of faith and good young priests, I have never encountered before or since anything like the wave of conversions that ran and reran through those young believers in those days.

We could say Mount Carmel was the start of it all.

August 10, 2008
Saint Mary's Cathedral, Sydney

AMOS THE PROPHET

Amos 7:12−15; Ephesians 1:3−10;
Mark 6:7−13

TODAY'S READING from the prophet Amos prompts me to say a few words generally on the role of the prophets in the Old Testament and more particularly on Amos, who is the first of the so-called minor prophets, the first whose message was written down and preserved for us. He began to teach and prophesy about 760 years before Christ's birth, when Jeroboam II was king of Israel, then at the peak of its prosperity. His message is a tough one, not balanced by beautiful references to God's faithfulness and love as you find in Hosea and Micah, whose "reproaches" are used in our Good Friday liturgy.

The three greatest of the prophets were Ezekiel and Isaiah, who wrote during the Jewish people's exile in Babylon, and Jeremiah, who was active immediately before the Babylonians captured Jerusalem. Incidentally in Jerusalem they have excavated ten or twenty meters below the present surface of the walls and discovered one narrow gate through which the Babylonians entered. Spear tips and other odds and ends there have been dated to about this time, early in the sixth century B.C.

The beginnings of Jewish prophecy are found from about the time of Saul and then David, the first Jewish kings, more than one thousand years before Christ. There were two types: (a) the seers or clairvoyants, like Samuel, and (b) the ecstatics, associated with a local shrine, who would often utter words they felt were not their own, under the influence of music and frenzied dancing. Amos was at pains to explain that he did not come from one of these groups but was a shepherd from a small village on the edge of the desert of Judah, who had been called by God Himself to give out His grim message of impending doom for the Northern Kingdom of Israel. For us today, a prophet is someone who foretells the future, and Our Lord certainly saw Himself as the Messiah whom the prophets had said was to come. Many prophets and righteous people had desired to see what the disciples were seeing (Mt 13:17), Jesus explained.

In their own day, the prophets preached, taught, and often used symbolic actions to make their point. Jeremiah wore a yoke on his shoulders at one stage, and Isaiah went naked—something Francis of Assisi did briefly early in his career. They called their people to repentance, emphasizing what God wanted and often pointing out the unfortunate consequences of not doing God's will. The call to repentance and right conduct, God's uncomfortable demands in the here and now, was more central to their work than foretelling the consequences of present activity.

It is consoling to remember that we belong to such an ancient tradition, going back over three thousand years, dedicated to the worship of the one true God, belonging to a community that has enjoyed a special covenant or relationship with God since then; a community of individuals and families trying to do the right thing by God and one another, who often had to struggle with circumstances much more difficult than our own.

In today's reading, we hear of Amos' expulsion from the college of prophets at Bethel, the royal sanctuary, the national temple. He is not too perturbed, because it is God, not any group of humans, who has told him to prophesy to the people of Israel. Amos believes strongly in the importance of the one true God, Yahweh, as He is called, the Lord of the physical universe. The priests at the sanctuaries of Bethel, Galgal, and Dan are wrong on two important counts. They are encouraging lip service, a formal performance of worship rather than a true religion of the heart. They have forgotten that election as God's people brings with it significant obligations.

More significantly, foreign deities and false gods are being worshipped in these sanctuaries. A type of syncretism, a mixture of the true and the false, a smorgasbord, with the priests making a variety of offerings, is being practiced. Today the bits and pieces may be different, but we, too, know about à la carte religion.

Amos also vigorously denounces the leaders of Samaria for their oppression of the poor, their greed, and their sensuality. He believes they have no sense of justice, no awareness of the rights of the defenseless poor. Amos believes that if the sinners repented, God would save them. "Seek me that you may live" is God's central call.

However, he concludes that he is speaking to the deaf; speaking to a brick wall, as we used to say. As a consequence, the Day of the Lord is coming, a new and terrifying day of wrath. And, in fact, the Assyrians did come and destroy Samaria, the Northern Kingdom of ten of the Jewish tribes in 721. Only the southern remnant of Judah was to survive into the future as the Jewish people.

July 13, 2003
Saint Mary's Cathedral, Sydney

JOHN THE BAPTIST

J OHN THE BAPTIST, the son of priest Zachary and Elizabeth, cousin of
Our Lady, was born six months before Jesus. Luke's Gospel tells us
Gabriel the Archangel appeared to Zachary in the Temple announcing
that Elizabeth would conceive a son. Gabriel told Zachary to give his
promised son the name of John, which means "Yahweh is gracious."
He would lead many of the sons of Israel to their Lord and would walk
in the power and spirit of Elijah. In his canticle called the Benedictus,
Zachary sings of his son as "prophet of the Most High". According to
tradition, John was born in the town of Ain Karim, about three and
a half miles west of Jerusalem. Luke also relates that John spent his
youth in the desert.

John appeared in the region of the Jordan as an ascetic and a preacher
of penance. His principal task was to announce the arrival of Jesus
Christ as Messiah and to baptize Him. He appeared clothed in camel's
hair, the traditional garb of the prophets; just as Elijah had. John came
as "a voice crying in the desert", echoing Isaiah. According to the
fourth Gospel, the Baptist categorically denied that he was Elijah or
the expected prophet or the Messiah. But he was indeed the last of the
Old Testament prophets.

The message of John's sermons is rather forbidding and severe (Mt
3:7–12; Mk 1:7–8; Lk 3:7–18): "the axe is laid to the root of the
trees." But Luke also insists on the positive and humane aspects of
the Baptist's message. No profession is denied salvation; all are called
primarily to practice justice and charity toward their fellowman.

In John's Gospel, the Baptist describes himself as the friend of the
Bridegroom who must decrease as Christ must increase; he proclaims
Jesus as the Lamb of God. John gathered around him a group of disciples who remained faithful to him until his death. The apostles Andrew
and John had been disciples of the Baptist before joining Christ. While

the Synoptic Gospels and John record disputes between the disciples of the Baptist and those of Christ about fasting and baptism, the Baptist, however, seems to have counseled his disciples to follow Jesus.

The Evangelists further describe how "all the country of Judea went out to him, and all the inhabitants of Jerusalem." Josephus, the ancient Jewish historian, as well as the Evangelists record the reaction of Herod Antipas, who, fearing an uprising, had the Baptist imprisoned. John had fearlessly denounced Herod's sinful marriage with Herodias, his brother's wife. In turn, Herodias instigated her daughter, Salome, to request John's death; to please her, Herod had John beheaded, although he had regarded him as a religious and just man. While in prison, John had sent a delegation of his disciples to ask Jesus if He was the Messiah. According to some critics, John had found it difficult to accept a meek and merciful Messiah rather than an Elijah-like figure. In answer, Jesus pointed to His fulfillment of the Old Testament messianic expectation, especially as described by Isaiah. He then took the occasion to eulogize John as "a prophet, yes, more than a prophet. . . . Among those born of women there has not arisen a greater than John the Baptist."

The Dead Sea scrolls were discovered by a shepherd boy in 1947. They had belonged to the Qumran Community, probably a Jewish group called the Essenes. Many scholars think that the Qumran community of the Judean desert had an important influence on the Baptist, and some claim that John belonged to the community.

The similarities are striking. The Qumran community was a priestly one; John, too, came from a priestly family that manifested intense Messianic hopes. Both John and the sectarians of Qumran found inspiration in the text of Isaiah 40:3. John preached a baptism of repentance, and while the Qumran community practiced ritual ablutions, there is no indication that they attached any moral significance to these. Yet the Qumran ritual was frequently repeated, whereas that of John was apparently administered only once. John announced a second baptism with the Holy Spirit and with fire, that is, an eschatological judgment; the Qumran ascetics, too, preached a second baptism that would be the work of the Spirit of God and would be eschatological.

A striking difference, however, between John the Baptist and the Qumran community is the universality present in John's preaching in contrast to the closed character of the Qumran group, which regarded all outsiders as "sons of darkness". Since John spent many years in the desert, it seems probable that he knew the Qumran community. It has even been suggested that as a child he had been educated by them. But he certainly was not a member of the Qumran community during his active ministry, for his missionary life was not in keeping with the rule of that community.

December 7, 2003
Second Sunday in Advent
Saint Mary's Cathedral, Sydney

3

The One True God

WITHOUT GOD WE ARE NOTHING

Introduction

M<small>Y CLAIMS</small> this afternoon are simple. It is more reasonable to believe in God than to reject the hypothesis of God by appealing to chance; more reasonable also to believe than to escape into agnosticism. *Goodness, truth, and beauty call for an explanation, as do the principles of mathematics, physics, and the purpose-driven miracles of biology that run through our universe. The human capacities to recognize these qualities of truth, goodness, and beauty, to invent and construct, also call for an explanation.* The Irish philosopher Brendan Purcell cites the frequently used quotation from Einstein that: "The one thing that is unintelligible about the universe is its intelligibility."[1] And he might have added that the fact that human intelligences are able to strive to understand the universe is also unintelligible of and by itself.

By way of introduction, let me follow Purcell again to try to set the scene for the God hypothesis in a rather simple and then in a more developed way. Purcell quotes the grumpy response of the British physicist Fred Hoyle, a former atheist, to his own discovery of the very narrow temperature range that allows the emergence of carbon in nucleosynthesis: "The universe looks like a put-up job."[2] I believe it is!

From the beginning, it is also important to realize that in arguing for God, we are not claiming the existence of a super-quality physical cause or phenomenon, accessible to science, within the universe. God is not some fantastic UFO.

Purcell quotes the philosopher and atheist Thomas Nagel, who explains that the purpose of the God hypothesis is to claim that not all is physical and "that there is a mental, purposive or intentional explanation more fundamental than the basic laws of physics, because it

---

[1] Brendan Purcell, "Deluded by What? Richard Dawkins' *The God Delusion*". Typescript (publication forthcoming 2010), 12.

[2] Ibid., 12 n37.

explains even them".[3] By definition, God must be self-sufficient, the reason for His own existence, which is a statement that young children, initially at least, do not find a very satisfactory answer to their frequent question about who made God. However, just as youngsters generally cannot understand the lessons hidden in Christ's parables, so very few of the young before adolescence think philosophically.

In this paper I am not arguing for a covert atheism, where we retain Godly language but reduce Him to our ultimate human concerns (like the "God is dead" theologians of the 1960s); nor am I a Catholic atheist, someone who passionately loves and defends Christian civilization but cannot or does not believe in God, like the Italians Umberto Eco and Oriana Fallaci. I believe the one true God is real, not simply because I was born into the Catholic tradition, but because for over fifty years my childhood beliefs have been tested and I have probed their rational foundations.

Every Catholic priest is supposed to study philosophy for a couple of years to develop his capacity for clear thinking, to introduce him to the metaphysical tradition favored by the Church, which stretches from Aristotle via Thomas Aquinas to the present, and to enable him to dialogue with those around him who do not share his Christian or even religious presuppositions. The God question has always been one of my intellectual interests, and when I was a seminarian in Rome, I took classes in the Institute for Atheism then run at my Catholic university by the Italian philosopher Cornelio Fabro.

Because of my vocation and because of my personality and education, I have regularly encouraged my listeners and students over the years to ask and ponder the ultimate questions. Why are we here on earth? What is the point of it all, given suffering and death? What is the good life?

The existence of evil and suffering, to which I shall return later, is more of a problem for those who believe God is good than for those who see God only as the Supreme Intelligence, Creator, and sustainer of the universe. If God was cruel and capricious, or even indifferent, it would be especially disappointing and hurtful to those who understand justice, value goodness, and reject evil. Such human beings in a moral sense would be better than a cruel and capricious or an indifferent and

[3] Ibid., 13.

heartless God! Similarly, an "impersonal" God would be less than a human person.

When a religion encourages and legitimizes a "holy" war or when a religion approves a "just" war, it has to justify its positions. But this is different from religious people ignoring the religious teaching of their tradition to wage war or impose evil.

My task today is to talk about God, but if God is rejected because of the evil deeds of religious people, we should follow this claim to see where it takes us. While the fruits of religion might be mixed, I do not concede that religions are generally poisonous. Indeed, when people follow Christian teachings, human life is enriched immensely. However, even if we admitted that religions generally are poisonous, what difference would this make to the logical case either for or against God's existence? *God cannot be reduced to the activities of His followers. God and religion are two different realities.*

In daily life, personally and psychologically poisonous religion might induce victims to curse the god who inspired his followers to commit such evil or to reject the possibility that such a god could exist. Such evil can be an effective counter witness against the existence of God. The suffering of innocent children is always terrible.

But scientifically and philosophically, does this abolish the God question? The discussion of God's goodness and concern for us would need to be reframed, but many of the ultimate questions would remain. *Who or what triggered the Big Bang? Are the astonishingly beautiful principles of physics and mathematics the products of chance? Why is there something rather than nothing?*

Whether we are interested or disinterested, happy or unhappy, good or evil, and despite recurrent natural disasters, the ultimate questions will always remain to be asked and to be pondered. These questions have meaning, logically and psychologically, as thousands of years of such enquiry attest. In fact, in the Western intellectual world, which is unique in the extent of its skepticism and agnosticism, God is still traveling more safely than He was one hundred years ago. Today, hardly anyone of any persuasion expects that religion will soon disappear.

Pierre Manent, a French social philosopher whose work I have come to admire, in his book entitled *An Intellectual History of Liberalism*, has advanced the thesis that the French Revolution of 1789, with its explicit hostility to religion, was the first example of the secular state.

One consequence of this is that Western democracies now follow the doctrine of the separation of Church and State, which finds a generally benign expression in the English-speaking world, following the example of the United States, and often an explicitly antireligious form in Europe.[4]

More significantly for our purposes, Manent claims that secular states discourage the discussion of ultimate questions, where religious bodies enjoy an enormous advantage. In a certain sense, ultimate questions are a religion's core business![5]

Here in Australia, public discussion and debate often proceed as though most of the population were godless, atheist, or agnostic. In fact, only 17 percent do not accept the existence of God.[6] However, the absence of God in Australian public discussion is generally due, not to any English-language political theory, but more to the secularist hostility to Christianity that remains the most formidable barrier to their program for an ever broader personal autonomy. Often God gets caught up in the secular hostility to the Christian defense of human life, especially at the beginning and the end, the Christian defense of marriage, family, and the linking of sexuality to love and life. Here in these culture wars lies the origin of most of the hatred of God and religion, while the violence of a minority of Islamist terrorists has given Western secularists new grounds to attack all religions. However, it is much safer to attack the Christians!

There are many more monotheists today than there were one hundred or one thousand years ago, both in absolute terms and as a percentage of the world's populations. The proportion of people belonging to the world's four biggest religions rose from 67 percent in 1900 to 73 percent in 2005 and may reach 80 percent in 2050.[7] Even more startling is the fact that "where pain, hardship and distress are far more prevalent, we find the highest rates of faith", even in those places in Africa where atrocious barbarism has recently occurred.[8] It is the reli-

---

[4] Pierre Manent, *An Intellectual History of Liberalism* (1987), trans. Rebecca Balinski (Princeton, N.J.: Princeton University Press, 1995), 79–83.

[5] Ibid., 114.

[6] Australian Bureau of Statistics, *Census of Population and Housing, Australia, 2006*.

[7] John Micklethwait and Adrian Wooldridge, *God Is Back: How the Global Revival of Faith Is Changing the World* (New York: Penguin, 2009), 16ff.

[8] Justin Thacker, "God on Trial", *Guardian*, September 7, 2009.

gious situation in Europe today that is unusual throughout the world and equally unusual when we glance back through history.

I willingly concede that general beliefs, even when they endure for centuries, need not be logically compelling, and such beliefs are regularly even less persuasive when they are popular for a limited period of time, for years or decades. Over the centuries, many approved of slavery. Today many believe that before Galileo most believed the earth was flat, which is quite untrue. Plato recognized the earth was round. Today, also, public opinion can continue to be quite mistaken: for example, in the majority approval of the moral legitimacy of abortion or in its enthusiasm for expensive scientific mythology. *Most Australians for the moment seem to believe in global warming primarily induced by humans or even in humanly induced catastrophic global warming.*

There is not sufficient scientific evidence for either of these claims; less evidence that we could influence or reverse such climate outcomes, and less evidence again that we could afford to attempt this. Religion has no monopoly on truth or on human folly!

Let me then conclude this introductory section by highlighting the extent of God's popularity throughout the world and through much of history. Present trends indicate that this will continue and even intensify so that, for example, China by the end of the twenty-first century could have the largest Christian population of any country in the world!

It is useful to acknowledge this context to belief and unbelief, while recognizing explicitly that such popularity does not prove God's existence. Both popular and elite opinion can be wrong over long periods. More people come to know God through the kindness and witness of others than through logic. But reason and logic remain important, even if we accept A. E. Housman's two lines:[9]

> Malt does more than Milton can
> To justify God's ways to man.

I will now examine what we mean when we speak of God; moving on to a discussion of the relevance of today's scientific knowledge for the God question, a few words about the achievements of the pre-Christian Greek philosophers in recognizing the existence of God, and

[9] A. E. Housman, *A Shropshire Lad* (1896), Poem LXII: "Terence, This Is Stupid Stuff".

concluding with a section on the contribution of Judaeo-Christian revelation to our knowledge of God.

Naming God

Different thinkers approach God from different directions, often emphasizing different Godly attributes, but all concede that we face enormous problems of language when we set out to explain something of what we mean by God. It was the fifth-century North African Saint Augustine of Hippo, one of Christianity's finest theologians, who spoke of our "learned ignorance of God".

Some claim that every notion of God is so incoherent that somehow this means that God does not exist, while others claim that we cannot say anything useful about God. One traditional response to these problems is to explain that our terminology for God is analogical, that it does not fit God as well as human language describes physical or human reality. Human beings are "good" in very different ways and to different degrees, but when we claim God is good, the term has a radically superior meaning that does not contradict the basic human meaning. God is not only good but better than we can imagine.

Different categories of believers believe in different types of God. Deists do not accept that God is in any sense personal, but believe Him to be a Supreme Being, a Creator who does not intervene in the universe. Pantheists identify God with the universe, regarding the universe as a manifestation of God. The mighty, often uncontrollable forces of nature often provoke awe in every type of person. Monotheists believe only one God exists, and traditional monotheists such as Jews, Christians, and Muslims believe God to be transcendent and personal in some superior sense. In other words, the transcendent God is not on our level of reality, not even as a thermonuclear trigger or giant rocket that sets off the Big Bang at the start of the universe. God is beyond space and time, not part of the natural order and, therefore, not open to observation by the natural sciences.

We often use apophatic or negative terminology to speak of this transcendent God. God is infinite—that is, cannot be measured, immutable, and immaterial or spiritual. God is spiritual, not material, and therefore has no parts. The spirituality of God means that God is not human, is neither male nor female. Once when I gave this explanation in a radio interview, the host enquired whether this was only my personal view or Christian teaching. He seemed surprised when I explained that this was a basic monotheist doctrine.

I follow Christian convention in referring to God as "He" or "Him", accepting Jesus' teaching that we pray to God calling Him "Our Father", but this is an example of the use of analogical language. *When trying to explain to senior primary and junior secondary students what we mean when we say God is spirit, I ask them to start from their parents' love for them; a real, powerful, and invisible force in their lives, very important to them, before I move on to the Christian teaching that God is love.* The children rarely object to this sort of argumentation. In Australia it is easy to be a de facto materialist, so we often have to argue for the importance of the spiritual. While it would be somewhat confusing to argue that our spiritual God has many faces, this Sublime Mystery can be approached in different ways as we glimpse hints of different facets of the Immortal Diamond, which has a heart of love.

His publicists claim that Antony Flew, a professional philosopher, was the world's most notorious atheist. He certainly was an influential and widely read unbeliever, and he has recently changed his mind and written an excellent, clear, and accessible book called *There Is a God*, explaining that his story is a pilgrimage of reason and not of faith.

Flew has collected a number of shorthand terms that prominent scientists and philosophers have used about God. He quotes Albert Einstein's avowal that he was neither an atheist nor a pantheist, although he did not believe in a personal God. For Einstein, God was a "superior reasoning force", an "illimitable superior spirit", the "mysterious force that moves the constellations".[10] The philosopher Richard Swinburne is cited for his defense of God as "an omnipresent incorporeal spirit".[11]

Even the well-known atheist and scientist Stephen Hawking, author of the best-selling *A Brief History of Time* (which I struggled unsuccessfully to read), wrote the following question: "What is it that breathes fire into the equations and makes a universe for them to describe?" In a later interview, Hawking conceded, "You still have the question

---

[10] Antony Flew, *There Is a God: How the World's Most Notorious Atheist Changed His Mind* (New York: Harper Collins, 2008), 99–102.

[11] Ibid., 72.

why does the universe bother to exist? If you like, you can define God to be the answer to that question."[12]

Two other quotations from different parts of the theistic spectrum will round off this section on naming God. The first is from the Scottish Sydney-based philosopher Hayden Ramsay, and the second is from Saint Augustine's *Confessions*, the oldest surviving autobiography in Western literature, a quotation Ramsay himself cites.

Ramsay writes that believers in God are not committed to any particular explanation of how the universe came about. However, he also writes:

> they are committed to believing in the radical incompleteness of cosmology and astrophysics. The Universe's history does not explain why the Universe exists. Such an explanation is wrapped around in mystery, since it is not for any person to explain it. But if we can ask the question, we must ponder the answer and, bewildering though it is, that answer "all men call God".[13]

Ramsay introduces the extract from Augustine as expressing the "unique reconciliation of complexity and simplicity that is God".[14] Saint Augustine wrote of God:

> you are most high, excellent, most powerful, omnipotent, supremely merciful and supremely just, most hidden yet intimately present, infinitely beautiful and infinitely strong, steadfast yet elusive, unchanging yourself though you control the change in all things, never new, never old, renewing all things yet wearing down the proud though they know it not; ever active, ever at rest, gathering while knowing no need, seeking although you lack nothing.

Although written about sixteen hundred years ago, these thoughts are one beautiful result of the interplay of Greek philosophy, especially Plato, Judaeo-Christian revelation, and the lived experience of the monotheistic tradition, which was then already about two thousand years old. I willingly concede that Augustine's description of God represents more than the fruits of reason alone.

[12] Ibid., 97.
[13] Hayden Ramsay, "God and Persons", in Craig Paterson and Matthew S. Pugh, eds., *Analytical Thomism: Traditions in Dialogue* (Burlington, Vt.: Ashgate, 2006), 257.
[14] Ibid.

Science and God

As well as being an accomplished philosopher, Antony Flew is also an excellent popularizer, able to express controversial thoughts forcefully and pithily. The most controversial claim in his recent book is "that of all the great discoveries of modern science, the greatest was God".[15] This is provocative for unbelievers, especially unbelieving scientists, and provocative for believers, who know that the roots of monotheism are found with Abraham about thirty-seven hundred years ago.

Although much of public opinion still regards science as an enemy of religious understanding and therefore of God, recent developments in physics and now in biology have strengthened the case for God the Creator as a first-rate mathematician as well as being prodigal and unpredictable in His creation.

We cannot arrive at God within the framework of science, because God is outside space and time. Flew explains neatly that when we study the interaction of physical bodies, such as subatomic particles, we are doing science. When we ask how or why these particles exist, we go beyond physics to metaphysics. We are doing philosophy.[16]

I should repeat that the God for which we are arguing is not a God of the gaps, not a God who is brought in to paste over the gaps in our present scientific knowledge, which might be filled later as science progresses. It is the whole of the universe that is not self-explanatory, including the infrastructure and elements we understand scientifically.

Many people over the ages have found evidence for the Mind of God in the laws of nature, in their regularity and symmetry. The law of the conservation of energy, Newton's first law of motion, and Boyle's law, mathematically precise regularities, universal and tied together, are the examples Flew gives as he asks how nature is packaged in this way.[17] Flew shows that as well as Einstein, the great scientists who developed quantum physics, Max Planck, Werner Heisenberg, Erwin Schrödinger, and Paul Dirac, were all theists.[18] Even Charles Darwin

---

[15] Flew, *There Is a God*, 74.
[16] Ibid., 89.
[17] Ibid., 96.
[18] Ibid., 103–6.

rejected blind chance or necessity as the cause of the universe and looked to a First Cause with an intelligent mind.[19]

A number of writers espouse a theory called the Weak Anthropic Principle, which is that "matter evolved in an elaborate, finely tuned conspiracy to produce air-breathing, carbon-based life forms possessed of self-consciousness."[20] Others have claimed as much by saying that the universe knew we were coming!

The universe is finely tuned. If the value of even one of the fundamental constants—the speed of light or the mass of an electron—had been slightly different, then no planet capable of producing life could have formed.[21] Other examples abound. If the nuclear strong force had been slightly weaker, no element heavier than hydrogen would have been formed. If the Big Bang had been more vigorous, matter could not have formed into stars and planets.[22] The one-force strength of electromagnetism enables carbon synthesis to occur in stars, allows stars to burn steadily for billions of years, and atoms to exist and ensures protons behave in such a way that chemistry is possible.[23]

All this is too much for blind chance. Neither do we have any satisfactory naturalistic explanation for the origin of life from nonliving matter, for the fact (for example) that every animal for six hundred million years has the same body plan; only the jelly fish is an exception![24] Living matter, or living beings, are purpose driven and directed. Aristotle was right, since living beings are defined in such teleological terms, as is evident in the innate activity of a child feeding on its mother's breast or a caterpillar developing into a butterfly. On top of this, all forms of life are able to reproduce themselves, and new and different species emerge in some mysterious way, which I suspect is more than random mutation and natural selection.

Another mystery of life is the origin of the coding and information

[19] Ibid., 106.

[20] Bryan Appleyard, *Understanding the Present: Science and the Soul of Man* (London: Pan Macmillan, 1992), 184.

[21] Flew, *There Is a God*, 115.

[22] T. Dixon, "Design Features", *Times Literary Supplement*, December 22 and 29, 2006, 3–4.

[23] Flew, *There Is a God*, 116.

[24] Purcell, "Deluded by What?" 11.

processes in all life forms. The cell is a system that stores, processes, and replicates information. Flew became a theist, changed his mind, after studying the directive capacity of DNA,[25] whose genetic message is replicated and transcribed to RNA. This message is conveyed to the amino acids, which are then assembled into proteins. How blind and purposeless forces could spontaneously produce such a process is unknown and, I believe, both unknowable and metaphysically impossible. Even atheist Nobel-prize-winning biologists like Jacques Monod and DNA codiscoverer Francis Crick regard the emergence of life from chemical realities as almost miraculous.

Nor is this the end of the succession of miracles. I remember Sir Hans Kornberg, a distinguished biologist, asking me about the intelligence level of dinosaurs. I replied that it was low, as we had no evidence they had produced anything worthwhile and they had a small brain. He said that they also had no voice box and that the development of the voice box, which enabled human speech, personal communication, the exchange of thought and information, was a development as spectacular as the development of life itself.

Some have alleged that life might have arisen by chance, but calculations and experiments have shown the odds to be impossibly high. In the 1980s, Fred Hoyle and the astrophysicist Chandra Wickramasinghe decided to calculate the odds on whether random shuffling of amino acids could have produced life. They found the odds were one chance in $10^{40,000}$, an unimaginable number, as the number of subatomic particles in the entire universe is about 10^{81}.[26]

Flew also recounts Gerry Schroeder's refutation of the "monkey theorem". What were the odds against a group of monkeys thumping away on computer keyboards and so producing a Shakespearean sonnet? Six monkeys banging away in a cage for one month did not produce a single word, not even "a"! The odds against a sonnet were calculated by Schroeder as one in 10^{690}, not as high as moving from amino acids to life, but still impossibly high.[27] Life has not come about by chance.

[25] Flew, *There Is a God*, 75.
[26] *Time*, January 18, 1982.
[27] Flew, *There Is a God*, 75–78.

Greek Philosophy on God

We have inherited our love and respect for reason, via the Romans and Christian civilization, from the great pre-Christian Greek philosophers, especially Plato, Socrates, and Aristotle. Plato quotes Socrates' insistence that "we must follow the argument wherever it leads." This still should be our aim, and it will always be a noble ambition.

None of the major philosophers in the leading Greek schools were atheists, although they came to God by reason alone and were critical of the irrational myths of the traditional Greek religions of the time. Xenophanes (565–470 B.C.) was the first philosopher to develop the concept of God as "the One", helping to purify the earlier mythological accounts of God from human projections and wishes. He criticized Homer and Hesiod for ascribing human weaknesses such as stealing, adultery, and cheating to the gods. For him, "One God is greatest among gods and men, not like mortals in body or thought." "The One", he said "is the God."[28]

Parmenides was the first to formulate a philosophy, as opposed to a religious expression, of Being, about the year 475 B.C., but he spoke of God as IS, not being:

> One way only is left to be spoken of, that IS, and on this way are many signs that IS is uncreated and imperishable, whole, unmoved and without end. And it was not, and it will not be, for it is altogether Now.[29]

The two greatest Greek philosophers were Plato and Aristotle, but the tradition of Saint Thomas Aquinas in which I was educated via the later writings of the Scholastics drew heavily on Aristotle. It is interesting to note that Aristotle's writings were largely unknown in Christian circles for the first thousand years of our era, existing only in Arabic translation made by Syrian monks before the Islamic conquest. The philosophy of Plato was dominant. It was only in the last quarter of the twelfth century that a number of Aristotle's texts were discovered in Toledo, Spain, hidden in old pottery jars. The local bishop, Nicode-

[28] Purcell, "Deluded by What?" 6.
[29] Ibid.

mus of Toledo, encouraged Jewish, Christian, and Muslim scholars to translate these works and distribute them around Europe.

Therefore, it was in the thirteenth century that Aristotle's thought became influential with Aquinas, Dante, Bocaccio, and Petrarch. The Church leadership, despite fierce opposition from the Platonists, came gradually to accept the "this worldliness" of Aristotle rather than the unworldliness of Plato. The historian Richard Rubenstein has written: "Farsighted popes and bishops . . . took the fateful step that Islamic leaders had rejected. By marrying Christian theology to Aristotelian science, they committed the West to an ethic of rational enquiry that would generate a succession of scientific revolutions, as well as unforeseen upheavals in social and religious thought."[30]

It was in the thirteenth century that we saw the beginnings of the great Western universities that continue today: Paris, Bologna, Salamanca, Oxford, and Cambridge. The slow rise of Western civilization to world dominance had begun. The famous five ways of Saint Thomas Aquinas, the five proofs (or attempted proofs) for God's existence, draw heavily from Aristotle. For Aristotle, God is pure Act, "the Understanding of understanding", and drawing on his philosophical conclusions, not on religious belief, he ascribes the following attributes to God: immutable, immaterial, omnipotent, omniscient, one and indivisible, perfectly good, necessarily existent.[31] All of this is eminently compatible with the Judaeo-Christian notion of the one true God, and it has been incorporated into our theology.

The Christian God

For Jews and Christians, the one true God is the God of Abraham, Isaac, and Jacob, while the Christians also see God as the Father of Our Lord Jesus Christ. Moses was told that God's name was "I am".[32] Accepting such claims does not require abandoning the reverence for

---

[30] Quoted in Michael Novak, *No One Sees God: The Dark Night of Atheists and Unbelievers* (New York: Doubleday, 2008), 242–43.

[31] Flew, *There Is a God*, 92–93. See also Purcell, "Deluded by What?" 7.

[32] Ex 3:13.

reason that I have been advocating, but it does mean accepting a world that is wider than the physical and criteria that are not scientific.

To accept that God has intervened directly in history by choosing one people as His own, His special agents to whom He has revealed more about His nature and plans than could be recognized philosophically, does require a leap of faith. But such a leap need not be irrational, although this leap can never be taken with mathematical certainty. Christians have a further challenge with their belief that Christ is divine as well as human. Christ should be accepted or rejected on the quality of His teachings, the integrity and plausibility of His actions during his lifetime, and the goodness and courage (or otherwise) of His followers as they strive to live out His teachings and defend their central doctrine that Christ rose after His ignominious public crucifixion.

As well as these intellectual challenges, the Christian concept of God immediately offers a formidable personal stumbling block. Unlike many strands of Judaism, traditional Christianity has a clear doctrine on life after death, where the good are rewarded and the self-centered evil are punished, either for a time (according to the Catholics) or even permanently. This is a two-edged sword, attractive to the victims of violence and oppression, but off-putting to the unreflective and threatening to the hard of heart, the obdurate who refuse to repent.

In a provocative inversion of Karl Marx's condemnation of religion as "the opium of the people", the Polish poet Czesław Miłosz, himself a victim of Communism, in his essay "The Discrete Charm of Nihilism", explains that the roots of twentieth century totalitarianism are found, not in religion, but in its nihilist antithesis. For Miłosz "a true opium of the people is a belief in nothingness after death—the huge solace of thinking that for our betrayals, greed, cowardice, murders, we are not going to be judged."[33] I think he is right.

A just God needs an afterlife of reward and punishment, including purificatory punishment to balance the scales of justice, because history shows too many innocent victims. Suffering, whether it comes from natural disasters or from human evil, is the greatest problem for those

---

[33] Czesław Miłosz, "The Discrete Charm of Nihilism", *New York Review of Books* 45:18 (November 19, 1998).

who believe in a personal, loving, and just God. We find no entirely satisfactory intellectual answer.

However, for those who believe that existence is purposeless, that the universe is the product of blind chance, the problem of evil and suffering is submerged in the larger intellectual problem of why anyone should be happy, of why there should be goodness, truth, and beauty. If the universe is only a brute fact, why did it emerge as good as it is, why does it not revert to chaos? Evil is a problem for theists, but the good things of life are a larger problem for atheists. Often those who claim God is dead silently assume the presupposition of the theist to criticize the sufferings in the world or the inadequacy of creation. One needs to assume, at least tacitly, that life should be good or just or peaceful before criticizing reality on these scores.

Conclusion

The God of the monotheist religions is much richer and more powerful than the same God recognized by the philosophers, which is certainly one, true, and good, but pale and thin in comparison. A martyr is someone who is prepared to accept death rather than reject God, and the twentieth century had more martyrs than any other century. Billions of believers continue to pray, live decent lives, love their families, contribute quietly to society in every monotheist tradition. But the militant in every tradition have gone to war in God's name. On the other hand, no previous century has witnessed the systematic hatred and oppression of religions like that perpetrated by Hitler, Stalin, Mao, and Pol Pot.

Even in tolerant societies, God can and does provoke strong feelings, hatred, and loathing. In some ways this is mysterious. Why be provoked by an absence? God provokes the forces of evil, and attacking the One, the True, and the Good can bring out the darker side of the assailants, poisoning honest doubters and turning atheists into anti-theists. A person who is confident of his case does not need to be abusive, should try to answer objections, does not need to portray his opponents in the worst light always and in every circumstance.

It is an intriguing question why so many in the Western world today are unable to believe, especially those culturally attached to Christianity and Judaism. For me the issue is too important for polemics and self-indulgence. I will continue to believe in the one true God of love, because like André Malraux I maintain that "no atheist can explain the smile of a child."

Against this the tsunami also reminds us brutally of the problem of innocent suffering. But such suffering is worse if there is no afterlife to balance the scales of misfortune and injustice, and worse again if there is no innocence or guilt, no good or evil, if everything has the moral significance of froth on a wave.

Without God we are nothing.

October 4, 2009
Festival of Dangerous Ideas,
Sydney Opera House

THE MYSTERIOUS TRINITY

Deuteronomy 4:32–34, 39–40; Romans 8:14–17;
Matthew 28:16–20

T HE TRINITY is a difficult topic to preach on, and this difficulty has
to be contrasted with the fact that we hope and pray that we will
spend eternity contemplating the Trinity—the greatness and the goodness of God—and in fact will be happy beyond all our imagining in
doing that.

I like to ask the primary school children what God is made of. Sometimes I ask them whether God is a man or a woman, and with the grade
six confirmation class I always ask them to imagine a good friend of
their own age, who knows nothing at all about religion and asks them
what is God like. I started to do this regularly because I stumbled onto
the fact that when we came to talk about God, some of the kids at least
had no idea whatsoever what they might say, although they had many,
many other bits of religious knowledge.

When I ask them this question, they will often begin by saying that
God is good, kind, caring, and forgiving. Then they will often move
on to saying that God is invisible or God is a Spirit; sometimes they
might use the word ghost. I ask whether the good God is like Casper,
the friendly ghost, and they all know that this is not a very useful point
of comparison.

And eventually I explain that love, especially their parents' love,
which is real and powerful and invisible, is the best place to begin
to understand the essence of God, because love is spiritual. Love always needs an "other"—another person, or at least something different from the agent who is loving. Here we can begin to understand in
some small way why God is Trinitarian: Father, Son, and Holy Spirit.

God is a great mystery of love beyond our imagining. If we can reduce God to our understanding, if we think we have done that, we
have missed the bus. God is not only stranger than we imagine, but
God is stranger and more beautiful and more powerful than we can
ever imagine. The Father is the originator and the Creator; the Son
is the Redeemer; and the Spirit is the go-between God, the God who
is present in our hearts everywhere. We also know what God is like
from Christ Himself; from His living, from His dying, and from His
teaching. That is our best point of entry, our best insight into the nature of God.

We share the one true God with all those who are monotheists,
especially the Jews and the Muslims who explicitly worship the one
true God. Obviously, they do not speak of the Trinity. Each race or
tribe or language group does not have its own God. God is not like a
patron saint or a football mascot. There is only one God. Very early
on, even the Jews were tempted to think of a whole pantheon of gods,
with their God being the most powerful.

Is there any God who has looked after a chosen people like the Jews
the way our God has looked after us, they wondered? And eventually
they moved on beyond that to the deep conviction that there is only
one God and all the other gods are false.

We begin to understand God by using human points of comparison.
We cannot invent God, of course; we cannot shape God to our own
needs and desires; God is a given. Christian language about the Godhead: Father, Son, and Spirit, can never be abandoned by Christians.
This language does not say everything, it does not exhaust the mystery,
but, for example, it is not legitimate to replace father by mother or
son by daughter or spirit by matter. The traditional Christian language
gives us a unique insight into the nature of God. Other images are
helpful—Christ the Good Shepherd, Christ the King. It is even useful
to talk about the motherliness of God, but the terms that Christ gave
us are not negotiable.

It is very interesting, while believing in the equal dignity of men
and women before God, to try to work out why Jesus used the term
Father while speaking of the Spirit, of God—because God is neither
man nor woman; God is completely spiritual, not material. Why did
Jesus use the term father rather than mother or life force or something
like that? Certainly, Jesus wanted to emphasize that God is personal,

and I think he also wanted to emphasize that God is beyond nature and the source and the giver rather than a recipient. Significant consequences from the idea of fatherhood follow in the way we understand the relation of God to nature, the nature of the ministerial priesthood, and the relationship of God and the Church community.

God is perfect fatherliness—we shall never be deserted. A good father never abandons his children, especially when they are in trouble. This father loved us so much that He gave us a brother, His own Divine Son, and we know Him as Jesus Christ, that is, the anointed or the chrismed one, the Messiah. And God's love for us is shown particularly in Jesus' life and especially in His death on the Cross. It reveals to us that the love of God is a giving. It is self-sacrificing. It is not something that is possessive and taking and self-satisfying.

That is the most basic fact to be learned about God—that God loves us, especially when we are in trouble and when we are suffering. Remember the Beatitudes: Blessed are those who mourn, Blessed are those who weep. God is not half-hearted about us or distant from us, interested only in obedience.

The Jews knew that God loved them, and Jesus insisted upon it. Perhaps the greatest Christian poet of all, Dante Alighieri from Italy, wrote that beautiful line that God is "the love that moves the sun and all the other stars". So let us thank God for our faith. Let us pray that we will understand just a little bit more deeply the basic fact that God loves us.

June 18, 2000, Trinity Sunday
Saint Patrick's Cathedral, Melbourne

DIFFERENT CONCEPTS OF GOD

Deuteronomy 4:32–34, 39–40; Romans 8:14–17;
Matthew 28:16–20

M ANY PEOPLE TODAY, especially if they are not well informed on the topic, will claim that all religions are pretty much the same, with similar teachings. Usually they go on to claim that these religions are not particularly useful, and some of them even choose different teachings or practices that suit them from the different traditions. The so-called New Age religions are like this.

One important difference among religions follows from the presence or absence of a belief that there is only one God. God, or gods, are not absolutely essential to the nature of religion. The Buddha himself wrote nothing about God and was probably agnostic. We come into a special category, of course, as we are monotheists, while those who believe in many gods are polytheists. Most people in the ancient world, including those in ancient Greek and Rome, were polytheists, and many Hindus today believe in many gods, although some also believe in a supreme God.

In Moses' time, the Jews were surrounded by polytheists, and often a nation would have a preferred god to whom they showed allegiance, recognizing that other peoples followed a different god, just as we follow different national soccer teams today! This is the background for Moses' claims about Yahweh, the one true God revealed to the Jewish people. Such was the Jewish reverence for God that they never pronounced His name. In Hebrew, the vowels are not written, so that some mistakenly today call God "Jehovah" rather than "Yahweh".

Yahweh is God, explains Moses, "He and no other"; He is above heaven and earth, the Creator of man, who has spoken to the Jewish people in the burning bush. They heard this voice and remained alive, because they are the one people God has chosen as His own, the people whom He led out of slavery in Egypt with many signs and wonders.

We take it for granted that the one true God has given us laws and commandments, but the idea that God would be interested in our moral lives and in fact requires us to live in a certain way would have been a complete novelty to the ancient Greeks and Romans. Their gods were capricious and selfish themselves and never prescribed moral duties.

Implicit in the notion that God has told us how we should live is the possibility that this same God will judge our personal performance during life when we die. For some, this is a terrible burden, and some neopagans today reject this notion that we shall be judged at death and often also reject the notion that there are moral truths, knowable standards of right and wrong.

One contemporary intellectual, George Steiner, even claims that the real reason why Hitler and the Nazis hated the Jews so insanely and with such malevolence was because the Jews brought us the news there is only one God. There might be something in this, because the Nazi hatred of the Jews was diabolical and economically counterproductive, as well as being monstrously evil.

Muslims are strict monotheists, but some Muslims and some Christians deny we worship the same God. When I have been asked about this, I reply that as there is only one God; no monotheist has anything else to worship, but the problem can be posed in another way. Are the descriptions of God found in the Qur'an compatible with the descriptions of God found in our New Testament? There are important differences because the Muslims do not believe in the Trinity of Father, Son, and Spirit, whose feast we celebrate today. Nor do they accept Our Lord as divine, believing Him to be an important prophet only, who in fact did not really die on the Cross.

Another important difference is that there is nothing like the emphasis on love in the Qur'an as there is in the Christian Scriptures. There is no equivalent to the passage in Romans explaining that we are sons and daughters of God, not slaves and more than servants. We can call God "Abba"—better translated as "dad" than the more formal notion of the word "father". *We are children of God, in some real sense brothers and sisters of Christ, heirs to his glory in the next life just as we are called, at least sometimes, to share his sufferings in this life.*

These perspectives are so important, these teachings bring such life

changes to our living, that we can understand why Our Lord commanded His apostles to take this message and preach it through the
whole world, inviting everyone to be baptized in the name of the
Trinity: Father, Son, and Holy Spirit. Imagine how different our self-
understanding would be if there were no God to forgive our sins, or
if the one true God did not believe in forgiving sins but followed the
principle of "one strike and you are out"! For all serious adult Christians, life would be totally different.

The foundation of all our religious understanding comes from the
conviction that the one true God loves us, and this belief is so much
easier when we accept that by understanding Jesus and His teachings
we are shown God's heart at work, when He sent His only Son to
suffer and die so that we would be saved.

June 6, 2004, Trinity Sunday
Saint Mary's Cathedral, Sydney

IS GOD CHOOSY?

Jeremiah 31:31–34; Hebrews 5:7–9; John 12:20–33

FOR MANY YEARS it was not too much of an intellectual puzzle for me that God had made a special pact or covenant with the Jews, so that they became His people in a way no other people were. I knew of course of the English writer Hilaire Belloc's little verse "How odd of God to choose the Jews"; and I realized that it was odd, because the Jews did not have too much going for them culturally against the ancient Egyptian and Persian civilizations, whatever might be said about the Babylonians and the fierce Assyrians.

And I realized, too, that the Catholic Church was now the chosen people (or was it all Christians, or was it mainly Catholics and Orthodox?) and that the Jewish people retained something of their special position. But my pondering over the usefulness and justice of God's being choosy, of His choosing one people among many peoples for His own, was prompted by another set of changing attitudes.

When I started to work in parishes forty years ago, there existed a group who identified themselves to at least some others as "bad Catholics". They might have admitted this, for example, when talking to priests later in the evening at wedding receptions. I am not sure whether that mind-set survives any longer in Australia (despite the fact that the Mass-going rate is about one third of what it was fifty years ago). Today in Australia, many feel that they do not have to worship every Sunday, or believe all of the Creed or seriously attempt to follow all the commandments to be as good a Catholic as the pope. Some claim to be okay because they are "following their conscience".

Alongside the decline in discipline and religious knowledge, another group of Catholics concluded from the Church's support for ecumenism that one Christian Church was probably as good as another, while in another area there was a great weakening across many parts of the Western world of the enthusiasm for missionary expansion. Some religious missionary orders no longer felt it necessary to preach Christ, especially to those who belonged to the other great religious traditions such as Buddhism and Hinduism and devoted themselves to working for human development or to listening and silent witness. We all realized deeply that God loved everyone, just as we fell silent on hell and purgatory disappeared into limbo!

While I welcomed the Second Vatican Council teaching on ecumenism and on the importance of dialogue with other religious and with those of no religion, I realized that the extreme positions mentioned above were wrong and a betrayal of our tradition. The whole of the New Testament is united in its conviction about the importance of preaching Jesus Christ, the Messiah and Son of God, and equally united in the conviction that it is a partner in a new pact or covenant with God.

But if God loved everyone, why did He make a special covenant with the Jewish people first of all and now with His Church? Was this just? Should we still be working strenuously to encourage others to join through baptism? What obligations follow from membership, and how do the Scriptures approach these problems, if they grapple with them at all?

The beautiful first reading from Jeremiah is conscious of the ancient covenants and that there will be a new covenant when God's law will be written on the hearts of the covenant members, when all from the greatest to the least will know God and their sins will be forgiven. Both Old and New Testaments believe in God's election of His chosen people. I can only conclude that God realized in His love for us that if something was to happen, it was not useful to ask everyone but much better to call or appoint individuals and a group to begin and expand this work.

I think Saint Paul has written about these problems better than anyone. Paul believed that the Jews were the chosen people of the Creator, despite their sins and corruption and despite the fact that they had been victims of the Egyptians, Babylonians, Greeks, and Romans in turn. Paul believed that Israel was called for the sake of the world and was

God's answer to evil. In other words, the covenant was God's way of dealing with idolatry and sin. Through His people, God would deal with the problems affecting the whole of creation.

In the letter to the Hebrews, whose authorship is contested, we hear Saint Paul's explanation of the next stage in the covenant story. Through the death of Jesus the Messiah, the redefinition of God's people was effected, because through His death and Resurrection, Jesus rescued His people just as Moses had rescued the Jews. Christ Jesus in the flesh learned obedience and acquired perfection through His suffering, so that He became "the source of eternal salvation for all who obey him".

God's work is still done best by us, His chosen people, when we do as we should. And this includes the duty to preach the gospel to those near us as well as to the ends of the earth. Nor does this new covenant call us to political power, to smite our foes and oppress their descendants. In fact, we are called to be like the grain of wheat that must die to produce fruit, to remove ourselves as a top priority, to serve others rather than ourselves. God often writes straight with crooked lines, but it always remains a mighty privilege to be a member of God's chosen people, just as it remains an awesome responsibility as ministerial priests to preach Christ crucified and risen and to serve the people of God in the world.

April 2, 2006
Graduate House for Priests
North American College, Rome

4

Jesus Christ, Our Redeemer

JESUS CHRIST, OUR REDEEMER

Who Is Christ?

A T ONE STAGE Jesus asked his followers, "Who do people say the Son of Man is?" (Mt 16:13–16). Son of Man was the way Our Lord most frequently described Himself. Before Peter answered, the other disciples suggested Jesus was one of the Old Testament prophets or John the Baptist. Everyone genuinely seeking religious truth in Australia today has to ask the same question: "Who is Christ?" Those who refuse to pray can never find the answer.

Was Jesus a fraud? Frauds are not prepared to die for their deceits. Was Jesus neurotic and deranged, especially in His claims to a unique relationship with the one true God? But His teachings are full of wisdom and beauty, and His life was courageous, dignified, and sinless.

Was Jesus a holy, original Jewish thinker, whose activity and teachings the New Testament writers exaggerated and distorted? Some Christians today claim to be unconcerned about many of the facts of His life; all that matters is to believe in the "Christ event". This is a bit like being in Wonderland with Alice and holding on to the grin after the Cheshire cat has disappeared.

Believing in Jesus Christ means believing in the Church, because it was writers from the Church communities who wrote the Gospels and Epistles. We only know the Lord through those who knew and loved Him and treasured His memory. Jesus Himself wrote nothing. But when we believe in our friends, we trust what they say.

Believing in Jesus also means joining a long tradition, acquiring a sense of history, acknowledging the need for memory. A community without tradition is like an individual with amnesia. This is why so many worship at Christmas and Easter, why Australians, young and old, celebrate Anzac Day. Where there is no memory, there is no culture and no conscience. We cannot deny that the memories of Christ transmitted across the generations by our ancestors are strange. We have heard them many times.

Christians claim that their founder and leader was born of a virgin and had no human father. Apart from being a political refugee soon after birth, Jesus' life was poor, ordinary, and hidden, except for the last three years or so when He performed some spectacular miracles, started to gather a nucleus of followers, gave out sublime moral teachings and extreme and unusual spiritual claims about Himself and God His Father. His opponents organized His death to put a stop to His "blasphemous" nonsense.

Who is Christ? Important consequences follow from our answer. If Jesus is simply another religious genius, limited by the common understandings of His age and the enthusiasms of His followers, then His teachings can be improved by later generations and His life story only has exemplary value. If Jesus is something more; if as well as being born of Mary, He is also the only eternally begotten Son of God, "God from God, Light from Light, True God from True God", then His teachings have a unique authority and His life and death might have culminated in His Resurrection and Ascension into glory.

Who is Christ? The answer is not like reciting that two plus two equals four. The answer is more like saying: "Yes, I love you." Jesus does not only offer us something to think about. He says: "Come, follow me" (Mt 19:21), and He acknowledges that this is not cost free, not even at a cut price. "Take up your cross and follow me" (Mk 8:34). Have we the courage to renounce sin and the spirit of evil, the strength to accept the one true God on His terms? This is Christ's question.

Who is Christ? Can we take His strange and demanding teachings at face value? Can we believe Him when He claims "He who sees me, sees the Father" (Jn 12:45)? Today we find it easier to accept Jesus' central teaching that we should love one another, but why is the first and greatest commandment that we love an unseen God (Lk 10:27)? This can be a problem for those who find it difficult to believe. Christ needs to be divine for us to accept that even the greatest criminals can be forgiven, if they repent—even ethnic cleansers. So too, we need faith and hope to believe that our sins are forgiven, that our worth and goodness have been restored through the sacrament of penance and genuine personal sorrow, even when we sometimes continue to feel guilty and ashamed.

It is interesting that for many young people today, Jesus' teachings are more impressive than most of His miracles, many of which can now be performed by modern medicine and science. For those who are hurt, lonely, or have known little love, Jesus' promise that God loves us is a revelation. For all of us, it is the only foundation.

Most countries date their calendars from the year of His birth. Even some Christians do not realize this, and some are even striving to replace the description B.C. (before Christ) with B.C.E. "before the common era". This is a task better left to unbelievers.

Today, even in some Catholic schools, sincere young Catholics can feel isolated, fearing that showing their faith might separate them from their friends or see them branded as crazy or strange. *All of us, young and old, need to be assured that our deepest personal needs can be met by the riches of the Christian spiritual tradition.*

Popular youth culture is powerful and relentless. Advertisers sell their products by insinuating that young people today are the first generation in history able to think for themselves; that older believers were brainwashed, unaware of alternatives. The influence of parents, teachers, and priests, the traditional mentors, has been diminished by those who wish to access the buying power of the youth market. No generation in history has been the object of such relentless propaganda to buy and consume. Is advertising helping us to think clearly, to choose for ourselves? Or is the television-induced "majority opinion" simply artificial peer pressure created by the retail industry?

Life forces all of us to make decisions about practical issues, about work, budget, leisure, even marriage. But all who love young people encourage them to confront and ponder the deeper questions. What is life for? Do the beauties and patterns of creation point to a Creator God? Does that Creative Intelligence love us? Why do people suffer, even good people? Why does death come sometimes to the young, innocent, and unsuspecting? Why is there so much evil? Is there life after death? What is there to hope for?

The Catholic Church cannot force anyone to consider these questions, much less force anyone to answer in a particular way. Everyone, in his heart of hearts, answers for himself. The Church is not a dictatorship because she points to truths, any more than a doctor or scientist is when he explains how to avoid disease or lead a healthy life.

But Christians do make remarkable claims. Christians do present Someone with a set of answers and prescriptions, to be accepted or rejected or ignored. The Catholic Church offers Jesus Christ to be loved and followed and has done so for nearly two thousand years. Half the job is done if we choose to believe in Jesus. Jesus gives meaning to our life, provides a focus, and is a source of strength. Jesus is our way to God and God's love, because Jesus brings God down to our level.

When the pastor proudly announced "Jesus is the answer", a cynic scrawled underneath "But what is the question?"

Death and Resurrection

In other ages, good Christians have found it difficult to believe that Jesus was truly man. Because they believed so strongly in Jesus' Divinity, they were tempted to think of His humanity as only a mask. By and large this is not our problem today. Many agnostics have little trouble in ranking Jesus among the prophets or acknowledging His goodness and the attractiveness of much of His moral teaching.

On the other hand, even young adults from Catholic families can find it hard to confess with Saint Peter, "You are the Christ, the Son of the Living God" (Mt 16:17). It is Christ's Resurrection, not His death, which is hard for us. Yet this is essential and central to the Catholic tradition.

Ultimately, being a Christian is not a matter of feeling, although believing often brings peace and a sense of purpose. Saying Yes to Christ is an answer to a call, a decision to follow a way of life, a commitment to a set of beliefs, founded on a succession of facts and historical events and on the power of Christ's spirit.

Faith is not like a hall of mirrors. The Incarnation (that God became man), the redemption (that He saved us), and the Resurrection (that He rose from the dead) are not sophisticated myths, devised early on by clever and imaginative writers to inflate the experiences of the early Christians. For many centuries in Eastern European Christianity, Christians have greeted one another after Easter with the words

"Christ is risen." And the correct response is "He is risen indeed." These words cannot be both true and false. As Saint Paul wrote in one of the earliest New Testament writings "If Christ is not risen, then our preaching is empty, then our faith is in vain" (1 Cor 15:14).

Christians stand or fall on the claim that a young Galilean rose from the dead after a brutal crucifixion in Jerusalem about 1,970 years ago. *If we discovered Jesus' earthly remains, Christianity would be false*. It is this Christian faith which enables us to join in the Easter hymn: "The power of this holy night dispels all evil, washes guilt away, restores lost innocence, brings mourners joy; it casts out hatred, brings us peace and humbles earthly pride." These are large claims, and there have never been better reasons for hope; provided they are true.

Love's Two Challenges

Those who believe that Christ rose from the dead accept two challenges (among many): to battle against evil and to believe in reward and punishment after death. Both are central to Christ's teaching and life story.

The spirit of evil cannot be ignored or conjured away, as the history of the twentieth century demonstrates through the crimes of Stalin and Hitler, Mao Zedong and Pol Pot. In the Gospels, the spirit of evil has a fiercely personal existence, seeking new slaves, searching to corrupt and pervert. Each of us, too, must resist the glamour of sin, refuse to become desensitized to lies and depravity and badness. Long sinful journeys in pride can follow from small initial steps.

Christ told us that it is difficult for the rich to come into God's Kingdom (Mt 19:23), and many of us, as Australians, are rich in comparison with most others in history. Perhaps this is why a growing minority of Australians doubt whether there is life after death, whether the scales of justice are balanced in eternity through reward and punishment (while acknowledging that this does not always occur during this life). The afterlife is becoming a blind spot.

The dead are very silent. Some reject hell as an invention, a tool of fear and oppression. For others, it is simply not an issue. It is as though by refusing to consider these unpleasant possibilities, they are projected into nonexistence.

Jesus' vision of the Last Judgment, the final separation of the sheep from the goats, the givers from the self-centered (Mt 25:31-46), points to a different picture, where reward and punishment begin in this life, where we construct our own personal heaven or hell by accepting or rejecting God's call and grace.

Heaven is a gift from God, a state of being beyond our earning capacity, but we can only come to heaven with the abilities we develop in this life. Hell is not "truth seen too late", but truth clearly seen and clearly rejected. Hell is only for those who refuse to enter the heavenly kingdom of love. We get what we choose, with interest and forever, but only the evil, not the weak, reject Love.

Life is a continuum from conception to eternity. The community of the saints with us is real, and purgatory as a necessary prelude, a merciful state of preparation for entry into God's presence, is one important reason why we pray for the dead.

The Answer

Who is Christ? How is Christ our hope, now and forever? The Book of Revelation gives us the answers: that Jesus is the alpha and the omega, the beginning and the end, the Lord God who is, who was, and is to come; the faithful witness, the Firstborn from the dead, the Ruler of the Kings of the earth, who loves us and washed away our sins (Rev 1:4-8).

Early in the third millennium, this is the faith that sustained the first Christians. We say "Amen" to it in Christ Our Lord. This is our faith. This is the faith of the Church. We are proud to profess it.

Pentecost Pastoral Letter
Melbourne, 2000

AN UNLIKELY PLACE

Love is born with a dark and troubled face,
Love is born when hope is dead and in the most unlikely
*   place.*

T HESE LINES of Michael Leunig come from a cycle of nine poems,
Southern Star, set to music by the Jesuit composer Christopher
Wilcock and performed by the Saint Mary's Cathedral Voices as a
preparation for Christmas. Later during Mass, the dean of the cathedral, Father Neil Brown, mentioned in his sermon that one of the
young choristers had asked how love could be born if hope was dead.
He reported his honest reply that he was not quite sure what Leunig
was saying but would study the whole text and come back to them.

After the Mass, a young American tourist approached, telling Father
Brown that love can return when hope has gone. She had come to
the cathedral despondent, full of negative feelings, but surrounded by
prayerful people united in an act of worship, with good music and a
thoughtful sermon, her burdens lifted and love returned.

She felt liberated and wanted the dean to tell the choristers what had
happened to her. He duly did so and provoked a wonderful twenty-
minute discussion with them on the poet's view of Christmas.

See the peace of God upon his newborn skin
Glowing with the fragrances of milk and flowers
Put your arms around the paradise within,
Hold the miracle of love and all its powers.

After forty years of priesthood, I find most Christmases more beautiful than ever, although occasionally things might go wrong. Saint
Francis of Assisi's invention of the crib was an act of religious genius
still loved by children today, and I do not like even the best choirs
omitting the most favored carols, which congregations love to sing.
I do not want the traditional routine at Christmas changed much at

all, still preferring the roast turkey and plum pudding of my childhood for dinner, rather than seafood, which is better suited to the Australian summer.

As is apparent from this list of likes and dislikes, which stretches from the sublime to the almost ridiculous, Christmas can mean many different things to different people and even for the same person: folk festival, family gathering, a celebration of birth and motherhood, a religious feast calling for gratitude and worship. There are many ascending layers of symbolism.

Christians are generally not asked to explain the significance of the Melbourne Cup (although most Catholic schools still stop to watch) or Test cricket, but if they cannot or will not say what Christmas celebrates, they should not complain if Christmas is "secularized", if "season's greetings" prevail. Those who view Christmas simply as the best time for food, booze, and electronics miss out on a lot and always wake up after the hangover as empty as when they set out on the binge.

Christian sympathizers who admire Jesus Christ as a great teacher and exemplar, but balk at accepting His Divinity and perhaps at the constraints of His harder teachings, can still celebrate the mystery of motherhood, birth, and new life at Christmas; an easier celebration than when death and resurrection are the central events. For mainline Christians of faith, the feast implies more than all this. Both friends and foes can be distracted from Christianity's central platform: God is love.

Christmas proposes that God loves each of us and sent His Son, the Eternal Word, to live and die with us. An astonishing claim, which needs to be celebrated with prayer, music, and solemnity. It is no coincidence that most optimists are religious, while the pessimists do not rate religion highly.

> Go your way now,
> All shall be well.
> Leave the day now,
> All shall be well.
> Go into the darkness
> Where the spark is,
> Real and right and true. (Michael Leunig)

Christmas 2006
The Sydney Morning Herald

JESUS' FOSTER FATHER, JOSEPH

I N TRYING TO SPEAK to the general population, the challenge for priests, bishops, and ministers of the Christian religion generally is to direct attention away from the holly and the ivy and away from Father Christmas (who was originally Saint Nicholas, an ancient bishop in southwest Turkey whose true story is lost in the mists of history. Legend has it that he paid the dowries for three young women, which enabled them to marry and avoid a life of degradation). The task is to focus attention in another direction onto the Christ Child, His mother, and onto Christ's teachings.

For those who are already Christians and regular worshippers, whether they are weekly churchgoers or "C and E Catholics"—those who come only at Christmas and Easter—the challenge might be different. One of our tasks is to resist the temptation to place the whole Christmas story in the world of fantasy and mythology and view it as beautiful poetry without any historical foundation whatsoever. While we are not constrained to accept every detail of the Christmas stories literally, we are talking about a historical event. Mary and Jesus and Joseph were individuals from Jewish history of two thousand years ago.

It might help us to understand the feast of Christmas better if we follow the story of Joseph, Mary's husband, who was not the father of Jesus. Catholic belief follows the ancient Christian teaching that Jesus is divine as well as human and that God is His father.

Joseph was a common name among the Jews of Jesus' time, honoring the patriarch Joseph, son of Jacob, who was the reason the Jewish people migrated into Egypt about seventeen hundred years before Christ.

Mary's husband, Joseph, certainly traced his ancestry back to King David, although Matthew's Gospel lists his father as Jacob, while Luke calls the father Heli. Both texts validate the claim that Jesus was entitled to be called a "Son of David".

97

Joseph was probably born in Bethlehem or at least had some property there, so explaining why he traveled to Bethlehem for the census under Quirinius, the Roman governor of Syria. The Greek text of Matthew's Gospel describes Joseph as a *tekton*, which means literally a tradesman, a worker in stone, metal, or wood. Therefore the tradition is well founded that describes him as a carpenter.

Joseph became "betrothed" to Mary, something more than a modern engagement but less than a full marriage. It was a formal contract, and infidelity by a betrothed woman was regarded as adultery. After a betrothal of some months, the bride was usually then received into her husband's home and the marriage was consummated.

Joseph therefore had both a personal and religious problem when he realized during the betrothal period that Mary was pregnant through some other cause. He is also described in Matthew's Gospel as a "just man" (*dikaios*), a man who scrupulously followed the Jewish law, which forbade him to consummate marriage with an adulterous woman. The penalty for a woman guilty of adultery was stoning to death.

The theologians have debated Joseph's state of mind at this stage, but the most obvious conclusion is probably the correct one. He thought well of Mary, did not understand her pregnancy, and decided to divorce her quietly and informally to avoid publicity. It was then that the angel appeared to him, reassuring him about the conception through God's Spirit. He took Mary into his home, and they were together when she gave birth in Bethlehem to Jesus, her child.

We know the rest of the story, but Joseph reminds us that faith does not bring with it a full and clear understanding or mathematical certainty. Nor does following Christ guarantee that confusion and indignity are excluded. Doing God's will does not even guarantee us a happy ending in this life. That comes in the next life for those who love faithfully.

As always, Christmas takes us farther than an unreflective acceptance of appearances, calling us to a deeper reflection, so that we go beyond the Christmas wrappings to search for the gift inside. The birth of a child is always mysterious and wonderful, bringing out the best in all of us, even if that goodwill sometimes fades quickly. But it requires an honesty, a readiness to set aside our self-centeredness, our imperial egos, to accept that this newborn Jewish child was and is the Son of God. Joseph was present for the birth of his Redeemer.

This claim turns everything upside down. The world's fulcrum is not the financial centers of New York's Wall Street or London's City, but a cave in Bethlehem. The most important currency is not the dollar or the euro, but loving service.

The children of the great are born in grand palaces and generally suffer in hidden places. Jesus Christ was born in a cave in an obscure village called Bethlehem in a small, foreign-ruled state, but he suffered and died a humiliating public death in the capital city of Jerusalem. The world is not as it seems at first glance, and Christmas is a time for us to renew our sense of wonder. Not just wondering how the international captains of finance could have got it all so wrong, but wondering about the daily blessings we take for granted: friends, family, a decent society, and the one true God who lies hidden in all this ordinary life.

I wish everyone the peace of Christmas, especially those struggling with sickness, sadness, or the consequences of our financial woes.

Christmas 2008
Saint Mary's Cathedral, Sydney

THE EVERYDAY AND THE UNSEEN

Glad, that night, of the metalled clubs, when jackals
cried on the hills and the dog snarled, they waited,
shaggy under keffiyehs, the heavy cloaks
rucked high for the wind, nibbling at olives,
one of them tossing his pebbles, one of them flirting
at reed pipes, all of them stinking of sheep,
in the eyes of the law none of them worth a damn.

It was the messenger who broke the spell
banality had spun for them, his pinions
gleaming under the drizzle, eyes bright
with news and laughter, talking of the glory
come over them and himself, spieling away
about rescue, and making a king of a shepherd, and signs.
*   Even the dog for once recovered his temper.*

And then it was raining angels like cats and dogs,
every last one of them choiring of praise and of peace,
the shepherds gawping, a son et lumière
put on for nothing, the night aspill with music.
Heading downhill to the swaddled child in the feed-box,
giddy with melody, flarelight still in their heads,
man and boy they loped as if to a dance.

CHRISTMAS BRACKETS TOGETHER the two dimensions of creation; the everyday world that surrounds us and the unseen world of the spiritual, of persons and forces far beyond the surface of things. It is not an everyday event when God visits His people, comes and stays for a short lifetime.

The first reading from the Old Testament prophet Isaiah captures the truth beautifully: "a people that walked in darkness has seen a great light"; and then "a son is given to us and dominion is laid on his shoulders." But we have all, or most of us, heard this passage many times, and it washes over us.

So we need fresh ears and eyes to hear these ancient refrains; something that is often difficult to achieve. Or we go searching, those of us who have to preach every year, for a poet or a fine religious writer like Pope Benedict to express these sublime truths in different words and images that will provoke us to stop, pause, and ponder the wonderful news that God is with us, that God's son was once a newborn baby.

In some years I struggle more than in others to express freshly the important truths of the central Christian feasts, and 2009 was one such year. But last Sunday a good friend brought to my attention the beautiful poem I began with, written by Father Peter Steele, the Melbourne Jesuit priest and poet. Sometimes his poetry is difficult to understand, but especially when he writes on religious themes, it is not only beautiful but generally accessible.

Luke's Gospel recounts the familiar story of Mary giving birth in a manger in Bethlehem, followed by the terror of the shepherds as the glory of the Lord shone around them and they heard the news that a Savior had been born. Steele captures their excitement as well as the mixture of the sublime and ridiculous. Shepherds lived a hard life and enjoyed a dubious reputation as petty thieves and standover men for travelers. Steele fills out the picture.

One shepherd had a reed pipe, most had metal clubs, they all stank of sheep, and none of them was worth a damn religiously. Such were the people who received the news of salvation. No wonder "it was raining angels like cats and dogs" and "every last one of them [was] choiring of praise and peace." There is a message of hope here for every one of us that you do not have to be a philosopher, you do not have to belong to the middle class to be offered the truth of things.

God became man out of pity for His people when He saw the mess of sin and folly that is human history. In His wisdom, God decided that the best way to provoke a yearning for goodness and a surge of hope was to come as a helpless newborn baby. We acknowledge in awe the innocence of any newborn, and our awe redoubles before this manifestation of Godly innocence and vulnerability.

Many more people pray than those who come to worship at Mass every Sunday, and I must say in passing that Christ came not just to be admired once or twice a year, but to be followed in our daily lives and to be worshipped regularly. His birth is also a call to conversion, especially for those who do believe but have let the situation slip or have become too relaxed, even lazy, to do their duty. We are all called to follow.

But there probably are people who rarely pray at other times and do pray at Christmas. Prayers to the Christ Child are honest prayers, because Jesus the newborn reminds us that God is neither threatening nor boring.

During Lent we emphasize repentance, thanksgiving at Easter, and the search for wisdom at Pentecost. But at Christmas we pray for faith, and we bow low before Godly innocence. All this is good.

Let me conclude with the Gospel acclamation of Christmas Eve:

> Alleluia, alleluia!
> Come Radiant Dawn,
> Splendor of eternal light, sun of justice:
> Shine on those lost in the darkness of death.
> Alleluia.

We make this prayer through the same Christ Our Lord. Amen.

December 25, 2009
Saint Mary's Cathedral, Sydney

PALM SUNDAY

Isaiah 50:4–7; Philippians 2:6–11;
Matthew 26:14—27:66

H OLY WEEK HAS BEGUN once again with the celebrations for Palm Sunday, the blessing of the palms, the small procession, and the reading of the Passion account for the Gospel. It appeared to be a happy occasion for Our Lord. Certainly the crowd was delighted to welcome Him into Jerusalem. Jerusalem was not a big city by our standards, and the crowd of welcomers would have been even smaller. Not a grand final crowd, not like the number who attend each day at the Easter Show, but closer to the small enthusiastic crowds that greeted Princess Mary of Denmark during her recent visit.

Jesus Himself would have been preoccupied, because He knew that His opponents were gathering for the kill; He would have anticipated His likely fate. In a few days there would be the agony in the garden.

Some have claimed that this crowd of well-wishers would have contained many of the people who came to mock him later on the way to Calvary. I prefer to think, and it seems much more likely, that they would have been basically two different groups of people, with a smaller number of hangers-on, idle and curious, who were present on both occasions. I cannot believe that most of these enthusiasts were turncoats who abused Him some days later.

I suppose that Palm Sunday followed by Good Friday reminds us that we have no lasting city. No matter what our situation, good or bad, it is not likely to last forever. The Latin text runs "sic transit gloria mundi" —and so passes the glory of the world—which when translated into Australian runs as "rooster today, feather duster tomorrow". We have no lasting city.

You are invited to take your piece of palm home and place it on your crucifix. Every Catholic home should have a crucifix on the wall somewhere. Your house does not need to be like a Catholic school with a crucifix in every room, but if you have no sign of your Catholic faith anywhere in your home, then you should ask yourself why that is so. Our faith should not be entirely private, especially today where there are so many contrary forces.

We should not be too saddened by the hostile pressures that surround us. Christ's followers were a much smaller minority than we Catholics are today. We are saved by the Cross as an essential prelude to the Resurrection rather than by this happy procession. It would be strange to claim that this happy little procession redeemed us; but it is even stranger to claim that this inglorious death is the centerpiece of our redemption.

A final word: this is the most important week in the Church's year, containing Holy Thursday, Good Friday, and Easter Sunday. Whether we are busy, half-busy, or following a more relaxed schedule, we should not let this week slip by like every other week.

March 20, 2005, Palm Sunday
Saint Mary's Cathedral, Sydney

LIFT HIGH THE CROSS:
MARK'S PASSION

"For me, kind Jesus, was thy incarnation,
Thy mortal sorrow, and thy life's oblation;
Thy death of anguish and thy bitter passion,
For my salvation."

T HE CROSS is still one of the most powerful symbols in the Western world, even for people of little Christian or religious understanding. I have even wondered whether centuries of believing have seared the Cross into the subconscious of the majority of our population, who might be unsure what the Cross stands for exactly, but do understand that it is somehow a symbol of life's victory over death, a symbol of Transcendent Power.

In Australia, the sites of fatal accidents on the roads are often marked by simple crosses and flowers. Last year in Australia, we celebrated World Youth Day, a Catholic gathering, with Pope Benedict, which attracted 110,000 overseas pilgrims and an attendance of four hundred thousand at the final Mass. For twelve months beforehand, a plain wooden cross, five or so meters high, without any figure, journeyed all around Australia. Four hundred thousand young people came to pray and pay their respects. Many were deeply moved, even adolescent young men.

What were they celebrating or lamenting? I can never hear a reading of the Passion without being stirred and touched, and in this ancient chapel sanctified by centuries of student prayer, fervent or tepid, compulsory or voluntary, and accompanied by some of the finest examples of Western sacred music, including Gregorio Allegri's incomparable "Miserere", it is easier to understand that we are watching a specially sacred event, something much more important than another example of innocent suffering reenacted in another TV or radio account. To the students I say that as you get older, provided you worship regularly, you will also find that repetition does not make the story stale, but that you enter into the series of events more and more with every telling.

> For me, kind Jesus, was thy incarnation,
> Thy mortal sorrow, and thy life's oblation;
> Thy death of anguish and thy bitter passion,
> For my salvation.

What do these beautiful words mean? Why are we exhorted in to-day's final hymn to "lift high the cross, the love of Christ proclaim"? Let me try to spell out three constituent elements of the Passion narrative.

Christianity is basically about faith, hope, and love, and all three are needed to understand the triumph of the Cross. The Passion can only be believed in by those who pray, because faith in an unseen God of love by those who live in a world of sorrows can be difficult to attain and is easily lost. We need faith to accept that Jesus is not simply another good man who was an innocent victim, but is also God's only Son. As He shares our common fate of death and undergoes more than His share of suffering, we need faith to accept that this fellow human is the Son of God, the only Son of the omnipotent God. I can still recall a Muslim taxi driver saying to me that he could not believe in a crucified God who was so weak!

Despite the fact that the Scripture message is about the triumph of love and the persistence of hope, the mystery of evil is not banished from the scene. We cannot avoid choosing between good and evil, between faith and fear. Christ Our Lord not only brings out the best in people, but He also reveals the worst. Simeon had prophesied about the baby Jesus that He would lay bare the secret thoughts of many and that He was destined for the rising and falling of many. This worked out in surprising ways. During the Passion, Peter was full of bluster and bravado initially, but succumbed to human frailty and denied his Lord three times. At the house of Simon the leper, the woman with an alabaster jar of expensive ointment, often identified as a public sinner, defied the best religious opinion to anoint His head. Judas, probably among the most capable of the apostles, their treasurer, became so em-bittered and disillusioned that he betrayed his Master with a kiss, the traditional sign of friendship. Too proud or too ashamed to repent, he later committed suicide. The Cross reminds us that life is a struggle for meaning and against selfishness.

My final point is that the Passion and Resurrection, the triumph of the Cross, have ensured that our sins will always be forgiven if we repent and seek forgiveness. Christ balanced out the scales of justice, which had been weighed down by all the terrible crimes and sins of history. Many lifelong Christians take Godly forgiveness for granted, but this is a mistake. Those who do not know the one true God are unable to ask for God's forgiveness, and they are enormously disadvantaged in comparison with Christian sinners.

> For me, kind Jesus, was thy incarnation,
> Thy mortal sorrow, and thy life's oblation;
> Thy death of anguish and thy bitter passion,
> For my salvation.

March 8, 2009, Evensong
Merton College Chapel, Oxford University

WHY IS CHRIST'S DEATH GOOD?

W E CALL TODAY Good Friday, a strange title to commemorate that day long ago when the man we call "Lord and Savior" was executed by evil men. Other peoples use other but similar titles "Dear Friday" or "Holy Friday" (*Kar-Freitag, Vendredi Saint*), but they all express the same strange idea. We are used to the title "Good Friday", but the death of any young man at thirty-three years of age is sad; the killing of a good young man of that age is a double tragedy.

Everywhere in the Catholic world the death of Jesus is being remembered. In Asia and Africa, in Rome and in Peru, in Sydney and in New York, the same ritual is being followed. John's version of the Passion is read, and everyone, without exception, is invited to come forward to kiss the wooden cross, the instrument of our salvation; a practice that dates from the fourth century.

Good Friday is also peculiar for another reason. No Mass is celebrated. We have the paradoxical situation that Christ's atoning death, the once and for all redeeming sacrifice of the New Covenant is remembered without any Eucharist, without the true, sacramental reenactment of our atonement. As early as the third century, a great North African theologian, Tertullian, wrote: "It is not fitting that we should celebrate a feast on the day in which the bridegroom is taken from us."

Neither should we forget another essential dimension of this mysterious day. That innocent and sensitive young man who sweated blood in anticipation of His ordeal, who became too weak to carry His Cross by Himself, who asked in His death agony why His Father had abandoned Him, was the only Son of God. As the ancient Council of Constantinople in A.D. 553 defined it: "He who was crucified in the flesh, Our Lord Jesus Christ, is true God, Lord of glory, and one of the Holy Trinity."

Why was it necessary for God Himself to suffer in this way (Jesus is the Son of God, one of the Trinity as the Council explained)? Obviously we confront layers of meanings here that we cannot understand, but the many crimes, terrible crimes as well as personal sins, that abound in history had to be balanced out; not simply ignored or forgotten. And Jesus suffered and died so these terrible crimes and our sins could be forgiven.

No one can buy forgiveness, which is not like a patch placed over a tear in a garment. Reciting a formula cannot guarantee forgiveness. Only those who admit to sinning can be forgiven by God, and they have to regret that they sinned. And even this would be beyond our capacity without Jesus' redemptive gift from the Cross.

Everyone has a basic sense of right and wrong, an understanding that some actions are evil, unless the goodness in their hearts is squeezed out by repeated sins when they are old, or by cruelty and lack of love when they were young. A sinful action is one that lacks proper order, that violates the order of creation that derives from the Maker of heaven and earth. Some call this natural law, and the situation is further clarified by the Ten Commandments.

The divine order of creation is an order of love, the universal love of the two great commandments, love of God and love of neighbor, which is violated by sin. Sin always involves an action that is heading in the wrong direction, away from God, and usually against the proper rights of others. Sin is always an improper assertion of self.

When Christ was dying on the Cross, He said about his persecutors; "Father, forgive them, they know not what they do" (Lk 23:34). He was practicing what He had earlier preached when He taught: "But to you who hear I say, love your enemies, do good to those who hate you" (Lk 6:27).

Some crimes cannot be forgiven by any human beings, because no one remains with the right to forgive. Murder provides such an example because the victim is no more. But God always forgives the repentant, including repentant murderers. Many people today still find it hard to forgive themselves; harder to forgive themselves than to ask God for forgiveness. God can help them, too.

When Christ forgave those who killed Him, He showed us that forgiveness is available to everyone who repents, and the beautiful story of the good thief confirms this. We all know that Our Lord was crucified between two thieves, both probably members of a band of brigands,

violent robbers who preyed on travelers in particular and retreated to
the mountains for safety. One thief abused Jesus: "Are you not the
Christ? Save yourself and us as well." The good thief rebuked him,
saying they deserved the punishment they were receiving, but Jesus
had done nothing wrong.

Then we have the celebrated exchange between that honest man of
violence and our crucified Lord, two of the most beautiful lines in the
Scriptures: "Jesus, remember me when you come into your kingdom",
said the brigand. The Lord replied: "In truth I tell you, today you will
be with me in paradise."

Here we have one of the most important consequences of Good Friday. The warm hand of God is always extended in friendship to those
who repent. Forgiveness is always available, even to the most hardened
sinners. We thank the Son of God for this fruit of the Passion.

Good Friday 2009
Saint Mary's Cathedral, Sydney

THE LIGHT OF OUR REDEMPTION

A T THE CONCLUSION of the introductory Service of Light, which begins the Easter Vigil celebrations, where Christ is described as the light of the world, the Alpha and Omega, the beginning and end of all history and the unimaginable space of the cosmos, we prayed in these words: "May the Light of Christ, rising in glory, dispel the darkness of our hearts and minds."

I cannot imagine anyone of goodwill, whatever the strength or weakness of his faith, who would not make that prayer his own. Unless we are blinded by hate, pleased to have enclosed ourselves in darkness, we all want to see, to understand many things: how reality hangs together, what we are meant to do now, what we should do with our life, how we should cope with adversity great or small, and how we should prepare for the afterlife.

The whole of life is seen in a different light when we accept the teachings of Jesus the Nazarene, who suffered, died, and rose again nearly two thousand years ago. Our claim is that the light of the risen Christ does dispel darkness from human hearts and minds.

Everyone needs a modicum of goodwill, genuine if basic love, to recognize God, the beauties of His creation, and the account of the redemption. In Dante's classic poem "Paradiso" the heroine, Beatrice, explains that the knowledge of God "is buried from the eyes of everyone whose intellect has not matured within the flame of love". *Children who are not loved by their parents or other significant figures find it hard to understand God's love. Love is necessary for understanding.*

My task as a successor of the apostles is to bear witness to these ancient truths which we all have received from generations of teachers, guardians of the apostolic tradition. I make no claim to be a religious genius, no claim to be a prophet or a poet, no claim to be unveiling some fantastic new spiritual scheme. My message is not my own.

III

My role is more modest, and therefore I believe it is more credible: to announce to you what I have received from the Church, from the New Testament writings as they have been defended, deepened, and explained by the teaching authority of the Catholic Church.

Jesus was not just another wise teacher; not even a compassionate miracle worker who through His curing of the sick anticipated many of the wonders of modern medicine. He was more than a hero, who endured His particular and ugly fate with uncommon grace and dignity. He died and rose from the dead. The truth of His claims is vindicated by His Resurrection, and this triumph over death justifies our attention, our meditation on all His sufferings.

Jesus' Resurrection is the central fact in Catholic worship and prayer and the foundation of all Christian thinking. Neither is it simply a prodigious miracle, but the culminating event, short of Christ's ultimate return, in the framework of Judaeo-Christian history, which brought into being a new community of believers, the Church.

Most of the misunderstandings that tempt us today have appeared at some stage of Christian history. So we are not like the very early Docetists, or the Muslims of today, who do not believe that Jesus really died on the Cross. His suffering and death were real. Neither do we believe, like the Christians' first opponents, that Jesus' Resurrection was a myth put about by His early followers, so that His body always remained in the tomb to corrupt into dust, while it was only His memory, or perhaps His soul, that went marching on.

However, there is another vital dimension to our claims. We also believe and announce that Christ's death and Resurrection have redeemed us. The poet Edwin Muir put it beautifully:

> But famished field and blackened tree
> Bear flowers—in Eden never known.
> Blossoms of grief and charity
> Bloom in these darkened fields alone . . .
> Strange blessings—never in Paradise
> Fall from these beclouded skies.

Redemption is a strange notion. It is the further claim that all people of good heart and goodwill are saved by Jesus' suffering. Christians understand that redemption means that God will forgive our sins, no matter how terrible, if we repent, that all good or godly people will be rewarded in the next life, and that goodness will triumph finally over evil and suffering. In the meantime, not the end time, sin continues to abound, while wars, oppression, and family trauma remain constant.

Some early Christians were impatient for Jesus' return on the Last Day, when the redemption will be completed, but we have waited so long, this expectation has faded. Nonetheless, even in daily life we can find some hints of this final triumph of goodness, some small evidence of the mighty transformation that Christ will effect upon the entire cosmos. Let me give a few examples.

Many years ago I buried a teenager who died from a brain tumor. At his funeral, I mentioned the Christian teaching of redemptive suffering. A tragedy like this often places additional pressure on existing family tensions, but afterward, the father of the boy told me that while his marriage had always been good, the suffering and death of their son had brought the mother and father closer together.

The memory of the 2004 Boxing Day tsunami, with its hundreds of thousands of deaths, is still raw. But this catastrophe was followed by an outburst of generosity and compassion, unequaled in Australian history, toward the many victims of different religions and different races. I do not believe that even fifty years ago in Australia the generosity of so many people would have crossed such a double barrier.

I also ask you to pray for our pope, John Paul II, in his final illness. We have been told that he is joining his suffering to that of Christ, no doubt offering it up for the good of the Church. The Holy Father has let it be known that he has aligned himself to God's will, to whatever God has planned for him. We understand this.

The Christian approach to suffering, because of our belief in redemption, is very different from secular understandings, which are typically tempted to ignore suffering or hide it away as demeaning and pointless or bring it to an end by eliminating the sufferer. Much of this was behind those voices suggesting the pope should resign. A Catholic friend of mine answered this well. To such a suggestion he asked whether the speaker had ever had a parent who was old and sick. When he replied affirmatively, he asked, "Did you therefore ask your father to resign?" Of course he did not. I think it is a good point.

Such examples show good coming from suffering, small hints of the triumph of goodness and happiness when Christ will return in glory at the end of time, when there will be no more mourning or sadness.

Christ's Resurrection is the guarantee of love's triumph. The Easter message is that love is stronger; stronger than any hate, any evil, any suffering. To all those in difficulty, the Easter message is a consolation. To all those of us who are going well, Easter is a reminder to count our blessings and be grateful to the good God for them.

March 27, 2005, Easter Sunday
Saint Mary's Cathedral, Sydney

ONE FRUIT OF THE REDEMPTION:
EASTER SUNDAY

The man next to me speaks from time to time
He is thirsty
He cries out to his father in heaven
He asks mercy for those around him
Last night in the cells there were some who
said he might be a king
I find myself urged to speak to him
I say "Remember me when you come
into your kingdom"
In a clear voice he answers "You shall
be there before the sun goes down"
I am struck silent by this promise
His words take away my last fear
Before night falls I shall be far away from
this evil hill with its demons
I begin to feel like a bird about to be
released into a sky without ending

My strength is slowly leaving me. . . .

It is 3 o'clock and the sun has left the sky
Darkness is everywhere

Then suddenly I realise I am no longer nailed
to a dead tree
I have only to stretch out my hands
and they will be taken.

Neville Braybrook

I REGULARLY TELL primary school children, and especially the grade six candidates for confirmation, that Christ's promise of heaven to the good thief is the most consoling, among the most beautiful lines in the New Testament. I do not know how many of the youngsters will remember the claim. Many would be too innocent, some too irreligious, to know what I am talking about, but every adult can understand what I am saying.

The incident comes from chapter 17 in Luke's Gospel, which recounts the different attitudes of the two thieves crucified with Jesus. One remained embittered, hardened in sin until his end, and abusing Our Lord. Dismas, the good thief, rebuked the abuser, saying that they, unlike Jesus, deserved their punishment, but that Jesus had done no wrong. Then he asked to be remembered in Christ's Kingdom. By his own admission, the man was a serious criminal, probably violent, and yet he was the first fruit of the redemption, among the very first into paradise.

The Resurrection was the great sign that God does forgive our sins, that evil and death will not have the last word. Through the Resurrection, the Cross was transformed into a throne of mercy, and the first beneficiary was someone who had been a hardened evildoer before he turned. This should give great confidence to every one of us who is aware of his weakness.

The Resurrection was a subversive and explosive event, which Jesus' followers did not expect any more than his enemies. Through His death and Resurrection, Our Lord became the redemptive Lamb in the heavenly sanctuary. As an older translation of the Apocalypse expresses it graphically: "Worthy art thou to take the scroll and to open its seal, for thou wast slain and by thy blood didst ransom man for God from every tribe and tongue and people and nation."

The Christian claims about the Resurrection are not understated. The tomb was empty; Jesus appeared to many of His followers, embodied, eating, inviting Thomas to place his hand in His wounds. This is why the early Christians persevered through almost three hundred years of intermittent persecutions, why we talk today of death and evil being conquered in a world where evil and suffering are in some places only too apparent.

Another poet spelled out the challenge for us.

Let us not mock God with metaphor,
analogy, sidestepping, transcendence;
making of the event a parable, a sign painted
in the faded credulity of earlier ages;
Let us walk through the door. (John Updike)

Tonight there are many hundreds of people walking through the door in parishes across the archdiocese to be baptized and confirmed or to be received into full communion. We welcome them home with open arms and hearts; we wish them Godspeed and many happy grace-filled years among us. I believe that it is a sign of the vitality of our parishes, including the cathedral parish, and I thank all those who welcomed and prepared them.

God has always been with His people throughout history, even before He sent His only Son to redeem us. Let us pray that we will not continue like the disciples in the early part of their journey with Our Lord to Emmaus—that is, followers who know most of the facts but cannot make the necessary connections to grasp the full picture. May we understand more deeply the mysteries we are celebrating and be renewed by this feast of the Resurrection in mind and body so that we give wholehearted service in genuine faith, hope, and love.

April 16, 2006, Easter Sunday
Saint Mary's Cathedral, Sydney

REDEMPTION AND SUFFERING

O N ASH WEDNESDAY 2004, Mel Gibson's *The Passion of the Christ* premiered (for the first time, because of the dateline) in Sydney. It was attacked beforehand as anti-Semitic (often by those who had seen no preview); then for showing too much violence. And violent it was, at excruciating length, especially during the crucifixion. The cinema network tried to prevent distribution.

Some of the professed fear that it would be used by anti-Semites was genuine, but secularists feared that it would be effective Christian teaching (with all its imperfections, I believe it was), while Catholic radicals feared it would give a boost to traditional understandings of redemption, which they wish to destroy. For them, too, the redeeming Cross is an anachronism, an embarrassing reminder of what they have jettisoned. "Ave Crux, spes unica" (Hail the Cross, the only hope) is no longer a truth for them!

So a redemptive understanding of suffering is not only a radical point of difference between us and neopaganism, but it is a sore point of difference, very deep and important, in all the Christian communities and even our own Catholic Church. For pagans old and new, suffering is a brute fact, with no redemptive meaning. They cannot offer it up.

The English Catholic magazine *The Tablet* (March 27, 2004) did us all a service by listing a range of such views. There was a writer from *The National Catholic Reporter* in the United States: "*The Passion* over-individualizes the Christian message by portraying violence against Jesus himself as a central concern of Christian faith, separating this violence from violence in our own lives today." In this way, "we are kept from seeing the banality of his death as something suffered by thousands of other political prisoners in his day. For these reasons, *The Passion* cannot be called a Christian film."

More deeply, a Protestant theologian from Sydney asked a thought-provoking question: "How can a flogging literally equate to hundreds of thousands being vaporized in an atomic blast over a city? The relationship between these events is not of an outward 'like for like' kind." A priest theologian from Boston College claimed that the Resurrection, not the Cross, is the foundation of our faith and that "the film gives the wrong answer to the question: why God became man. It illustrates Anselm's atonement theory, which has held devotional meaning for a very long time but needs to be replaced."

Perhaps the worst of all was an Australian Catholic theologian at Oxford University. On the Passion and death of Jesus, he said: "There is no deep meaning to it; nothing to be gained from picturing it in our minds, or on the cinema screen. It is just the awful banality of evil, the utter predictability of the unfeeling cruelty human beings mete out to one another, and then justify by reason of statecraft or religion. And it still goes on today, and is still defended today, even by religious leaders, and by the leaders of the so-called 'free world'."

In some ways we have even moved beyond H. Richard Niebuhr's verdict in his 1937 book, *The Kingdom of God in America*,

A God without wrath
brought men without sin
into a kingdom without judgement
through the ministrations of
a Christ without a cross

because the United States remains one of the most religious in history; much more religious than Australia and most parts of Europe.

A recent work of Pope Benedict, *Truth and Tolerance*, explains something of this new concept where the renunciation of the claim to truth is seen as a fundamental condition for peace. The then-Cardinal Ratzinger quoted an Egyptologist, Jan Assmann, who claimed that Moses introduced the notion of truth into religion, rejecting false gods. Hitherto religions had been pure or impure, sacred or profane; people could have a number of religious enthusiasms! But Moses' destruction of the golden calf set an unfortunate precedent for monotheistic intolerance.

The "secular" task today is to return to ancient Egypt, to remove again the distinction between God and the world, a return to pantheism, a vague nature worship. With this reversion, there would be no more need for the notions of sin and redemption. Sin only came into the world with Moses, according to this theory. If there is no true and false religion, it is (almost) impossible to distinguish good from evil. "If there is no truth about man then he has no freedom, only the truth makes us free."

If there is no personal God, there is no possibility of judgment after death and therefore no need for Godly forgiveness, no possibility of reward or punishment. We know Karl Marx's claim that religion was the opium of the people, numbing them and taking them away from the class struggle for justice. In fact, the contemporary Polish poet Czesław Miłosz is closer to the mark; the opium of the people today is the mistaken belief they will not be judged after death by our good God.

Evil is real, evil is committed by persons. My group of pilgrims visited Auschwitz en route to Cologne; we saw again that evil is real and that the scales of justice often do not balance in this life. We need a just God to balance the scales in the next life, with the life, suffering, and death of His own Divine Son eliminating or balancing the sins of the saved. There are many dimensions to Christ's redeeming activity; indeed, a diversity of orthodox emphases as well as the radicals' rejection. But a Christian can only start from the scriptural evidence.

In Mark's Gospel it is made clear that the Son of Man came to give his life as a ransom for many (Mk 10:45). The Eucharistic words of institution (Mt 26:26–28; Mk 14:22–26) emphasize that Jesus' body is given and blood shed for the remission of our sins. And Saint Paul in his Letter to the Hebrews emphasizes that Christ is both priest and sacrifice, spilling His own blood and thus securing our eternal redemption (Heb 9:12). Peter speaks of Christ's suffering as an example for us to follow (1 Pet 2:19), while Paul in his Letter to the Colossians speaks of the cosmic and eternal consequences of Christ's death and Resurrection over principalities and powers (Col 1:16).

Many Christians today pass over Jesus' violent death quickly. In Australia, we have more at our Christmas Masses than at Easter. So, too, outsiders and even Catholics who believe in a one-dimensional, kind, and tolerant Jesus are disconcerted when reminded that Jesus was killed for His teaching and activities. They are uneasy about crucifixion Christianity.

But Jesus' suffering is a wonderful help to us in our suffering. Not only do we have his example, but we know that He, the Son of God, understands what great suffering is: God is not immune to human suffering. It is a consolation, too, to know that we can make up by our own suffering what is lacking in the suffering of Christ; that we can offer our sufferings, large or small, to Christ for a good purpose.

Redemption will stand us in good stead at the Last Judgment! Consider the promise of Our Lord to the good thief on his cross. Let me conclude with last three verses of the *Dies Irae, dies illa*:

> Prepare me a place among the sheep,
> and keep me from the goats,
> standing at your right hand.
> With the slanderers silenced,
> sentenced to piercing flames,
> call me with the blessed.
> Kneeling I plead,
> (my) contrite heart like ash:
> carry my trouble until the end.

August 17, 2005
Juventutem Vespers and Talk, World Youth Day
Düsseldorf, Germany

PREACHING CHRIST

BROTHERS AND SISTERS IN CHRIST, I want to begin with a few words of thanks: thanks for the contribution that the Neocatechumenal Way has made to the life of the Church throughout the world. I have already expressed my gratitude so many times for you, especially for your contribution here in Australia, with the priests, with the brothers and sisters, and especially the families in mission. We are very, very grateful for this.

You have passed through every part of Australia before this World Youth Day preaching the gospel of Jesus Christ. In almost all the dioceses of Australia, certainly in all the provinces, you have gone preaching in the streets the person and the teaching of our Brother and Redeemer, Jesus Christ.

Young people in Australia, so many of them, understand very little of religion. But, in many ways, I think that many of them are like Zacchaeus. They are rich enough, interested in the person of Jesus, and want to hear what we have to say about Jesus. And they will listen when we are preaching the gospel.

I visited a number of countries before this World Youth Day, inviting the young people to come to Australia, but I always said that one goes on pilgrimage to reinforce one's own faith. However, I told you to come to Australia to reinforce the faith and goodness of the young in Australia, especially the young Catholics of Australia. And you have done exactly that. A thousand, thousand thanks!

It is an interesting thing, but the Neocatechumenal Way has not made as spectacular progress among the English-speaking peoples as it has in other parts of the world. The ways of Providence are strange. But it is wonderful to see so many Australians from the Way among the forty thousand here this afternoon and in such good voice. Here in Australia, I think the tide is changing. I think our fellow Catholics are understanding that you are not people with two heads, that you are not a threat, but that you are truly people of the gospel, followers of Jesus Christ, trying to do His will in our somewhat difficult situation.

It is not the worst of times. It is not the best of times. But I believe that the finger of God is upon the Neocatechumenal Way, and I believe that the breath of the Spirit is blowing through you.

The ways of Providence are mysterious. I do not understand them, but I do know that the pressures against our Christian way of life are so strong that we need extra community strength—to strengthen one another and especially to pass on the treasures that we have received to the next generation—and in your communities we have that presence.

I want now to say a word or two about Zacchaeus. I think I would have liked Zacchaeus. Zacchaeus was rich, and he was probably unpopular—I think he was a tax collector or something like that. The people did not like him. But he had no fear. He wanted to see Jesus. Despite the fact that he was a rich man, he just went up the tree. He did not worry about his human dignity. He wanted to do something, and he did it. Now I think, as I have said earlier, that a lot of us are (or perhaps we like to think we are) something like Zacchaeus. If we have something to say, we usually say it. And if we want to do something, we are usually not too worried about our dignity. And Zacchaeus underwent a conversion and decided to follow Christ, and Christ came and stayed with him and lived with him, just as Christ and the Spirit have come and visited us here in this World Youth Day.

I also recall hearing one preacher adding to the Gospel story and suggesting that, when Zacchaeus went home, Mrs. Zacchaeus was furious because Zacchaeus had become converted and had promised to give fourfold money to all the people he had defrauded. I remember once a rich man was listening in my congregation when I said that. And he came to me later, smiling, and said "I am sure there is a lot of truth in that story."

And that is one of the things that has always convinced me that the people of the Neocatechumenal Way are gospel people—the regular contributions they make at different stages to help the poor and the very poor. And I thank God for that.

There are many ways to God within the Catholic Church. And all of us are united in proclaiming the love of the one good God for us all. This conviction that God loves each one of us is the foundation for all religious belief and all religious living.

Secondly, of course, we proclaim our brother Jesus Christ, who lived and died and rose for us to redeem us. And we are members in what is primarily and substantially the one Church of Christ united around the successor of Peter and the apostles.

I often say this: "Jesus did not say: 'There are five or six good and different holiday packages. It does not matter which one you choose.' He did not say that. Jesus said: 'I am the Way, the Truth, and the Life. Come, follow me. I bring the treasure, the pearl of great price and the treasure hidden in the field.'"

I just remind you that there is no organization in the world, other than the Catholic Church, that could have brought together so many beautiful and wonderful, good young people to a gathering like World Youth Day. I do not say that to make you proud or arrogant, but to remind you that we do have this precious truth which is knowledge of Jesus and the love of His Father—and also to remind you, in all humility, that of those to whom much is given much is required.

We know and understand that Jesus does not expect us to live just like people who never really heard or understood his mission. That is the reason for the theme of World Youth Day: "When the Holy Spirit comes upon you, you will receive power, and you will be my witness to the ends of the earth."

Many people from other countries say that we in Australia are at the end of the earth. When even Cardinal Ratzinger said that to an Australian bishop, Archbishop Eric D'Arcy, who had been a professional philosopher, D'Arcy replied: "Your Eminence, it depends where you start from." And Cardinal Ratzinger said: "We do not want that type of relativism here!"

No matter where the ends of the earth might be found, I pray that with the power of the Spirit, through the power of the Spirit, all of you will in fact be true witnesses to God's love everywhere and especially to the ends of the earth.

July 21, 2008
Meeting for young people
of the Neocatechumenal Way
The Domain, Sydney

TRIUMPH OF THE CROSS
AND THE BEAUTY OF FLOWERS

Numbers 21:4–9; Philippians 2:6–11; John 3:13–17

C OMMON SENSE, defined as good practical judgment in everyday affairs or the general feeling of the community, changes over time.
Common sense in Australia has been influenced by our geography and
history, including many centuries of Christian teaching. Australians
who support a "fair go" for all are an example of this.

But Christian and secular versions of common sense differ on some
points, such as the importance of forgiveness and the potential value
of suffering. Secularists, who share many decent convictions with us,
would never celebrate a feast such as the Triumph of the Cross. The
death of a good man on a cross (the form of punishment used for slaves
and prohibited for Roman citizens) at the hands of evil opponents was
a tragedy. Any God who took on the condition of a slave, emptying
Himself of His Divinity and accepting such a disgraceful death, was
going against the canons of common sense.

By another coincidence, this feast occurs during the flower festival,
celebrating the beauty of God's creation. How do we reconcile this
light and darkness, blessing and curse, Christmas and Easter, health,
decay, and death and their aftermaths—oblivion, regeneration, or resurrection? The short answer is found in the life and teachings of Jesus
Christ, Son of God and Mary's son, who lived, suffered, died, and rose
again to give us life. The Cross gives eternal life. The Cross is not an
end in itself. Christians are not masochists, who enjoy suffering. The
Cross and all forms of Christian penance are means to life and goodness. Christians are extreme optimists because we believe in heaven.

Jesus was not a fatalist, who accepted illness and misfortune as God's
will. He battled against illness and suffering. He cured the sick, dumb,

blind, and lame and urged us to help all those in any type of misfortune. And always over two thousand years, good Christians have battled against evil and sickness.

Jesus was not self-centered, proud, or arrogant. His aim was service, not domination, the genuine humility of a genuine helper. Virtue is beautiful. *Vice is deforming, but evil can be fascinating. While there can be no demonic truth or goodness, there is demonic beauty, beguiling us to evil ends.* When we recognize this, it is quite clear that Our Lord understood the beauty of nature as a blessing, a Godly gift. Solomon in all his glory was not clothed like the lilies of the field, which neither toil nor spin (Mt 6:28–9).

Love and flowers are both gifts from God. Love reflects God's very essence; *flowers are the work of His creative will, and their beauty has its origin in God's perfect beauty.* It is therefore most appropriate for a cathedral dedicated to worshipping the one true God to celebrate the arrival of spring with this Festival of Flowers, lovingly arranged. In doing so we celebrate the gift of life, the wisdom and Providence of God, and we express our thanks to our Creator. Even those who are unbelievers, or simply unsure about God, are still touched by the beauty of nature, and indeed many people in countless generations have been led toward God by contemplating these beauties.

The Bible tells us that the human race was born in a paradise, Adam and Eve in the Garden of Eden. The gardener there was God Himself, and the garden had in it everything that we needed: little wonder that ever since we were expelled for breaking the rules of conduct, humanity has longed to return to that garden. That longing for paradise is reflected in our delight in the beauty of plants, their flowers and fruit, their comforting shelter, their strength and their usefulness.

Because we no longer live in a paradise garden, we have had to learn how to select and sow, fertilize and water, weed, cultivate, and prune. We construct gardens for food, gardens to walk in, beautifully patterned gardens to admire. Such gardens and their cultivators provide nourishment for body and mind, and they should awaken in us deeper, spiritual feelings. Little wonder that herb gardens and kitchen gardens and flower gardens have long been important features of convents and monasteries. I suspect it would be difficult for someone who is a serious gardener to be a bad person, because he is too much in tune with what is good in nature, producing and nurturing life and beauty.

Gardeners also realize that skill and hard work are necessary to produce regularly beautiful flowers in beautiful gardens. Even in this wonderful, fertile area around Sydney, so untypical of most of Australia, we are not in the Garden of Eden. Roses still have thorns. Sweat on the brow is still required.

Nature can be cruel and relentless in droughts, bushfires, earthquakes, volcanoes, or typhoons. Nature, too, needs to be redeemed. Nature is beautiful, but human beauty is of a higher, purer order than any flower, higher than anything in the lower orders of nature. And the highest human beauty, purifying the agent, is found in sacrifice for great and good causes. Only the Christ who suffered, died, and then rose was able to open the gates to eternal happiness in paradise. That is what we mean by the Triumph of the Cross.

September 14, 2003
Saint Mary's Cathedral, Sydney

CORPUS CHRISTI

Exodus 24:3–8; Hebrews 9:11–15;
Mark 14:12–16, 22–26

NATURALLY WE SHARE the feasts of Easter and Pentecost with all other Christians, and generally, now that all followers of Christ celebrate the feast of Christmas, we also share the birth of the Christ Child. Extreme Protestants such as Cromwell in seventeenth-century England, after dethroning and then executing King Charles I, abolished the public celebration of Christmas. Naturally the abolition did not last beyond the return to power of the Stuart kings. Until recently, however, Scotland had no public holiday on Christmas Day.

Today's feast of Corpus Christi, Latin words meaning the Body of Christ, is not celebrated in the other Christian traditions. It is a specifically Catholic feast that grew up in Belgium in the thirteenth century and spread later throughout the Catholic world. The custom of celebrating the feast with a public procession through the streets or countryside began in Germany in the fourteenth century and is now one of the best-known examples of Catholic popular piety.

The feast stresses the extraordinary fact that through the priestly words of consecration, the bread and wine become the Body and Blood of Christ, despite the fact that the appearances of bread and wine remain. The Church has solemnly declared, for example at the sixteenth century Council of Trent, that Our Lord meant literally what He said for the first time at the Last Supper on the night before He was killed on the Cross: "This is my Body. This is my Blood." We are not merely talking about symbols.

All the Christians of the Orthodox traditions, such as the Greeks and the Russians, believe in the Real Presence of Christ in the consecrated species. By a strange irony, it is especially Evangelical Protestants, who are often tempted to fundamentalism—accepting the literal meaning of Scripture passages—who are the keenest to deny the literal meaning of Jesus' words at the Last Supper. It is useful to remember that differences over the nature of Holy Communion (a real or merely symbolic presence) and the sacrificial nature of the Mass were among the fundamental differences during the Protestant revolt, or Reformation, against the Catholic Church, started by Luther in the sixteenth century.

Many of the Old Testament rituals as well as Old Testament teaching prepare us for Christ and the New Testament. One of the constant refrains in the Scriptures is that God expects the partners He has chosen for His covenant, for a unique relationship, to keep His commandments, follow His instructions. This sacred moment with the twelve tribes of Israel when Moses told them of these commandments was consecrated by the slaughter and burning of bullocks, with half of their blood being poured upon the altar. It was the blood offered to God that symbolized the covenant, or pact, He had made with the Jewish people.

In many other cultures there were somewhat similar offerings made to particular gods. Jesus' unique sacrifice goes infinitely beyond these pale anticipations. The author of the Letter to the Hebrews explained that Our Lord's suffering, death, and Resurrection had replaced the slaughtered animals, giving us a perfect and all-sufficient sacrifice. This is what we make present in the celebration of the Eucharist, first celebrated on Holy Thursday night, when Jesus left us His Body to eat and Blood to drink. His blood became the Blood of the New Covenant.

Bread and wine are food, and the fundamental significance of the Eucharist is that the Sacred Species are to be eaten. It is the Mass that is the source and summit of Catholic life, and adoration of the Eucharist at Benediction or in a procession through the streets is a subordinate celebration, an event that springs from the Mass and brings us back to the Mass. That is how we celebrate the fact that Christ has redeemed us and chosen us as His special people with our own set of particular duties. Catholics are not expected to conduct their lives just like everyone else, especially those with little knowledge of God and no Christian formation.

The feast of Corpus Christi therefore is a celebration of Christ's triumph, His victory over both evil and death. In a 1981 article, the then-Cardinal Ratzinger compared the Corpus Christi procession to the official visit of a head of state, who is often taken through the streets so that the local population can pay him due honor. He also noted then that the Council of Trent, defending this custom, cited the practice of the ancient Romans in giving victorious generals a triumphal procession, especially through the streets of Rome to the forum and the Capitoline Hill.

Joy, the cardinal explained, is the basis of every feast, and Corpus Christi claims that Christ has made genuine joy possible through His demonstration that love is stronger than evil and death. We receive Christ by giving Him the public reception and recognition that is His due.

About 450 years ago, the Council of Trent claimed that in the face of the magnificence and joy of the Church at Corpus Christi "the enemies of the truth will either fade away or, stricken with shame, attain to insight." This was a bit optimistic, short of the Parousia.

But love is stronger than death; in Christ Jesus, God is among us. The Corpus Christi procession is a symbolic expression of our claims that genuine Christianity always acts in society like yeast in a loaf of bread, like a beneficent ferment, like an electrical power station pumping out faith, love, and especially hope to the wider community.

This is the meaning of the Corpus Christi procession.

June 14, 2009
Saint Mary's Cathedral, Sydney

5

The Body of Christ

Prayer and the Eucharist

THE EUCHARIST:
HEART OF OUR FAITH

S INCE EASTER, the Catholic Church has received unusual press coverage, unusual in its volume and in its tone. The death and funeral of Pope John Paul II and the election of Pope Benedict XVI were celebrated by two Masses in Saint Peter's Square, Rome. The funeral brought mixed emotions; sadness at the death of a great pope, relief that his suffering was ended, hope because of our belief in life after death. Pope Benedict's inaugural Mass was a joyful occasion.

Saint Peter's Square provided a grand setting. There were hundreds of thousands of worshippers, many national leaders, and representatives of other Christian churches; but at the center of it all was the same simple rite of the Mass, the same celebration of the Eucharist that we have in our parish churches.

What Is the Mass?

The Eucharist is the heart of our faith. It is an act of worship, of prayer to the one true God through Jesus Christ, His Son. It is a memorial of the death and Resurrection of Jesus, a sacrament of love, a sign of worldwide unity, a bond of charity, and an anticipation of eternal life.

Outsiders, those without Christian faith, can admire this ancient ritual, but only those who believe can understand fully and be said to participate. We will always be disappointed if we think of the Mass as a concert or performance, where we regularly need a fresh angle or a new act. The Mass draws its strength from tradition, repetition, and familiarity.

Today it can be difficult, especially for young people, busy with study, sport, work, family, and friends, to believe in the reality of an unseen

God worthy of our worship; or even to believe that love is of first importance, that it will prevail over evil and suffering. These pressures can distort our understanding of the Eucharist and our willingness to give it proper time.

Peer pressure against Christian faith can sometimes seem relentless, urging us that God is too distant, that Christian teachings are too demanding, too old fashioned. To give in to these pressures is a mistake. So, too, it is a mistake to believe that by abandoning Christ or redefining sinfulness, we escape from feeling guilty.

A person who feels no guilt or shame is not fully human but a psychopath. We all make mistakes and should regret this. The only true escape from guilt is to repent of our sins, to believe through faith that God forgives us, and to begin again on the right path. In the Eucharist we rejoice in the availability of God's forgiveness, because we commemorate the liberation achieved by Christ's suffering and death on the Cross. Eucharist means to give thanks, especially for this.

Symbols and Reality

When Jesus Christ was conceived and born, the Son of God took on a human nature. God became more accessible to us, so that in Jesus we see God the Father.

God respects and loves the universe that He has created, especially man and woman, who are the centerpiece of this immense masterpiece. Material creation is not second-rate and certainly not sinful. Matter is good and important. Therefore it comes as no surprise that in all the sacraments Christ and the Church have decreed that symbols should be used. Water and oil are used at baptism and confirmation, while bread and wine are used at Mass and turned into the Body and Blood of Christ.

There is another deeper level to this symbolism when we eat the Body and Blood of Christ that the priest has consecrated. Many Jews left Jesus when He told them they would have to eat His Body and drink His Blood. They were scandalized (Jn 6:48–66). Similarly, today, even good Christians can be surprised to hear Catholic teaching that the bread and wine are not symbols but become the Body and Blood of Jesus Christ Our Lord. So we speak of the "real presence" of Jesus in the host.

We receive Jesus into our hearts at Communion spiritually and into our bodies as we consume the host. Women of faith have explained that after Communion they feel like Our Lady herself at the Annunciation, when Jesus was conceived and present in her body.

Backward and Forward

The origins of the Eucharistic prayers and actions derive of course from Jesus' Last Supper, celebrated with the apostles on the night before He died. This ritual in turn was rooted in Jewish customs from the Old Testament. The unleavened bread eaten each Passover feast commemorates the Jewish exodus from Egypt. We also remember the manna they received to sustain them in the desert. We recall, too, the priest Melchizedek, from the first book of the Bible, offering bread and wine (Gen 14:17–20).

But there would have been no point to the Last Supper on Holy Thursday without Jesus' death on Good Friday. We are not having another restrained and old-fashioned community celebration at the Eucharist. It is not a quaint party with unusual readings and, often, music. In faith we are celebrating the death of the Lord until He comes again. The Power of the universe has acted through His Son, the sacrificial Lamb of God who takes away the sins of the world. It is this gaining of salvation through Jesus' unique sacrifice that we commemorate in every Mass.

But we also look forward because Holy Communion is what Saint Ignatius of Antioch, who was martyred in the Colosseum in A.D. 107, called "the medicine of immortality". Holy Communion in particular, and all the sacraments, give us the spiritual energy or grace to enjoy happiness after death. In fact, the Eucharist is a foretaste of the heavenly banquet to come.

Because the Mass is such an important event, we need to work to participate properly. Mass is not an opportunity to relax and daydream, to let our minds wander wherever they might. We are called to participate with our hearts, minds, and bodies. Such participation must be internal and spiritual; it requires periods of silence and listening, but above all it requires prayer. A Mass is only a "good Mass" when it is prayerful.

The Eucharist and the World

There is always tension between good and evil, and, sometimes, there is open and even terrible conflict. We have only to look at the world around us, at the terrorism, the wars, the activities of drug rings, the waves of pornography.

From Old Testament times, marriage imagery has been used to describe the relationship between God and His chosen people. So, too, the New Testament speaks of Christ as the bridegroom and the whole Catholic community as His bride. We can accurately speak of Jesus facing death to save His bride, the Church, just as we speak of Christ as a warrior dedicated to defeating the power of evil. The Eucharist is a kind of celebration of this marriage and of this total giving unto death.

The Eucharist in particular should give us the strength and energy to take God's love into the world. But for this to be effective, every lover must be a fighter. We cannot follow Christ without a struggle, without fighting and battling to control and purify our selfish instincts. We are called to fight and battle against evil in its many forms. We know that evil will triumph if enough people do nothing.

Good parents will battle to protect their children. People will even give their lives for great causes, to defend their country. I do not think a Christian can say "I'm a lover, not a fighter." The Eucharist gives us energy for this essential struggle. It is no coincidence that Catholic people pray the Mass at important times: for marriages, deaths, at times of tragedy and times of challenge. There were many more people at Mass after September 11, 2001, and the Bali bombings.

Adoration

The last decade has seen a revival of the ancient medieval practice of prayer before the Blessed Sacrament. Increasing numbers of parishes now have a weekly period of such adoration. There is a hunger in our busy, distracted society for silence and contemplation, and an encouraging number of young people feel that the celebration of Benediction and quiet prayer meet this need. Such devotions enrich us personally and prepare us better for participation at Mass.

Attendance at Mass is not an optional extra for Catholics but part of the obligations we assume by being followers of Christ. If the Power of the universe is made available to us through the sacraments, and especially the Mass, we have to realize that going to Mass is not like visiting a distribution point for tea and biscuits. Participation requires a level of faith and understanding, a serious effort to repent of our sins so that we are in a worthy state, able to participate truly and honestly, rather than making a show. Those in serious unrepented sin should not receive Communion, although all are welcome at Mass to pray.

Talk about the Eucharist highlights the debt of the Catholic community toward their priests, and as archbishop I gratefully acknowledge the wonderful support the Catholic community gives to them, as I acknowledge the faith and fidelity of the priests themselves. I ask Catholics to continue to pray for their priests and to pray for more seminarians and priests. The Eucharist is the heart of our faith, and for the Eucharist to be celebrated we need more priests.

Pentecost Pastoral Letter for Youth,
Sydney, 2005

PRAYER: MAKE A STRAIGHT WAY
FOR THE LORD

Isaiah 61:1–2, 10–11; 1 Thessalonians 5:16–24;
John 1:6–8, 19–28

J OHN THE BAPTIST is back in today's Gospel from Saint John. He has
central casting during Advent, because he pointed the way to Christ
and called His followers to repent and believe. These are still the central demands for anyone today who wants to be judged a follower of
Christ.

In today's Gospel, with the theological terminology typical of Saint
John (somewhat different from the personal and local imagery used in
most of the other three Gospels), John the Baptist describes himself as
a witness to the Light. He was not the Light itself; neither was he the
Christ, the one who was anointed (and therefore the Messiah); nor
Elijah, nor the Prophet who was expected. In fact, he was not fit to
undo even the sandal strap of the One who was to come, who would
baptize with the Holy Spirit rather than mere water.

John the Baptist described himself as "a voice crying in the wilderness", urging everyone to "make a straight way for the Lord". What
are we called on to do, especially in Advent, to make a straight way
for the Lord? We are called to repent and believe. Regular repentance
of our sins as we go through life is essential, and the sacrament of
reconciliation, going to confession, is part of the best preparation for
Christmas.

As regards the other half of the challenge, the call to believe, faith
is not something we acquire once and for all, that we can put in our
pocket or list as one of our possessions and then retain without doing
anything about it. Even a possession like a house needs to be contin-
ually maintained and repaired, while a garden needs a lot of regular
work to keep it beautiful.

In some periods of history, I suspect it is easier to believe than in others, because of the changing pressures of elite or popular opinion. In Australia, the pressures for unbelief are probably waning, but in parts of western Europe, including England, unbelief is still very strong. At different stages in our lives, God can seem near, and at other times He can seem distant. After the untimely death of a loved one, perhaps with intense suffering, God can seem hidden, and we have to struggle through this darkness by continuing to pray.

We make straight the way of the Lord through regular prayer, because if we decide to continue in faith or if we want to believe, we need to pray and pray regularly. Every Sunday Mass-goer should pray every day, even if it is only an Our Father and a Hail Mary. Morning and night prayers are a good and easy habit to follow, and grace before family meals is also appropriate as well as easy and practical. Saint Paul urged the Thessalonians to pray constantly and give thanks to God for all their blessings.

Recently, an English Catholic writer, Paul Johnson, had a beautiful article on Advent prayer in the British magazine *The Spectator*. Advent, he explained, is a time for prayer, for the ascent of the mind to God. There are four elements to prayer: the praise of God, thanksgiving for His benefits, asking pardon for our sins, and of course praying for what we need. Like immature children, we can be always asking God for something and neglecting the other elements of prayer, especially saying thanks and praising God.

Over the ages, Christian writers have disputed what things we might properly pray for. One or two claimed we should only pray for spiritual things, but Our Lord Himself in the Our Father urged us to pray for our daily bread. How widely that might be interpreted is a matter of dispute. Saint Augustine put it nicely: "It is proper to pray for anything that may be lawfully desired."

Johnson then explained that he prayed for those who have died, fifteen persons in particular, and the welfare of the living, his current list containing thirty-two names. He knows it is not lawful to pray for the destruction of his enemies, though he longed to do that for four in particular! He also gave a marvelous example of how we should not pray, citing an ex-member of parliament, "a successful pill manufacturer" who allegedly prayed like this: "O Lord, Thou knowest that I have nine houses in the City of London and that I have lately purchased an estate in Essex. I beseech Thee to preserve the counties of Essex and

Middlesex from fires and earthquakes. And as I also have a mortgage in Hertfordshire, I beg Thee to have an eye of compassion on that county too, and for the rest of the counties Thou mayest deal with them as Thou art pleased."

As we examine our consciences, we should ask ourselves: Do we pray regularly? Do we attend Mass every Sunday? Are we improving or slipping in our prayer life? Do we pray more or less than we did in the past? Is our prayer stronger or weaker? Whatever our answers, prayer makes straight the way of the Lord, especially in Advent.

December 11, 2005
Third Sunday in Advent
Saint Mary's Cathedral, Sydney

AN EMBER DAY AND
POPE LEO THE GREAT

Today's is the Mass of the Saturday Ember Day after the feast of Pentecost. In the past, Ember Days were days of fasting and abstinence; four groups of three days, Wednesday, Friday, and Saturday after the great feasts of the Church year. They were common to the Western Church, and their origins are obscure, perhaps making sacred the celebrations of harvest, vintage, and seeding time. This is uncertain, but the practice spread from Rome. We have evidence of these Ember Days from the time of Pope Callistus (A.D. 220), and I was able to look up a couple of Pope Leo the Great's Ember Day sermons from around A.D. 450.

Leo the Great is something of a parallel figure to our present Holy Father, John Paul II. His was a time of barbarian invasions into the Roman Empire. In 452 Leo persuaded Attila the Hun to withdraw north from Rome, and in 455 he parleyed with the Vandal leader, Gaiseric, and while the pope could not dissuade him from taking Rome, the city was spared from fire, torture, and massacre. The parallel with our pope's central role in the collapse of European Communism, a modern form of barbarism, is quite striking.

Pope Leo the Great was also an important figure in the articulation of the Christian tradition, being a strong defender of the humanity of Christ. With Leo's consent, the Council of Chalcedon in 451 defined the doctrine that Jesus Christ was a single person, with both a divine nature and human nature.

Pope John Paul II heads a Catholic community much larger than Leo ever dreamed of, even though there was no split then between the Latin rite and Byzantine Christians; moreover, the challenges to the apostolic tradition today, in morals as well as in faith, are far more profound and menacing than the theological divisions in Leo's times.

141

I suspect that Pope Leo came from a moral stable similar to Malcolm Fraser's in that he would have agreed very readily that life is not meant to be easy.

His sermon certainly highlights a religious difference between now and then. Today, very few people fast for religious reasons; while many people will diet to maintain or improve their health. This is paralleled by the fact that many people spend a lot of time and money planning their retirements; it is a smaller number who spend equal time preparing to meet their God and give an account of themselves!

Very sensibly and accurately, Leo saw the Christian life as a struggle, a type of spiritual warfare between good and evil, not just in society generally, but as a struggle at the heart of every man and woman. He knew, as we know, that evil is more radical, more deeply rooted than we can imagine; evil has not merely produced unjust or sinful structures, evil has also touched and corrupted our hearts from birth. Original sin is not a myth, but a primary challenge; probably the easiest Christian teaching for a skeptic to accept. As the old pre-Vatican II atheist claimed, original sin was the only Christian teaching on faith he believed!

For Leo, prayer and fasting prepared us for this spiritual struggle. Fasting, he wrote, "is a healthy practice for the healing of soul and body". Even the great figures of the early Church, he claimed, "began the rudiments of Christian warfare with holy fasts". As they had to fight against spiritual wickedness, they put on the armor of abstinence so they could slay all incentives to vice. Although divine grace gives daily victory to His saints, "He does not remove the occasion for fighting" (sermon LXXVIII).

We now live in an age of great physical comfort and magnificent health care. We should not romanticize the past: they were tough people, who knew much more about sickness, death, and struggle than we do. While they had love in their hearts, they also had fire in their bellies. That is one reason why the faith has been handed down to us, why it has survived for so long.

As the readings of today remind us, some of them predating Christ from the Old Testament, we must realize deeply that God is with us. We are God's people, just as surely as the Jews were God's people and led by God when they escaped from Egypt into the Promised Land. God will care for us, just as surely as he preserved the three youths from the fiery furnace, just as surely as he helped the old men to dream and the youngsters to see visions—provided we remain, in faith and hope, the sons and daughters of God.

There has been some considerable media interest in this traditional Latin Mass. "What is its significance?" I have been asked. It is significant, of course, primarily because it is an act of Christian worship.

The Catholic Church has a history of nearly two thousand years; there are many different rites in the Catholic Church, the Latin rite to which we belong, Maronite, Melchite, Ukrainian, Syro-Malabar, with different expressions of worship, piety, organization, and Church law. There have usually been competing schools of theology in the past, as there are now, different schools of church music, and an impressive variety of personal styles and political viewpoints. In other words, there is an immense pluralism within the Church in many areas, and it is not too strange to celebrate again, as is done regularly in Melbourne, that form of the Mass which predominated for nearly fifteen hundred years in the Western Church.

But all this revolves around a central core of belief and practice, around Christ the Son of God, whose essential teaching has come down to us in the Catholic and apostolic tradition, spelled out for us, not merely in the great creeds, but in the early rules of faith, in the early baptismal formulae. This is a precious inheritance; it is not ours to improve or to prune. It is the source of faith and repentance, the source of everlasting renewal. To the extent that we depart from this central tradition of worship and conversion, that we damage or pollute this core, we are weakened and enfeebled. "Without me," says Christ, "you can do nothing."

We must remember this. The world that first produced Gregorian chant at the end of the sixth century is gone from us. So too is the world that witnessed the Tridentine reforms in the sixteenth century, the Catholic reforms, so long delayed, that saved the Church in the face of the Protestant breakaway; a breakaway only made possible by Catholic weakness and corruption and a worldly papacy, little interested in religion.

These worlds are gone, but the Christian mystery that inspired these great moments is still with us. Christ is still the unique source of religious vitality; the Catholic Church, gathered around the pope, the successor of Peter, the rockman on whom Christ built the Church, and the bishops, is still the core and axis of the Church of Christ, the focus of God's work in the world.

I cannot promise you a second spring. I can only promise you a hard slog. The external pressures on us will remain formidable. The Counter-Reformation discipline that applied in the Church from Trent until the 1950s is gravely weakened. Our situation is closer to the theological variety and turmoil that existed in the Middle Ages, while the external threats are a bit like the Gnostic crisis in the second and third centuries that nearly destroyed the Church; when a bewildering variety of movements, both puritan and laxist, deriving both from philosophy and the Eastern mystery religions, struggled to make the Christian message contemporary, to improve it, to make it appropriate for the times. Even then in the second and third centuries, the chattering classes thought Christianity old fashioned and irrelevant!

However, I can do two things. I can remind you once again who you are, and I can request that you work and pray for the maintenance of the apostolic tradition and for the increased vitality of the Catholic communion.

I hope and pray that this Mass strengthens you for this long struggle. The Tridentine Mass has many virtues; it is part of a noble tradition of worship. Through prayers, ritual, and music, it attempts very explicitly to convey the beauty of holiness, and especially through its decorum and dignity it helps to bring us to bow in worship before the invisible God, the All-Holy One.

Every Catholic Mass seeks to inspire among priest and people an appropriate "interior and spiritual participation in the Paschal Mystery of Jesus Christ", to bring us to a prayerful awareness of the mighty sacrifice made by the God-man when he redeemed us. The Tridentine Mass helped millions of men and women achieve this for nearly one and a half millennia. May it achieve as much for all of us.

June 13, 1992
The first pontifical High Mass in the Tridentine Rite
in Australia since the post-Vatican II liturgical changes
Saint Patrick's Cathedral, Melbourne

MUSIC IN THE CHURCH

Psalm 67:4−7, 10−11; Hebrews 12:18−19, 22−24

THE SCRIPTURE READINGS of the twenty-second Sunday of the Year (Cycle C) are not ideally suited for a celebration commemorating fifty years of worship and music from the cathedral choir. Certainly the psalm urges us to rejoice and sing to the Lord, to make music to his name, to exult in his presence. This is the task of us all this morning, just as it has been the task of our cathedral choir since the Vienna Mozart Boys Choir, under Doctor George Gruber, was stranded in Melbourne by the outbreak of World War II.

However, my preferred point of entry comes from the reading from the Epistle to the Hebrews. In the Mass we come before God Himself, the Supreme Judge, and Jesus, our brother, our mediator, and our Savior. In other words, we come to "nothing known to the senses; not a blazing fire, or a gloom turning to total darkness, or a storm; or trumpeting thunder or the great voice speaking which made everyone that heard it beg that no more should be said to them." We come to none of all this.

In the Mass, we come before the silent mystery of God, brought among us through the symbols of bread and wine. Through our prayer and song, we worship this one great God, and especially through the masterpieces of our Church music, we gain some hints of God's beauty and majesty, and sometimes we can hear God whispering to us of love or hope or lost innocence; sometimes calling us to repentance.

The struggle between faith and the music of the world has been very fruitful, but it has been a struggle, and the tension took on a new form after the Second Vatican Council. Indeed the place of music in worship, or even in a civilized society, has been debated since the origins of Western society.

The Greek Philosopher Plato banned most types of music from his ideal Republic. Aristotle was more tolerant, but even he banned "the orgiastic and pathetic" music of the Phrygians from education, only allowing it to adults for relaxation and the relief of tensions.

The early Christians therefore inherited a Puritan musical tradition from the Greeks, but also from the Jews and especially the Pharisees. They saw life as a struggle between the law and the gospel, between the spiritual ideal and the sensual. They placed music in this sensual and fallen world.

However, Christianity was a concrete faith rather than a philosophy, and singing, especially psalm singing, was an early tradition. However, it was something that had to be controlled and watched. Saint Jerome (ca. 420), who translated the Bible into the Latin vernacular, a notorious controversialist and ascetic (and probably the rudest man to be canonized), urged Church singers, especially the younger ones, to "sing to God with their hearts, not with their voices, not plastering neck and throat with ointments like stage-players, churning out theatrical tunes and songs in church".

The late-sixth-century pope Gregory the Great, who did much to promote church music (hence our "Gregorian chant"), was closer to the mark in my book when he banned all the higher clergy, deacons, priests, and bishops from any musical task except singing the Gospel. All the singing tasks were to be done by subdeacons or those in minor orders. Too much singing might distract the clergy from their proper work or make them proud.

The great Saint Augustine, who died in 430, was also suspicious of church music. He was a North African, and they were a bit like Queenslanders today, although Augustine, unlike many now and then, repented of his earlier sins! He was afraid of sinning grievously by being "moved more by the music than by the reality to which the singing refers" and would prefer "not to hear singing at all". However, when he remembers how he was reduced to tears, how "his frozen feeling for God began to thaw" when he heard the singing in Saint Ambrose's Cathedral in Milan at the time of his conversion, he does concede the value of church music by which "the soul that is still weak is encouraged to rise to the world of piety." Even Thomas Aquinas, more than eight hundred years after Augustine, still wrote of music summoning the minds of the weak to piety!

Music, of course, is like a Catholic school, because schools can help or hinder the development of faith, can coarsen or refine personal sensibilities. An exchange between Boswell and Doctor Johnson neatly captures this capacity of music to inspire good or ill. Boswell told Johnson that music made him want to weep or throw himself into the thick of the battle. "Sir," replied Johnson, "I should never hear music, if it made me such a fool."

It is no coincidence that some of our modern popular music is a regression, aesthetically and temporally; a crude enticement to lechery, seduction rather than purification, a search through primitive rhythms for escape, for an anesthetic. Many of us would also remember those terrible scenes in the film *Apocalypse Now* when the American helicopters flew into battle in Vietnam with "The Flight of the Valkyries" blazing from their amplifiers.

Our music has a different purpose, as it is an aid to worship. In the Eucharist, we do not have a community simply actualizing their highest powers. We are speaking with God. Therefore, the aim of liturgical music is to provoke prayer, not applause; it is for this reason that choirs are generally not too visible in churches.

We worship and glorify our God through our music, and those who listen, attentively and in faith, participate in this worship just as surely as the singers and musicians and celebrants.

Through this worship we ascend to God. Praise of God is a movement or path, so that our heart is purified and drawn away from what is opposed to God. Just as the heavens silently tell the glory of God, so our prayers and music become part of the cosmic proclamation of God our Father and Christ Our Lord and Savior. The most beautiful liturgical music at a Mass can never be simply entertainment or a cultural event. Such music is an invitation to bow down before the Transcendent God, to become aware of the sacred and the divine; ultimately to participate spiritually in the Easter mystery of Christ's death and Resurrection.

Therefore our celebration today is a celebration of religion as well as a celebration of cultural achievement. As Cardinal Ratzinger wrote recently about church music: "Next to the saints, the art which the Church has produced is the only real apologia for her history."

Therefore, we thank God for all these good things in the Cathedral of Melbourne. We note with particular pride the presence of Doctor

Percy Jones, priest and musician and choirmaster, who has contributed so much to the cultural and musical life of the Church in Melbourne and the English-speaking world.

We ask God's continual blessings on the choir and pray that it will continue to flourish and inspire us to prayer, weak men and women that we are, for many years to come.

September 3, 1989
Fiftieth Anniversary of Saint Patrick's
Cathedral Choir, Melbourne

Pope and Bishops

THE PAPACY

Matthew 16:13–19; 1 Peter 5:1–4

Gathered here in Rome as successors of the apostles, united in the worldwide college of bishops with and under the successor of Saint Peter, it is appropriate for us during this Mass to ponder the mystery of Peter in the Catholic scheme of things and the extraordinary history of the papacy over nearly two thousand years as a vital force for both the unity and the universalism of the Catholic Church.

We often take our universalism for granted, but it is a marvelous and providential attribute we should consider carefully and value. We are truly brothers, despite our many different national backgrounds. I studied here in Rome at the Collegio de Propaganda Fide, and sixty-three nationalities were represented among the students. Always during Australia's brief history we have been served by priests and religious from overseas and now by overseas missionary families. Many other Christian denominations are imprisoned in their local or national communities, but we transcend that, and the office of the pope enhances and enables this worldwide unity.

It is a consolation to me, and no doubt to you all, that the position of Peter as leader is so well established in the New Testament. The role of Peter is one essential element in God's plan for our communion.

Saint Peter plays an important role among Jesus' followers before and after the Resurrection. Originally called Simon, the son of Jonah, he was a married man and a fisherman from Bethsaida on the north bank of the Sea of Galilee. The brother of Andrew, he was among the first to be chosen by Our Lord and one of the inner circle of three with James and John. He is one who speaks for the Twelve; his family home was Jesus' base in Capernaum.

Loyal, impetuous, and outspoken, probably a born leader, his faults are also recorded vividly in the Scriptures. His celebrated denial that he knew Jesus during the Passion is nearly as infamous as Judas' betrayal. He objected strongly to the prospect of Jesus' suffering and dying. He was not at the foot of the Cross. His weakness and perseverance should encourage us.

It was Our Lord who renamed Simon as Peter, the man of rock, on whom he would build the Church that would never fail. Peter would share the solidity and stability of the one true God who is our fortress and our rock. Jesus also gave him the keys of the Kingdom of heaven and the power to permit and forbid, to acquit and condemn (Mt 16:18-9).

Just before the Passion, Luke describes Our Lord prophesying Peter's denial, telling him that "once you have recovered, you in your turn must strengthen your brothers" (Lk 22:31-32). At the conclusion of John's Gospel, we also have the beautiful scene by the Sea of Tiberias when the risen Jesus three times asks Peter whether he loves Him. Peter is upset by the repeated question, energetically protests his love, and is commanded to feed the Lord's lambs and His sheep (Jn 21:15-17), an instruction recalling Jesus' own parable of the good shepherd who lays down his life for his sheep (Jn 10:7-18).

It was Peter, in particular, who kept the followers of the Lord together in the aftermath of the Resurrection. He preached to the crowds after the coming of the Spirit at Pentecost and supervised the appointment of Matthias as the twelfth apostle, to replace Judas Iscariot, the traitor who had committed suicide. Even Saint Paul, in his clash with Saint Peter, acknowledged Peter's special role as a pillar of the Church and preacher to the circumcised (Gal 2:7-14).

Society in the first centuries of Christianity was not as geared to the future as we are. The advances of science and technology make us value what is modern and up-to-date and look forward to new developments. The ancient world looked more toward the past, reverencing the heroes of history, reverencing the myths of golden ages. Within the early Christian communities, especially while there was still uncertainty about the nature and limits of the New Testament (which books were inspired, what should be excluded and why?), the overwhelming preoccupation was to ensure that contemporary teaching was the same as the teaching of Christ and the apostles.

To ensure this continuing identity, Christians looked to the local community Churches founded by the apostles to guarantee their orthodoxy: Jerusalem, until it was destroyed, Antioch, Alexandria, and especially Rome, where the Church was founded by both Peter and Paul. For many centuries, Rome was not a great theological center. These were in the East, as we know from the rivalry between the two great schools of Alexandria and Antioch. But Rome always claimed the last word on questions of orthodoxy, and this preeminence was widely accepted. Parallel to this we had the development in Saint Irenaeus, an Easterner but bishop of Lyons in France, of the theory of the apostolic succession of bishops as the local guarantors of the genuine apostolic tradition.

As bishops, we are the vital centers of unity in our local communities, but we also have a vital role in preserving worldwide unity by our loyalty and obedience to the successor of Peter. The pallium that is given by the pope to the metropolitan archbishops is another reinforcement of this unity. Unity in Catholic terms does not mean uniformity, and undoubtedly the governance of souls, which Pope Gregory the Great described as the art of arts, is based not only on the Gospels but on the lessons from the history of the pagan Roman Empire.

Business executives are amazed that the Catholic Church's organization is so flat; that individual bishops basically answer to the pope, that they have such scope for individual decision making as there are no general managers for Europe or the United States or Southeast Asia. Within the constraints of orthodoxy, bishops under the pope have remarkable freedom to serve through governance. *The office of the papacy, strengthened by the Holy Spirit, is much more than the individual capacity of any one pope, no matter how saintly or capable he might be. It is also a mystery of faith; sometimes a sign of contradiction.*

The papacy was a principal point of division in the split with the Orthodox Churches in 1054 and when the Church of England and the Protestant communities broke away in the Reformation of the sixteenth century. Papal leadership has been exercised in different ways and has been accepted or resisted to different degrees by the local Churches. Opinions about the popes differ among us, too.

Some popes have been saints, most have been capable religious leaders; some were inept, a few were public sinners. But the office is more important than the person, and the office remains, no matter how deficient the officeholder. Today, each pope is called to be the public champion of the Catholic tradition and the best known symbol and protector of Church unity.

Opponents of the Church realize, often better than we do, the strengths of Church unity. Conquerors and tyrants feared and opposed the papacy. Napoleon imprisoned two popes, Pius VI and Pius VII, before he was defeated by the Quadruple Alliance in 1815. Hitler boasted at table that when he won the Second World War, he would destroy the papacy and set up a pope in each country. In every nation the Communists took over, they tried to set up a national Catholic Church and separate bishops, priests, and people from the pope.

Let us thank God for the immense pastoral, doctrinal, and spiritual strengths the institution of the papacy brings to our work as the servants and teachers of the Christian tradition. Let me conclude with a well-known and beautiful passage from Thomas Macaulay, the late-nineteenth-century British historian, not a Catholic, but the author of a wonderful testimony to the historical achievements of the popes.

> The proudest royal houses are but of yesterday, when compared with the line of the Supreme Pontiffs. That line we trace back in an unbroken series, from the pope who crowned Napoleon in the nineteenth century to the pope who crowned Pepin in the eighth; and far beyond the time of Pepin the august dynasty extends, till it is lost in the twilight of fable.
>
> [The Catholic Church] was great and respected before the Saxon had set foot on Britain, before the Frank had passed the Rhine, when Grecian eloquence still flourished at Antioch, when idols were still worshipped in the temple of Mecca. And she may still exist in undiminished vigor when some traveler from New Zealand shall, in the midst of a vast solitude, take his stand on a broken arch of London Bridge to sketch the ruins of Saint Paul's.

London Bridge has been sold, transported, and rebuilt in Arizona in the United States. But the rest of the quotation remains as true today as when it was written.

September 22, 2009
In-service course for newly consecrated bishops
Legionaries of Christ Seminary Chapel, Rome

SAINT IGNATIUS OF ANTIOCH

Philippians 3:17—4:1; John 12:24-26

PAUL TOLD THE PEOPLE of Philippi to be united in following his rule of life and to take as their model those who have already done this "and study them as you would study us". We therefore have good reason to look briefly at the strange Syrian whose feast day we celebrate, Bishop Ignatius of Antioch.

Probably born around A.D. 35, he died a martyr in Rome around 107, perhaps in the Colosseum. We know of his life only from his seven surviving letters—six to local churches such as Rome and Ephesus and one to Polycarp of Smyrna, another martyr. He was the second or third bishop of Antioch after Peter. We have five different surviving accounts of his martyrdom, none of them, alas, worth the paper they are written on. He is therefore a contemporary of the writers of the New Testament. Passionate and extreme, at least in his language, his letters are colorful pamphlets, urging the small Christian congregations to stand firm under persecution and to have nothing to do with the heretics.

He is reputed to have been a writer of hymns and the inventor of antiphonal music; the latter claim probably a pious and harmless exaggeration! He certainly uses many musical terms in his letters. His presbyters (priests)—a fine group these and "justly famous"—are attuned to the "bishops as strings to a harp"!

The levelers in every age have always found him disconcerting. Not only was he the first to speak of the "Catholic Church", but he had an alarmingly high theology of bishops and priests, who took the place, not of the apostles, but of God and His Son Jesus. One or two today are trying to date his letters a half century later, mainly because of his unedifying certainty about the role of the bishops as the "hub" of the community and the "immovable rock". The Church did not follow all his ecclesiological theory, which was one reason why his writings were not included in the New Testament body of writings.

Ignatius (once described by a former staff member of Corpus Christi College as the "real Ignatius" to distinguish him from Ignatius of Loyola, who founded the Jesuits and to whom this college owes so much) is one of the sons of thunder, a lineal descendent of Saint John, part of that scarlet thread of aggressive men and women who have curbed and directed their unruly instincts to do great things for the Kingdom of God. Paul was such a man. So were many others: Athanasius, Thomas Becket, Ignatius of Loyola, and giants of our own age like Mindszenty, Wyszynski, Slipyj, Romero, and Helder Camara. Ignatius urged his fellow martyr Polycarp to stand firm; not to give an inch, "firm as an anvil which is belted (by a hammer)". They were not pleasers of men but *"pleasers of God"*.

What might we learn from him today? First of all, Ignatius insisted that the clergy be men of the spirit; men for whom spiritual development was an imperative, not a rare luxury. They were to strive for every gift of grace. He described himself as "theophorus", a God-bearer, and all Christians were to be "Christ-bearers".

He well knew the text from today's Gospel, that the wheat grain has to die for there to be a harvest, and he incorporated this into his mystical view of Christ's suffering and his coming martyrdom: "I am God's wheat, ground by the teeth of wild beasts that I may become the pure bread of Christ; grant me nothing more than that I be poured out to God, while an altar is still ready."

We celebrate Ignatius' death and martyrdom because he followed the example of Jesus' death. Irreligious people find this shocking; irreligious people celebrate only birthdays. For us, a good death is birth to eternal life. This was why Ignatius, as he approached martyrdom, wrote that "the pains of birth are on me."

Christians are not wowsers or spoilsports. They cannot be anti-life, anti-beauty, anti-goodness. But it could be the particular vocation of Christians today to remind our society that growth, goodness, even happiness, only come at a price, even when we limit ourselves to this world—which Christians cannot. Paul Claudel, the French Catholic writer, once wrote that sacrifice is the crowning glory of the free man. Ignatius knew that. Many Aussies would not even understand what Claudel was talking about.

Secondly, Ignatius had a passionate attachment to the unity of the Church, a unity founded on Christ, rooted in eternity, with a cosmic, more than earthly dimension, despite the attacks of many heretics, those "who bear deadly fruit", those who mix their "deadly poison with honeyed wine". For the followers of Christ, there must be "one prayer, one petition, one mind, one hope in love in the spotless joy which is Jesus Christ". This unity is one of mutual love, of mutual service, where the variety of the Spirit's gifts are valued. There is a harmony, like a choir of many parts singing together.

Finally, Ignatius is a truly Catholic figure because he reminds us that in any genuinely Catholic Church there must be room for those who are not entirely respectable. This will have to remain true in Australia if the Church is to have any future at all!

Ignatius' zeal for martyrdom was excessive: "I long for the beasts that are prepared for me. . . . I will even entice them to devour me promptly." Listen to him describing his travels as a prisoner to Rome with the soldiers: "From Syria to Rome I am fighting with wild beasts, by land and sea, by night and day, bound to ten leopards [that is, a company of soldiers], and they become worse for kind treatment." There is nothing of Dale Carnegie in Ignatius; very little of the cautious and reluctant approach of Thomas More before martyrdom, which we understand so much more easily. I could not help thinking of my classmate Father Peter James, who was buried on Monday, as I prepared this sermon. I could not imagine Jamesie in any Australian Church except the Catholic Church. His errors of judgment like his virtues, his love and generosity, were of magnificent proportions. At his funeral, I wondered how long it was since the cathedral had seen such a mixed bag of people in the congregation; probably not since Mannix was in his heyday in the conscription struggles.

Ignatius and Peter James were one of a kind, although they certainly had different theories about bishops. Battle might have been joined already on the issue in the heavenly regions! Ignatius knew his people, cared passionately for them, served them at great personal cost and inconvenience. So did Peter James. They both loved Christ and the

Catholic community around Christ. They were great Catholics. They were far from perfect. Let us remember them, let us be inspired by them, as we follow at a distance!

October 17, 1986
Corpus Christi College,
Melbourne regional seminary
for Victoria and Tasmania

POPE SAINT GREGORY THE GREAT
ON THE ROLE OF BISHOPS

Luke 22:24−30; 2 Corinthians 4:1−2, 5−7;
Jeremiah 1:4−9

T HE ORDINATION OF A PRIEST is always a happy occasion. Years of
preparation and testing flower into the prospect of a lifetime of
service. The consecration of bishops produces different reasons for rejoicing. The friends and parishioners of the bishops-elect rejoice that
their years of hard work have been recognized. They pray that the
leadership of the Church is being entrusted to wise hands as the wheel
of apostolic succession turns slowly and inevitably into the future.

I welcome Fathers Julian Porteous and Anthony Fisher, O.P., into
the college of bishops, united around the successor of Saint Peter, Pope
John Paul II. They have both been at the head of life-giving institutions, the Good Shepherd Seminary and the John Paul II Institute for
Marriage and the Family. They are both Sydney men, baptized Catholic priests. Otherwise, there are significant differences. One, a priest
of the Sydney archdiocese, refused the chance of further study after
ordination to continue working in a parish and has been involved with
the New Communities that have sprung up unbidden in the Church
since Vatican Two. The other belongs to a medieval order of preachers,
who has devoted much of his life to study and teaching. In different
ways, they have both struggled for years to make God's light shine in
the darkness; have preached Jesus Christ, not themselves, in season and
out of season, and shown themselves to be slaves for Christ's sake, as
Paul recommended.

Six weeks ago, when their appointments by the Holy Father were
announced, there was a flurry of local press comment, unusual even by

157

contemporary standards for its misunderstandings and misrepresenta-
tion. One account announced them as new archbishops. Another account spoke of shock, worst nightmares, and an atmosphere of tyranny;
then worked up to a crescendo, where, almost breathless with dismay,
it was announced that one of the appointees was opposed to contraception, abortion, and euthanasia. Actually the situation is worse, because
both bishops-elect hold these positions. In fact, these truths express
official Catholic teaching, taught by all bishops in communion with
Rome and are not personal idiosyncrasies held only by Wahhabi Catholics.

We celebrate this ordination on the feast of Saint Gregory the Great,
Pope Gregory the First, who died in A.D. 604. From a rich senatorial
family of Rome, possibly even the grandson of Pope Felix III (the clergy
were then allowed to marry before ordination), Gregory entered the
civil service and became prefect of Rome. They were evil and disturbed
times. Even the center of the empire at Constantinople was embattled,
while Western Europe was regularly overrun by "barbarians" such as
the Lombards. At the death of his father, Gregory became a monk and
turned the family home into a monastery. At different times he was
one of the seven deacons of Rome and abbot of his monastery.

He then served as papal legate (*apocrisiarius*) at the Imperial Court in
Constantinople, before election to the See of Rome in 590. In 591 he
wrote his classic work on the duties of bishops, *Liber Regulae Pastoralis*.
His experiences entitled him to recommend that an officeholder should
have learned the required virtues, such as humility, before he assumes
office. I am not sure how often this is achieved.

The work itself was soon translated into Greek by Anastasius, the
Patriarch of Antioch. The Roman missionary Augustine whom Gregory sent to convert England, took it with him, and three hundred
years later, Alfred the Great, King of Wessex, who defeated the Danes,
had it paraphrased into West Saxon, sending a copy to each bishop
in his kingdom. In ninth-century France, Charlemagne, the first Holy
Roman Emperor, ordered that each bishop receive a copy during his
consecration ceremony.

Many images have been used over the years to bring together the
personal inadequacies of all bishops, on the one hand, and the high
sacramental dignity, the mightily important works of service bishops
must perform, on the other; to capture the competing imperatives in

the first reading from Jeremiah; the duty to be a prophet to the nations, speaking God's word, and the realization of personal inadequacy, inexperience, and lack of eloquence. In his memoir, *Milestones*, Cardinal Ratzinger quotes Saint Augustine meditating on Psalm 72 and comparing his work as a rural bishop in Hippo to that of a beast of burden, an ox. Cardinal Sin of Manila has often publicly compared himself to the donkey Our Lord rode on His entry into Jerusalem on Palm Sunday. Saint Gregory thought that God leaves rulers imperfect so they will not inflate their own importance or glory in their performances. He himself felt like a poor quality painter portraying a handsome man.

The bishop aspires to be a conduit, an open channel for the light and grace of the Son of God to flow through his works of sacrament, word, and service. He aims neither to distort nor to hinder this building up of the Body of Christ.

Many Australians think of the Catholic Church as a source of many things: nearly everything, in fact, except genuine religion, worship, prayer, and spiritual wisdom. For too many, their instinct is to look elsewhere, such as to New Age trickery or Asia for such qualities.

Gregory was disconcertingly blunt about the bishop's obligations. A man who is caught up in the darkness of everyday life and blind to the light of contemplation should not be a bishop. A person who is not in good standing with God can make the situation worse through his intercession, Gregory claimed.

The Second Vatican Council describes the first duty of the good shepherd, bishop and priest, as teaching the good news of Jesus Christ. Gregory understood that this is no easy task and listed the characteristics of forty different types of person who had to be reached in different ways. He was a splendid psychologist.

Our task in this age of change, technology, and advertising is to explain the apostolic tradition to an Australian society that yearns for the consolations of religion but is hesitant or hostile to restraint and sacrifice: to a society that still turns to the Church at times of tragedy and at Christmas but that is also partly tone-deaf to the call of the Spirit.

Bishops, priests, and teachers also have to compete against an influential minority that either denies God's existence or denies the need for God, if He happens to exist. With this cast of mind, there is no possibility of truth, much less of revelation; certainly no need for redemption. For them, all communities, and especially institutions, are reduced to exercises in power politics. Teaching is propaganda to protect the power brokers. The Church is not seen as a means to eternal life; the sacraments are not seen as worship of the Transcendent One, not seen as channels of spiritual energy for the worshippers, but as superstitions at best, or at worst as cynical and pretentious pageants.

None of this is entirely new, but there are contemporary particularities. Christian confidence has been weakened by the spread of irreligion, the decline of regular worship, and clerical scandals. Pope Gregory lived in a more confident Catholic age, despite its political turmoil. While he acknowledged that his listeners were like a harp that had to be played correctly (part 3 prologue), he also warned that the bishop would be assailed by a lust for pleasing people; by a desire to put a cushion under every elbow. This was as objectionable to him as excessively rigid censures.

Cardinal Avery Dulles put the contemporary question very well. "In the face of dissent, it might seem that the Magisterium should mute its voice. Does it not weaken its own authority when it teaches doctrines that many practicing Catholics will predictably reject?"

His reply is uncompromising and encouraging to bishops. The Magisterium "would forfeit all credibility if it taught only what people wanted to hear. The first and indispensable task is to bear witness to the deposit of faith."

Pope Gregory believed that "the government of souls is the art of arts." Is it not true that man's thoughts, sinful or mistaken, are more hidden than the sores in our bowels, he wrote. *He laments how often spiritually ignorant men profess to be physicians of the human heart.* The idiom is not ours, and the language is self-confidently hierarchical. But all in all, there is an important kernel of truth here. Even in the healthiest religious organization, leadership is not superfluous and incompetent leaders can cause damage more easily than good leaders can encourage growth.

Every leader, including the bishop, needs a clear set of beliefs; to know the direction in which he is heading. Without these, a bishop cannot inspire hope, encourage prayer, service, personal and community initiatives. In this way the young, especially, but also outsiders as well as regular parishioners will realize that the Church community is serious about its supernatural claims and hard at work. Community confidence and a sense of identity are essential foundations for enduring personal conversion; a necessary protection for the flame of faith. May our new bishops be leaders in this mold.

I ask you (and for once I feel this is a genuinely superfluous request) to pray for our new bishops, that they may be worthy successors of the apostles, true shepherds knowing and loving their priests and people, faithful stewards of those mysteries which carry us to judgment in eternity, and, above all, bishops who practice the lesson outlined in the Gospel text they have chosen tonight from Saint Luke: that Christ Our Lord came among us as one who serves, and we, all of us, are to do likewise.

September 3, 2003
Episcopal Consecration of Fathers Julian Porteous
and Anthony Fisher, O.P.
Saint Mary's Cathedral, Sydney

THE APOSTOLIC SUCCESSION

T HE JOINT FEAST of Saint Peter and Saint Paul has been celebrated in the city of Rome from at least the time of Constantine, the first Christian Emperor of the Roman Empire in the early fourth century. In the East, the feast was often celebrated on December 28, as evidence from Syria in the fifth century and Egypt in the sixth century demonstrates; but gradually, the date of the Roman commemoration took precedence.

We now take this apostolic partnership for granted; the apostle to the gentiles and the apostle to the circumcised; the greatest theologian of the New Testament (just nosing out Saint John for the honor) and the rock man on whom Christ promised to build His Church. Both traveled to Rome, the center of power and administration in a mighty Empire that endured in the West for four hundred years after their death and in the Christian East for another fourteen hundred years. Both were martyrs there in the sixties. Both made spectacular and public mistakes. Peter denied Christ three times, and Paul was a persecutor of Christians.

They represent different threads in the Christian tradition. Peter had been a Galilean fisherman, poorly educated. Paul was from Tarsus, a Pharisee of the Pharisees, a student of the famous rabbi Gamaliel, and a Roman citizen to boot. They were probably in different theological schools, as Peter would have lined up closer to James than to Paul, and they clashed publicly and deeply over the necessity (or otherwise) of circumcision for non-Jewish converts. Their unity in faith across these differences has important lessons for us.

One of the strangest aspects of Christianity is that Our Lord left no writings. We cannot even be sure that He could write, the only direct evidence being that He drew something in the sand when defending the woman accused of adultery. As the first generation of people who had contact with Our Lord aged and died, the New Testament Scriptures were written. But no written documents can completely answer changing contemporary problems, and who was to define what the Scriptures actually meant?

Especially in the second century, the Church was shaken and almost destroyed, not by the imperial persecutions, but by a vast and various movement, which we lump together under the label of Gnosticism, from the Greek term for knowledge. Like today's New Age movement, it had a bit of everything, in different ways, in different sects: philosophy and Eastern mystery religions, puritanism and promiscuity. The mood was for individualism and syncretism, and many of the Gnostic sects had secret traditions that were passed from master to chosen pupils, kept from the masses, from the unenlightened, those who did not know.

This was the second-century background that saw the rise of the doctrine of the apostolic tradition and the apostolic succession of bishops, which went back to the apostles themselves. The faithful could be sure that they had access to what Our Lord had taught, because the Church drew up a list of genuine new Scriptures (the New Testament for us), distinguishing these from the many other writings claiming this status (which we now describe as apocryphal), and because the bishops became universally recognized in the orthodox communities as the prime guardians of the teachings of Christ and the apostles.

Among those bishops and communities, Churches founded by the apostles themselves had a special authority as defenders of the tradition and arbiters in doctrinal disputes. The special claims of the Church of Rome came from the fact that it was the city where the two greatest apostles taught and were martyred. The bishops of Rome, successors of Peter, came to embody this supreme tradition of orthodoxy, this guarantee of the faithful transmission of Christ's teaching, which Peter and Paul had handed over to the Christians in Rome.

As we celebrate the feast of Peter and Paul, we should conclude by doing a couple of things. We might firstly thank God for the quality of leadership we have received from the individual popes during the last century and especially for the leadership of our present Holy Father, true successor of Saint Peter and one of the great popes of history.

Secondly, we should pray in thanks for the institution of the papacy. Conquerors and tyrants have often understood the importance of the office of pope much better than we do. Despite the bad popes, despite the Great Schism of popes and anti-popes around 1400, the papacy is a miracle of grace.

We remember Peter and Paul together because they founded this Roman tradition. As Pope Leo wrote fifteen hundred years ago, "we must not make distinctions [between them] because they were equal in their election, alike in their toils, undivided in their death. [It was God who] set them like the twin light of the eyes in the body, whose Head is Christ."

May Peter and Paul continue to guide our Church today and keep us faithful to the teaching of Christ and the faith of the apostles.

Feast of Saints Peter and Paul, 2002
Saint Mary's Cathedral, Sydney

SAINT JOHN FISHER

I T IS ALWAYS A PRIVILEGE to deliver a commencement address to a group of new graduates, to congratulate them on their achievements, and to thank their family, sponsors, and friends who supported them during their studies. We look forward with Christian hope and human optimism to the contribution they will make to society and the Church in the future.

I have been a long-term admirer of Saint Thomas Aquinas and was for eleven years the director of an Aquinas College in Ballarat, Australia, now a campus of the Australian Catholic University, but my Aquinas College was not a Great Books college like yours here in Santa Paula, California. Students here have an unusual advantage from their direct engagement for four years with the profound thinkers who have shaped our Western civilization. They have followed the traditional Socratic method of questioning and dialogue, continued their search for meaning and truth in a learning institution that is committed to the Catholic faith. Faith and reason are offered for their acceptance or rejection as they rigorously examine the intellectual claims of these great authors, religious or otherwise. I repeat that they have been unusually blessed and advantaged, because they have an ideal base for any professional course they might now choose to pursue.

His Life

A commencement ceremony is a happy time. Why then should I choose to speak of an obscure sixteenth-century bishop from England, who spent his episcopal life in Rochester diocese, England's poorest, and then so misjudged his political situation that he was executed by his king on some theological point of principle, without the support of even one of his brother bishops?

Saint John Fisher's life story is told simply. Born in Yorkshire in 1469, one of four children of a prosperous merchant, he went to Cambridge University at the age of fourteen where he was introduced to the currents of intellectual reform springing from the Renaissance. In 1491 he was ordained priest, gained his MA, and elected a fellow of Michaelhouse.

An appointment that was to prove crucial for his later career occurred when he became confessor to Lady Margaret Beaufort, the devout mother of Henry VII. Probably as a result of her patronage, he was appointed Vice Chancellor of Cambridge University in 1501 and in 1504, at the age of thirty-five, he became Chancellor at Cambridge, an office that he held for the rest of his life.

Even in his early years, he clashed mildly with the new King Henry VIII, who wanted to take the money his grandmother Lady Margaret had bequeathed for the development of new colleges at Cambridge and use it for his own purposes. Luther's Protestant Reformation had started in 1517, a development that Henry VIII strongly opposed, even earning from the pope for himself and his successors to this day the title of "Defender of the Faith" for his defense of the seven sacraments.

Fisher became the best-known defender of Catholic doctrines, selected by Cardinal Wolsey, then Lord Chancellor, to preach at an open-air rally outside the old Saint Paul's Cathedral in London against Luther, when Luther's books were burned publicly in 1526. Henry was so pleased with his two-hour address delivered in English, a primitive language then not spoken outside England, that he ordered it to be translated into Latin so that it could be read and understood in continental Europe.

This united front was broken by the inability of Henry's wife, Catherine of Aragon, to produce a male heir and Henry's infatuation with the formidable Anne Boleyn, who was eventually also executed by her tyrant husband. A good historian who specializes in the period claimed to me that a major reason for Henry's determination to eliminate Anne was his resentment at her bitter hostility to both Fisher and Thomas More.

We all know that Henry wanted his first marriage to be annulled, that this was refused by Rome, and that he responded by declaring himself to be head of the Church in England. After careful study, Fisher emerged as Catherine's most public advocate and a resolute defender of the essential role of the pope as successor of Saint Peter in Catholic life. His detailed study convinced Thomas More, former speaker in the House of Commons and briefly Lord Chancellor, to refuse to take the oath of kingly supremacy. A background piece of information that is often forgotten today (when we have been blessed with good popes for a long time) is that during the whole of Fisher's lifetime, the best of the popes were worldly with limited religious enthusiasm, while some others had disgraceful private lives. In short, the papacy then was a scandal, but Fisher was prepared to die for the Catholic truth embodied in the papal office and not for the personal qualities of its officeholders.

Most historians have now abandoned the view that Catholicism in England on the eve of the Reformation was weak and corrupt because Henry and his Protestant successors had to wage a bitter struggle for generations to strangle Catholic life. Henry was regularly extravagant and short of money, and in a masterstroke he commandeered the wealth of the monasteries not just for himself, but for many of the local nobility. In other words, he locked most of the establishment behind him with significant financial encouragement!

In those days when there was little effective separation of powers and no freedom of speech, Henry would tolerate no public opposition. In April 1534, Fisher was confined in the Tower of London, and the case against him proceeded slowly. In May 1535, Pope Paul III created him a cardinal in the hope of saving his life. Henry VIII was not impressed, declaring that Fisher would not have a head on his shoulders to wear the cardinal's hat. No head, no hat!

On June 22 of that year, he was executed by beheading, rather than being hung, drawn, and quartered; a remission due not to his age or office, but to his poor health. Despite his frailty, he announced in a loud voice that he was dying for the faith of the Catholic Church. His headless naked body was left on the scaffold until 8 P.M., when it was then placed in a shallow grave without ceremony. His head was boiled down and placed on London Bridge for two weeks, where his supporters were delighted by the fact "that it grew more florid and lifelike, so that many expected it would speak". His head was then thrown into the Thames to make way for the head of Thomas More.

Incidentally, Fisher's room in the Tower of London was renovated on Churchill's orders toward the end of World War II, not because of any reverence for Fisher's memory, but because, if Hitler had survived the war, Churchill was determined to imprison him, at least for a time, in the Tower of London.

Lessons

Before I began my brief resumé of Saint John Fisher's life, I asked why we might ponder his story on a happy occasion like this commencement. This question has been left hanging, although the simple telling of his story suggests many lessons for a Catholic audience. Let me spell out a few further considerations.

A preliminary reason is that as a bishop, I am keen to speak of a brave and farseeing fellow bishop, who was fated to live in a violent time of change, which laid the foundations for England's rise to greatness and, indeed, the foundations of our contemporary English-speaking world. Thomas More, the layman and martyr, Fisher's contemporary, has the best lines, is a more interesting personality, and has gained much more publicity through the film *A Man for All Seasons*. I want to redress this imbalance.

Saint John Fisher is remarkable for many reasons, but one might begin with a group of new graduates by reminding them that he was truly wise and that wisdom is not coterminous with learning or, indeed, with cunning. Wisdom brings insight, the ability to analyze and devise new syntheses, something akin to Cardinal Newman's criterion for an educated person, which is the ability to recognize the relative value of different truths. Wise people can evaluate public opinion, identify what is central, discard what is irrelevant, and downgrade what is secondary.

Cardinal Fisher was the only bishop to resist Henry, to acknowledge publicly that the issue was not merely a disputed annulment case, not just another quarrel with Rome, which would soon be over, to enable the situation to return to normal. In fact, the rejection of the crucial role of the papacy split the universal Church and set in train the destruction of Christendom. The subjection of the Church also opened the way to a royal despotism being exercised with fewer checks and balances.

A second point we should notice is that John Fisher was not only a learned man, but one who continued to study and learn throughout his life. In middle age he settled down to study Hebrew and Greek as well as wrestling with and answering the new challenges thrown up by the Protestant rebellion. He was also a patron of learning. As Chancellor at Cambridge University, he worked to attract the funds necessary to bring leading scholars from abroad and to introduce the new learning of the Continental Renaissance, the rediscovery of the ancient classical authors in Greek and Latin, as well as the study of Hebrew for the Old Testament Scriptures. He also played a major role in the establishment of Christ's College and Saint John's College, new foundations at Cambridge, which are still thriving today.

Saint John Fisher exemplifies the importance of courage, of a principled integrity, a determination to speak the truth whatever the consequences. Courage is not universal; indeed, it is rare and wonderful especially when the penalties, such as torture and execution, are extreme. It is marginally easier to be courageous in a crowd, not merely because courage is infectious, but because friends, family, and intellectual allies are great helps in times of trial, bolstering morale and providing reassurances on judgments and tactics.

Fisher and More were almost alone as they took their stand. As we have mentioned, no English bishop supported Fisher, and there was no family support for More, not even from Meg Roper, his favorite daughter. If courage is "grace under pressure", the pressures were not sufficient to destroy the resolve of this sick, elderly bishop.

It might also be useful to state the obvious even here at Thomas Aquinas College (it certainly would be useful in Australia) and point out that Fisher and More (indeed, the martyrs on both sides of the Reformation) did not die for conscience's sake, for the inviolability of personal conscience or the primacy of conscience. This is a contemporary way of speaking where public tolerance of different points of view is often regarded as the supreme virtue.

Fisher announced on the scaffold in a surprisingly strong voice: "Christian people, I am come hither to die for the faith of Christ's holy Catholic Church", and we well remember More's famous words that he was "the King's loyal servant, but God's first". They both died for the truth and, more particularly, the Catholic insistence on the essential role of the papacy.

The final lesson we might draw from the life of Saint John Fisher, and the most important one, is that we should be encouraged by his holiness, so that we imitate his faith and goodness, while we rejoice that we are not put to sterner tests. Erasmus, one of the greatest scholars of the Renaissance and no religious zealot, described Fisher "as the one man at this time who is incomparable for uprightness of life, for learning and for greatness of soul".

He was noted for the devotion he exhibited during the celebration of Mass, uniting himself with Christ's self-offering on the Cross. He had a replica of the severed head of John the Baptist on the altar in his episcopal residence, as he took very seriously indeed the teaching of Thomas Aquinas that the office of bishop requires a high degree of sanctity. While all Catholics are not called to be priests or religious, all are called to follow Christ in a serious way, to imitate Christ's wholeness of life, in what we traditionally call holiness. Fisher is a good model.

I wish all the graduates of Thomas Aquinas College my repeated congratulations on their graduation and hope they receive every appropriate grace and blessing as they commence their new lives. I am sure that you have already met many good examples and mentors in this environment and in your families. May you also be inspired by the learning, holiness, and courage of Saint John Fisher to devote your own life to some great and good cause.

May 10, 2008
Commencement address
Thomas Aquinas College,
Santa Paula, Calif., United States

Priests

MILITARY CHAPLAINS

A COUPLE OF YEARS AGO, I led the Anzac Day religious service at the Commonwealth War Graves Cemetery in Rome. It was a perfect spring morning with a light breeze, under the ancient Aurelian walls of the city built well over fifteen hundred years ago. As always, this sacred site was immaculately preserved, clipped lawns, beautiful flowers coming to bud around a large cross with the sword of honor at its center. Across Australia and everywhere there are significant numbers of Australians overseas, we gather to celebrate Anzac Day, as we gather on no other day for any national celebration.

I have visited the graves of our war dead in Port Moresby, Rabaul, the Middle East, and the vast military cemeteries in France. Most of those buried were little more than boys. Some of them were only boys, many with names like those of our neighbors and our relations. In all these visits, I have been struck by the tragedy of their young deaths, the powerful example of their sacrifice as they lie there in their hundreds, thousands, or even tens of thousands to await resurrection. Only the very young or the very foolish glorify war. I have never met an ex-soldier who did, and certainly this is not the purpose of Anzac Day, not the purpose of this commemorative service.

When the First World War ended, the nation of Australia was still a teenager, and about sixty thousand Australians died in this "The Great War" to end all wars—sixty thousand from five million people. About fifteen thousand New Zealanders died from a population of one million, two thousand more than Belgium with a population seven times as large as New Zealand's. Different Australian groups, English and Irish, Catholic and Protestant, were united after this common suffering in a way they had never been previously.

As an archbishop, it is appropriate for me to acknowledge the contribution of all the chaplains, Christian and Jewish, who went with our troops to war to bring support and help to anyone who was in need, whatever their creed or personal system of belief. They, too, were brave, shared the hardships, and a good number were prisoners of war.

A brother priest who was in the air force in the Second World War wrote that the conversation at reunions was much more about grandchildren, arthritis, and those who died recently, rather than the heroics of war. He explained that there is nothing as basic as facing the prospect of almost certain death. The bonds between those who did this together, once, a few, or many times (perhaps particularly when they were volunteers), are strange and remarkably strong. For many, nothing in their later lives reached that level of intensity. Some believed their later lives were lived on borrowed time.

Most Australians today have not known active service at war. We pray this continues. Why, then, do we gather on Anzac Day? The answer is simple. We gather to do our duty, to express our gratitude to those brave enough to put their lives at risk for our freedoms, to remind ourselves and especially the young that our freedoms have been won and defended the hard way and might have to be defended again. We also come to acknowledge publicly their bravery. Not all Australians are brave in every situation, but many of our soldiers were brave, sometimes brave beyond belief.

Only this week, *The Catholic Weekly* told the story of a well-known Sydney priest and navy chaplain from the Second World War, now deceased, Father John Roche, known as Cocky Roche. In the Philippines campaign, he was on the *HMAS Shropshire*, and in an engagement at the Leyte Gulf their flagship *HMAS Australia* was hit five times by kamikaze attacks. During this battle, Cocky Roche insisted on being taken to the *Australia*, where seventy men were wounded. The *Australia's* commander, Captain Dechaineux, was badly burned, but he ordered that every one else should be treated before him. He died as a result of this sacrifice.

Today we pay tribute to the brave from all our Australian forces and to the brave among those who were our enemies. We do not minimize, much less trivialize, the bitter divisions of the past, but we do not aim to remain there, locked in by the memories of suffering and death. We pray that in the blood of the fallen, all the fallen, we may find the seeds of peace.

At the Rome ceremony, I mentioned the booklet that contained the tribute written in 1934 by Mustafa Kemal, himself a famous commander at Gallipoli, to all the fallen Anzacs. We know him as Atatürk, the founder of modern Turkey. This is what is now inscribed at Gallipoli; also in Canberra, Albany, Western Australia, and Wellington, New Zealand.

> Those heroes that shed their blood
> and lost their lives. . . .
> You are now lying in the soil of a friendly country.
> Therefore rest in peace.
> There is no difference between the Johnnies
> and the Mehmets to us—where they lie side-by-side—
> here in this country of ours. . . .
> You the mothers
> Who sent their sons from far away countries,
> Wipe away your tears;
> Your sons are now living in our bosom—
> and are at peace.
> After having lost their lives on this land—
> they have become our sons as well.

These are beautiful and generous words written by a brave soldier and a renowned nation builder. As Christians, we should strive to be no less generous, sustained as we are also by the promise of eternal harmony in heaven for all good people, no matter what might have divided them here on earth. Lest we forget.

April 25, 2004
Anzac Day Service
Shrine of Remembrance, Hyde Park, Sydney

PRAYING THE PSALMS

I T IS GOOD for us to be here together in Malta, united by our common Catholic faith, by our priestly identity, and by our solidarity one with the other. We should thank God for all these blessings. Last night it was very encouraging to be swept up into the strength and faith of the responses, common prayers, and hymns. As we all know, it is good to pray with a church full of believers.

So we gather for the official morning prayer of the Church and insert ourselves into an ancient Christian and Catholic tradition, which the Early Church took over from the Jews. Many Jews had prayed at fixed hours of the day and the night for hundreds of years before Christ's birth. The monks of Palestine, Egypt, and Gaul were the first to organize a cycle of prayers using all the psalms, while cathedrals and parish churches used a simpler ritual of morning and evening prayers.

Late in the fifth century, the Roman basilicas compiled what became the traditional seven prayers for daytime as well as the "night office", or early morning office of Matins. Saint Benedict, the founder of Western monasticism, used these for his prescribed round of daily prayer, which he called "Opus Dei", the work of God. This spread through Western Europe during the following centuries and remained basically unchanged until the reforms of 1971, which we still follow today.

From the beginning, the Old Testament psalms have provided the backbone of the Liturgy of the Hours, the Divine Office. Part of the official Old Testament canon of Scripture, these psalms were composed under the inspiration of the Holy Spirit by many authors at different periods of history. Some might go back to the time of King David; many were written after the exile, while today's canticle of Tobit, probably written about 200 B.C., purports to tell of a young man when the kingdom was divided after the death of King Solomon.

Not just this canticle, but the psalms generally were not written as scientific or historical treatises, but as religious poems, to be sung in the praise of the one true God. Their imagery has helped form the Christian imagination and has contributed to the development of all European literature and those other literatures touched by European influence of East and West, Latin and Greek.

Naturally, we pray these ancient prayers as Christians with the benefit of revealed truths then hidden in the old dispensation. Therefore, it is important that as we pray we find Christ in the psalms, because He provides the key to the poetry of these beautiful prayers. The psalms are accessible to many types of people of any and every race, educated and uneducated, even the irreligious. They can offer us something, bring us to God, when we are well or sick, when we are exhilarated or depressed, feeling benevolent or battling black feelings of resentment, even revenge. A number of priests struggling through deep personal crises have told me how they were strengthened and helped by praying the psalms.

Thomas Merton wrote in *Bread and Wilderness* (1961) that the psalms are the simplest and greatest of all religious poems. My Old Testament lecturer in Rome who guided us through the psalms as seminarians made a similar claim that they had no equal in any religious literature. I was skeptical of this then but have found nothing in my reading to disprove his thesis.

It should also be a consolation to us that not only have Christians been nourished by these psalms for two thousand years, but that Our Lord Himself prayed them from His earliest years until His last moments on the Cross. He, too, was consoled and challenged by their praise and supplication, by their rhythm and imagery, which became part of His own preaching. He quoted them more frequently than any other part of the Scriptures.

Time and again we have that Semitic parallelism, the repetition of a basic thought in a similar image to reinforce the message.

> Benedicite, omnia opera
> Domini, Domino
> May the heavens bless
> the Lord, the waters of the deep,
> the sun and moon, the stars,
> night and day, frost and snow.
> All bless the Lord.

This is only one example of a technique that Jesus himself was to adopt.

Think of chapter 7 in Saint Matthew's Gospel, a text that is particularly appropriate for meditation by those of us ordained as priests for many years, perhaps even more than for young priests: "Ask, and it will be given to you; search, and you will find; knock, and the door will be opened to you" (Mt 7:7).

Is there any one request that might be appropriate for every one of us as priests, gathered from every continent in the world and representative of nearly every age group? I have one suggestion, from Psalm 23. May we always be men who regularly seek the one true God, priests "who seek the face of the God of Jacob".

I do not want to suggest for a moment that we priests do not know the one true God and His only Son. We would not be here if that were the case. Some time ago a well-known architect in Australia said that a Catholic church was a place for those searching for God. I felt that was profoundly wrong, because overwhelmingly a Catholic church is for those who have found the one true God in His Son, Jesus Christ. But we do not see clearly, and often we struggle to convey to others what little insight has been granted us.

> Who shall climb the mountain of the Lord?
> Who shall stand in his holy place?
> The man with clean hands and pure heart
> Who desires not worthless things.

These lines present an inescapable challenge to each and every priest. We fill a multiplicity of different practical roles as parish priest or assistant, teacher, administrator, builder or organizer, academic or bishop. No doubt the list could be continued. But each of us is called to be a man of God, because each of us is a priest, called to stand in God's holy place, called to be a formator of saints for the New Millennium.

C. S. Lewis, in *Reflections on the Psalms* (1958), claimed that a vocation such as ours is a terrible thing; not simply because we are priests, but because priests, like religious, like some lay Catholic leaders, are called out of nature into the supernatural life. This is a costly honor, the call to reject natural claims, to prefer God ahead of father, mother, children, and life itself (Mt 10:37–9). Ministerial priests are not only called to the service of all the people of God, but we are called to be listed among the pure of heart, who shall see God (Mt 5:8), one of the

Beatitudes from the Sermon on the Mount that Our Lord developed from rich Jewish teachings, such as Psalm 23.

Paul's personal history and conversion should always remain an encouragement to us in our work and in our personal struggle toward God. We are regularly tempted to reduce Paul into our own manageable categories, to reduce the scope and drama of his conversion.

Scripture scholar N. T. Wright, the Anglican bishop of Durham in England, said that he understood what Paul was really like when he saw on television the face of the young man who assassinated the Jewish Prime Minister, Rabin. Paul, too, was a persecutor of Christians, present at the martyrdom of Stephen, a zealot and a fanatic, a man of violence. God's grace turned him from this dead end, this hate, and slowly turned him into our greatest missionary; a spiritual giant who truly climbed the mountain of the Lord.

Whether we are young or old, fit or arthritic, we too can climb the mountain of the Lord. I am now convinced that technique is much less important in these things of the Spirit than persistence. If we persist, especially if we use a spiritual director, God will help us. If God occasionally brings us down to Hades, He also brings us up again, and none of us can escape from His hand.

No decline in our energy, no series of hurts and disappointments for us can mean that God himself is diminished or beaten or uninterested. God is always faithful, His works are to be trusted, He does fill the earth with His love, even when we see this darkly and even when we might not feel it at all.

In faith and as the years pass, may we always acknowledge with gratitude and enthusiasm that

> The Lord is our help and our shield.
> In him do our hearts find joy,

and may we always be able to pray

> May your love be upon us, O Lord,
> as we place all our hope in you.

October 19, 2004
Morning prayer, International conference of priests, Malta

THE ORDINATION OF
A BENEDICTINE MONK

Just before christmas, I was speaking to a young Burmese deacon who had studied for the priesthood at our seminary in Sydney. We are all aware in general terms of the oppressive political situation in Burma, and the seminarian's father, a catechist, had been killed years ago by the military. This young man told me he chose the feast of Saint Thomas Becket, December 29, as the date for his priestly ordination as he wondered whether a fate similar to his father's and Becket's lay in front of him. I was touched and impressed by his faith and simplicity.

I am not suggesting that any similar threat hovers over Brother Brian, but I could not push this earlier encounter out of my mind as I worked to prepare a few words for this priestly ordination on the feast of the conversion of Saint Paul. We all need conversion, and the Church needs converts if only to balance the departures!

Britain is not as post-Christian as our opponents would like to claim as they strive to bar us from participating in public discussion, but the decisions to follow the rule of Saint Benedict as a monk and accept priestly ordination are now countercultural, a provocation to many of today's opinion makers. And a ceremony like today's ordination gives all of us reason to pause, to thank God for the gift of our faith, for the monastic life, and for the ministerial priesthood.

It is always a happy occasion and a privilege for a bishop to ordain a priest and an unusual privilege for a bishop from the other side of the world to do so here. I am doubly grateful for the invitation of Abbot Cuthbert Johnson, because it enables me, as archbishop of Sydney, to acknowledge the debt of the Catholic Church in Australia to the English Benedictines, who provided the first two archbishops of Sydney—John Bede Polding and Roger Bede Vaughan. They came to us, not from Quarr, but from Downside. With a largely Irish flock and the harsh penal conditions in that distant colony, Polding's dream of a Benedictine Australia did not materialize, but they were our fathers in the faith. I gratefully acknowledge this debt.

Saint Paul and Saint Benedict make up an interesting pair of saints, demonstrating again that the word Catholic means universal. Paul's Epistles and Benedict's Rule reveal two very different personalities, who both dedicated their diverse talents to the service of the one true God and Christ His only Son. I am not sure that Paul was ideal material to become a monk. He had been a man of violence, religiously inspired violence, like some of our Islamic friends today, although he did not injure indiscriminately, as some terrorists do, but focused on those following Jesus from Nazareth, who had been crucified.

Paul was tireless and restless, a constant traveler for whom the vow of stability would have been a constraint. After conversion he was completely obedient to Christ but often found cooperation with his fellows difficult. Humility is not the first word that comes to mind when we think of him. I do not know the monastic world well at all, and experienced monks might claim that he is just the raw material needed to be molded by the wisdom and sobriety of Saint Benedict's Rule, but I suspect he would always have been something of a challenge for his abbot.

Certainly Paul and Benedict agreed on the basic task for true believers. The prologue to Benedict's Rule calls every monk "to give up (his) own will, once and for all, and armed with the strong and noble weapons of obedience to do battle for the true King, Christ the Lord". Paul would have endorsed this completely and agreed with Benedict that a monk and a priest should "run on the path of God's commandments (with) hearts overflowing with the inexpressible delight of love". Every one of us, and especially a new priest, "must run and do now what will profit us forever".

Through the long priestly years of service that lie ahead for the soon to be Father Kelly, he will remain true to his vocation only if he continues to turn toward Christ as the center of his prayer life and the basis of his teaching, community living, and service. Christ's teachings do not need to be improved; His more difficult challenges cannot be quietly ignored, and we cannot hope to improve or succeed if we place someone or something at the center of our lives other than Christ, the Son of God and Son of Mary. Therefore it is from this specifically Christian base that we can now move to speak on the ministerial priesthood, the order to which you are now to be raised.

For your part, you will exercise the sacred duty of teaching in the name of Christ the Teacher. Impart to everyone the word of God that you have received with joy. Meditating on the law of the Lord, see that you believe what you read, that you teach what you believe, and that you practice what you teach. Therefore, let what you teach be nourishment for the people of God. Let the holiness of your life be a delightful aroma to Christ's faithful, so that by word and example you may build up the house that is God's Church.

Likewise, you will exercise in Christ the office of sanctifying. For by your ministry the spiritual sacrifice of the faithful will be made perfect, being united to the sacrifice of Christ, which will be offered through your hands in an unbloody way on the altar, in union with the faithful, in the celebration of the mysteries. Understand, therefore, what you do, and imitate what you celebrate. As celebrant of the mystery of the Lord's death and Resurrection, strive to put to death whatever in your members is sinful and to walk in newness of life.

Remember, when you gather men and women into the people of God through baptism and when you forgive sins in the name of Christ and the Church in the sacrament of penance; when you comfort the sick with holy oil and celebrate the sacred rites, offering prayers of praise and thanks to God throughout the hours of the day, not only for the people of God but for the whole world—remember then that you are taken from among men and appointed on behalf of men for those things that pertain to God. Therefore, carry out the ministry of Christ the Priest with constant joy and genuine love, attending not to your own concerns but to those of Jesus Christ.

Finally, dearly beloved son, exercising for your part the office of Christ, Head and Shepherd, while united with the bishop and subject to him, strive to bring the faithful together into one family, so that you may lead them to God the Father through Christ in the Holy Spirit. Keep always before your eyes the example of the Good Shepherd who came not to be served but to serve and who came to seek out and save what was lost.

Let us all pray then during this Mass and ordination ceremony that Brian Gerard Kelly during his priestly and monastic life will "faithfully observe (Christ's) teaching in the monastery until death and patiently share in the suffering of Christ so that he may also deserve to share in his Kingdom".

January 25, 2008
Conversion of Saint Paul, Priestly Ordination
of Father Brian Gerard Kelly, O.S.B.
Quarr Abbey, Isle of Wight, U.K.

CELIBACY OF THE CLERGY

1 Corinthians 7:32-35

TODAY I WILL USE the second reading from Saint Paul's First Letter to the Corinthians to speak about the celibacy of the clergy, that mandatory discipline for priests like myself of the Roman or Latin Rite. We all realize that other families who belong fully to the Catholic Church such as the Maronite or Melchite or Coptic churches, do have married clergy. It is also true that probably most of the parish clergy in our Western Church for the first thousand years were married, and this was true in England and Ireland, too. Of course there were also many unmarried priests and brothers, but they were monks in monasteries, usually Benedictines, as the Franciscans and Dominicans were only founded in the thirteenth century and most other religious orders began after Saint Ignatius of Loyola founded the Jesuits in the sixteenth century.

Paul today is not talking about the celibacy of priests but about unmarried men and women who have more time and fewer distractions so they can devote themselves completely to God. Undoubtedly, the duties and cares of marriage and family can and should be directed to God, but only yesterday the wife of a very sick man said she understood better than she used to why priests are unmarried. Not every unmarried priest does use the freedom from family responsibility to give more time to God and the service of others, but that is the way it should be. Many unmarried lay men and women also lead wonderfully productive lives at both a human and a religious level.

At the 1990 Synod in Rome on the preparation of priests, which I attended, many journalists, a number of them ex-priests, were campaigning busily for a married clergy. One bishop remarked that if the theme for some future synod was to be agriculture, a goodly percentage of the press would want to talk about celibacy!

He was right. The celibacy of the clergy is newsworthy, an affront to the worldly and the irreligious. However, it follows the example of Christ Himself, Saint Paul, and Saint John and is, I believe, a principal reason for Catholic strength throughout the world and especially in Australia.

Most Australian Catholics appreciate the advantages priestly celibacy brings, but a majority, probably even among regular churchgoers, wonder why the discipline should be mandatory. Would we not quickly have more priests if they could marry before ordination?

Perhaps we would, but the Anglican and Protestant Churches have had married clergy for nearly five hundred years, and their situation is much weaker than ours. Nor do I believe that the apostolic vitality of the Orthodox Churches, who have always had married clergy, is higher than ours, and their missionary outreach is certainly much less.

A priest is supposed to be another Christ, an ambassador of Christ, a "pontifex" or bridge maker between God and humanity. As Christ was unmarried, I believe it is supremely congruent that priests, too, be unmarried.

I accept that in the future we might see a change of discipline whereby the Church allows the ordination of married men. This is different from allowing ordained priests to marry, which will never happen. But I do not favor the first option, because I do not believe it would strengthen the gospel vitality of the Church in the long run.

When a priest is unmarried, this is a provocative sign. Why would a young man sacrifice the possibility of the personal and generational fulfillment of marriage with a wife and children? Regulations urge bishops not to accept as seminarians those with long-term and deeply seated homosexual drives.

Priests are prepared to make this sacrifice for the Kingdom of God. It is something like pruning a tree so more fruit can be produced; so that people can be reminded that life is more than daily living, that we serve an unseen God of love who requires us to worship Him, and that we are destined for a life of reward or punishment after death. Life has an important supernatural dimension.

Mandatory celibacy has a powerful sign value, a capacity to teach about things unseen, but it also brings huge practical advantages to the Catholic people. The widow of a Catholic priest, who had been an Anglican priest, said that Catholic people regularly put more demands on their priests than Anglicans did with their married clergy. A wife and children need not only love, but regular time and attention, and certainly I could not have devoted the time I gave to my work if I had also family responsibilities. It goes without saying that it is cheaper to keep a priest in comfort than to keep a priest with a wife and family, so they can afford to have children, educate them, and live in decent comfort.

I am regularly asked about this in secondary schools but also at senior primary level. Even in grade six, they understand clearly the advantages of a situation where, for example, Karol Wojtyla, when Archbishop of Kraków and elected pope, did not have to ask Mrs. Pope and the little popes whether they would be prepared to live in Rome!

Let me conclude this brief sermon of support for the discipline of mandatory celibacy by quoting from an unlikely source, the nineteenth-century German philosopher and atheist Frederick Nietzsche, who famously proclaimed "God is dead." He was a writer of unusual power with unusual insights, who suffered a massive nervous breakdown and died in an asylum. Here is what he wrote on priestly celibacy:

> Today we see clearly that Luther was fatally limited, superficial, and imprudent. He gave back sexual intercourse to the priest: but three-quarters of the reverence of which the people are capable (and particularly the women of the people) rests on the belief that a man who is exceptional in this regard will also be exceptional in other matters. It is precisely here that the popular belief in something superhuman in man, in the miraculous, in the saving God in man, has its most subtle and suggestive advocate. Having given the priest a wife, he had to take from him auricular confession. Psychologically this was appropriate, but thereby he practically did away with the Christian priest himself, whose profoundest utility has ever consisted in being a sacred ear, a silent well, a grave for secrets. (*Die Frohliche Wissenschaft*)

The best way forward is not always the easiest way or that favored by worldly wisdom. Love and sacrifice, faith and service will take us forward. More good young priests, loving and celibate, are what we need.

February 1, 2009
Saint Mary's Cathedral, Sydney

Churches, Cathedrals and Chapels

SAINT PATRICK'S CATHEDRAL, MELBOURNE, CENTENARY RENOVATIONS

L AST WEEK I blessed the extensions and refurbishment in a Catholic secondary college. The new headmaster explained that he was there only to enjoy the occasion because all the hard work of planning and fund raising had been done by his predecessor. I know what the headmaster was talking about. My first task in inaugurating these centenary celebrations, after receiving the certificates vouching for the conservation and restoration works completed, is to thank and congratulate my predecessor, Archbishop Frank Little, and his team, led so ably by Mister John Ralph, Mister Ed Ryan, Mister Ted Exell, and Dean William McCarthy, for a huge job that has been done and done well. We are proud of what has been accomplished.

I must acknowledge also the gratitude of the Catholic community to our twenty-six thousand recorded donors, large and small. These include the governments of Australia and the State of Victoria. Support for the cathedral restoration fund has come from all quarters of society —the priests and religious of the archdiocese, charitable trusts, major donors, as well as the many thousands of Melbournians whose names have not been recorded.

Victorian Catholics of today and tomorrow will always be in debt to the generations who built this cathedral. When it was completed in 1897 after nearly fifty years of controversy, difficulties, and sacrifice, there were fewer than 125,000 Catholics in the City of Melbourne, with nothing like our levels of prosperity and education. They built for us one of Melbourne's great buildings; a cathedral that is not only loved by "ordinary" Catholics, but admired as preeminent by many architects and artists.

Our beautiful church was designed by William Wardell, the most successful architect in the colonies of Victoria and New South Wales at that time, who also designed Saint Mary's Cathedral in Sydney and our own magnificent Government House, with its ballroom bigger than Buckingham Palace's ballroom—a point that is supposed to have provoked Queen Victoria's explicit disapproval.

Wardell was born in England, became a Catholic convert, a disciple of A.W. N. Pugin and part of the Gothic revival movement that flourished in the nineteenth century in the English-speaking world. It is interesting to note that the word "Gothic", which we use to describe the style of our cathedral as well as buildings as different as Notre Dame in Paris and the British Houses of Parliament, was first used by Italian Renaissance artists as a term of disparagement, harking back to the barbarian Gothic tribes from the North who had helped destroy the Roman Empire. They were criticizing a style of architecture, especially church architecture, that originated in France in the thirteenth century and came to dominate much of Europe, but never flourished south of the Alps.

When I was in the seminary, some apologists claimed that the thirteenth century was the Catholic "golden age". Certainly it was rich in achievement; the time of Saint Albert the Great, Saint Thomas Aquinas, Saint Francis of Assisi, the rise of the universities, of Dante Alighieri, when the papacy was at the height of its political influence and France had emerged as the cultural center of the West.

The Gothic cathedrals embodied this militant energy that saw the leadership of the celibate clergy consolidated, the disappearance of married clergy in the West, and the triumph of a rationalist and tightly organized scholasticism. In many ways it was an intellectual climate very unlike our own, a period when nearly everyone believed the one true God was mightily important, an age of religious enthusiasm, especially in the monasteries, and extensive personal mysticism. Individualized responses to God and the beauty of nature were not uncommon and encouraged.

Many of the Gothic cathedrals took generations to complete, allowing a host of individuals, usually anonymous, to add quite different personal contributions. The next stage in this cathedral's history will see the other cultural traditions of the Melbourne church represented. But all of their churches were characterized by height and light; the builders wanted to remind us of the beauty of the transcendent God, not only through awe-inspiring immensity, but also through magnificent stained glass, which explained the Bible stories, especially for those who could not read, and which harnessed this light to symbolize the very Godhead itself, especially through the great rose circular windows.

Late last century, architects of the Gothic revival such as Wardell, sparked by the interest of the Romantic movement in the Middle Ages, but more importantly by their opposition to the spread of secularism or unbelief and the attacks on religion by confident scientists such as Darwin and Huxley, strove very explicitly to recapture and restate the God-centered energy and enthusiasm of those who designed and built the first Gothic churches. This is the intellectual background against which this cathedral was completed one hundred years ago.

This building is certainly enduring evidence of Irish Australian vision and determination; a proud statement to their fellow Australians. But what sort of a statement? The facts speak for themselves. *This cathedral is faith made visible, a rock and a fortress where people gathered for consolation and rejoicing, which also announces a confident hope of what is to come after death.*

The Irish Australians built beautiful schools; the occasional hall, but their centerpieces were their churches. They did not build museums or a concert hall; no mausoleums to their leaders. While they did contribute, with many others, to building our race tracks and our sporting fields, they built no casinos.

Here they built a house of prayer for all people. They knew in their hearts and bones that just as God took flesh in Jesus, so their frail human nature and ambiguous human activity could be transformed and sanctified to express the holy. However, they were not only celebrating the glories of God's creation; they were building a memorial to His redemptive action. All Catholic churches, indeed all Christian churches, throughout our city are fruits of the Cross, where believers gather to worship the Father in Spirit and truth.

Three thousands years ago, when David had consolidated his Jewish kingdom, he realized that it was incongruous for him to live in a palace of cedar, while the one true God was housed in a tabernacle dating from Israel's many long years of wandering and struggle after leaving Egypt for the Promised Land. God deserves the best.

This cathedral embodies our best efforts over nearly 150 years to build and maintain a suitable house of God. We are still glad each time we come to the house of the Lord, because we do see this place as being like a holy mountain where God dwells, especially through the Real Presence of the Eucharistic species. It is regularly a joyful house of prayer where God is worshipped through the celebration of the sacraments, where sins are forgiven. It is for us an image of the heavenly Jerusalem, the City of God, an invitation to, and a hint, an intimation of paradise. Christ is the keystone, and the mighty pillars represent the apostles and prophets on whom Christ built the Church. As the cathedral, the mother church where the bishop has his "cathedra" or teaching chair this church is the focus of unity for the Catholic communities of the archdiocese. Through its worship, its bells calling the community to prayer and its proud presence, this cathedral reminds the wider community of the Christian and Catholic claims that in Christ we have the key to understanding human history.

It was faith that shaped these stones and faith that inspired the generosity and dedication for the restoration. The three major appeals for this cathedral were all conducted during times of financial distress: during the crash of the 1890s, during the depression of the 1930s, which saw the addition of the spires (part of the building program Doctor Mannix encouraged throughout the diocese in order to create work), and during the 1990s. Despite this, the work prospered.

Neither money nor history nor legitimate community pride can replace the Spirit of Truth. If the time ever comes, and may God forbid this, that the flame of faith vanishes in our community, then these stones will fall silent and the Spirit of Truth will disappear to await recall.

Faith keeps this cathedral alive. Faith inspires our care for justice; faith explains our ambition to be people of integrity. Our faith enables us to worship in Spirit and truth in this magnificent building, which expresses our best efforts, just as faith enables us to live and worship, if that is necessary, in miserable surroundings and in the most difficult circumstances.

May this cathedral continue to bring peace to our homes for many generations, many centuries. May God reward the faith and generosity of all who built and restored this house of God. May a living Christian faith always burn within this church and carry it securely into the future as a true house of God.

March 16, 1997
Saint Patrick's Cathedral, Melbourne.
Centenary Renovations

A NEW CATHEDRAL ALTAR,
BALLARAT

A S SOMEONE WHO WAS BORN, bred, and educated in this city, who worshipped in this church as a teenager and seminarian, and who was a seminarian and priest of the Ballarat diocese for twenty-seven years, the consecration of the new altar here in Saint Patrick's Cathedral is an occasion that enables me to express my gratitude again to the diocese that formed me, to my two bishops, James Patrick O'Collins and Ronald Mulkearns, to the priests and teachers of my youth, the priests who worked with me, and the many people and friends I endeavored to serve.

As children of Abraham, we acknowledge that our forebears have been worshipping the one true God since about seventeen hundred years before Christ. When Cardinal Moran, the archbishop of Sydney, preached at the Sunday Mass on November 22, 1891, to celebrate the consecration of this cathedral by the second bishop of Ballarat, Doctor James Moore, the previous Thursday, he captured this very beautifully.

The cardinal began with Jacob, Abraham's grandson, the one who wrestled with the angel, who saw in a vision a ladder of golden light stretching from earth to heaven, a vision of God himself promising to Jacob innumerable descendants, like dust on the ground. When Jacob awoke from the dream, he was frightened, struck with awe. That place, he recognized, was nothing less than a house of God, the gate of heaven. And to commemorate this, he took the stone on which he was lying, anointed it with oil, and set it up as a monument.

So our rites of dedication tonight have their origins in the Jewish liturgy of the Old Testament, which, like Saint Paul writing to the people of Corinth, explicitly separated itself from paganism, from the reverence of false gods and demons, to worship the one true God of love. Our ceremonies have been enriched by the customs of the early

Church and succeeding centuries, especially from the times of the fierce Roman persecutions, and are centered, of course, around the figure of Christ, our Brother and Redeemer, in the celebration of the Eucharist.

Since the dedication of the cathedral in 1891, the rites have been simplified, but the Christian essentials, the source of our vitality, which enable us to continue worshipping in spirit and in truth, remain exactly the same. In many ways, though, it was a different world 109 years ago. Ballarat was then a very rich city, where gold mining still continued. At a celebratory dinner afterward at Holy Ghost College (predecessor of Saint Patrick's College), a Melbourne MLA praised Ballarat as "the Athens of the south". There was no Commonwealth of Australia, just a collection of different British colonies, which was why the archbishop of Wellington was listed among the twelve Australian bishops present.

The music at the consecration, with a full orchestra, a choir of one hundred voices, four principal soloists, and a rendition of Hummel's Mass in E flat, was "the finest ever heard in Ballarat", according to the Melbourne Catholic paper, *The Advocate*. By our contemporary standards, such music was exotic, predating the austere musical reforms introduced by Pope Pius X. But it is a blessing that good music remains a tradition here.

However, all this is secondary to the central concerns of those who built this cathedral—according to the original plan, incidentally, proposed for Saint Patrick's Cathedral in Melbourne. And the artistic surroundings tonight are secondary to the ambitions of Bishop Connors and all those who helped in some way to bring this cathedral back to its original beauty.

This building is a sacred place, which, since it was first opened in 1863, has been sanctified by the different prayers of hundreds of thousands of worshippers; the happy prayers of parents at the baptisms of their children; the excited and hopeful prayers of the newly wed; the heartbreak and sorrow of funerals; the grateful prayers of those forgiven in the sacrament of penance, grand public occasions, hidden private moments of prayer. This cathedral has seen them all.

And at the center of this cathedral, as in every Catholic church, lies the altar, the Eucharistic table of Christ's followers, gathering to celebrate again what He initiated at the Last Supper. The Christians first used two Greek words to describe their Eucharistic table; *thusiasterion*, meaning altar, to remind them of Christ's unique and redeeming sacrifice, which is made present at every Mass, and *trapeza* meaning table, the place where the sacred meal is celebrated.

Later, the Latin-speaking Christians moved away from the word *ara*, used for pagan altars, and adopted or devised the word *altare*, from which we derive our English word, altar. The altar was always placed in a special place, the sanctuary, separated in our churches in the past by a low screen, what used to be the altar or communion rails. Church authorities, too, liked to place the altar near the tomb of a martyr. As the faith spread and persecutions ceased, the supply of martyrs dried up, and so the relics of martyrs (who died for the faith) were often accompanied or replaced by the relics of saints, those who lived outstanding lives of faith and love.

According to Saint Ambrose, the late-fourth-century archbishop of Milan, the relics of the saints are "placed there so that the triumphant victims may occupy the place where Christ is victim; He, however, who suffered for all, upon the altar; they, who have been redeemed by his sufferings, beneath the altar". The long and beautiful prayer of dedication takes up the Old Testament themes we have mentioned: the rainbow, God's recurring promise to his people since the time of Noah and the ark that he would never again destroy the world by flood; the threatened sacrifice of Isaac by Abraham, and Moses sprinkling the blood of the sacrificial lamb on the altar.

Our altar will be anointed with the oil of chrism used at baptism, confirmation, and the ordination of a priest. It is as though the altar itself is being baptized and confirmed to ready it for its sacred functions. Cardinal John O'Connor of New York, when he anointed the new altar at the Melbourne Cathedral, took up another theme from the first Christian writers, explaining it as symbolic of the anointing of the dead Christ after His crucifixion. Christ was often described as the victim, priest, and altar of His own sacrifice.

In perhaps the most spectacular piece of symbolism, a lighted brazier will be placed on the altar. Fire is an ancient symbol of God and His presence; the pillar of flame that led the Jews through the night as they wandered in the desert; the burning bush that was never consumed. Even more than water, fire captures something of the mystery of God's purifying and energizing love.

Incense is thrown on the fire, with the hope in faith that our prayers will rise like the incense smoke, a ritual that the Jews themselves took over from the ancient Empire of the Persians, who liberated them from the Babylonians. And as always, especially with the Easter candle, we remember Christ the light of the world.

We will conclude with the customary celebration of the Eucharist, when the priest takes Christ's place to consecrate the bread and wine, to effect once again the everyday miracle of transubstantiation into the Body and Blood of Christ; to celebrate once again on the newly consecrated altar the death of the Lord until He comes again.

In 1891, Cardinal Moran's sermon was long, elegant, and brimful of confidence. My few words are shorter, less elegant, well aware of the pressures we are under, but, please God, just as confident, in faith, that the words of Christ Our Lord, the solemn teachings of the Church, and the faith and love at the heart of the Catholic community are as powerful and as true as they have been for two millennia.

Cardinal Moran spoke of the Church then being "assailed by innumerable foes"; of those at that time "guided by the spirit of the age", who "too often regard the Church as if it were a mere human institution". That was a fatal mistake then, and it remains a dead end for us today, as surely as it has been for every preceding generation. May God continue to bless the diocese of Ballarat. May God send an increase of vocations to the priestly life, because the Catholic Church in order to remain Catholic must be a sacramental community. May the good God, day by day, add to your congregation those destined to be saved, just as He did in early Jerusalem. May your parishes and schools continue to be quickened by the Divine Spirit, as you remain faithful to the teachings of the apostles. And may the renewal of this cathedral church be a true sign and symbol of the increasing spiritual strength of your wonderful diocese.

April 26, 2000
Saint Patrick's Cathedral, Ballarat

125TH ANNIVERSARY OF
SAINT MARY'S CATHEDRAL, SYDNEY

*2 Chronicles 5:6–11, 13 — 6:2; Psalm 83:3–5, 10–11;
1 Corinthians 3:9–11, 16–17; John 2:13–22*

T HIS WEEKEND in our beautiful cathedral is somewhat unusual, prin-
cipally because we celebrate the 125th anniversary of its opening,
but also because yesterday I ordained two young priests for our archdiocese, making a total of five for this year. Otherwise, however, it was
business as usual with the daily Masses on Saturday, Sunday Masses,
confessions, and weddings, and today we have the First Communions
and confirmations of some of our choirboys. A cathedral, even more
than the usual parish church, is a spiritual powerhouse where the one
true God is worshipped, the fruits of Christ's unique redemptive activity are made available to us, and the Church, the Body of Christ,
continues to renew herself through the nourishment of her members
in the various sacraments.

In the first reading we heard about the dedication of the first temple
in Jerusalem, Solomon's Temple, about 950 years before the Lord's
birth. It is the prototype of all our great cathedrals and was a building
loved by Christ Himself as He wept over its future destruction.

But we, unlike Solomon, no longer sacrifice innumerable sheep and
oxen. Our worship of the one true God, identical of course with the
God worshipped by the Jews, is centered on the life and redemptive
death of Jesus Christ, the Son of God. And in the sanctuary with the
main altar, we make present again Christ's unique sacrifice through the
celebration of the Eucharist, when we eat Christ's Body and drink His
Blood. It is the conviction in faith of the importance of the activities
we perform in this cathedral, a conviction shared by generations of

193

clergy and people, which explains its magnificence and our determination to complete the interior renovation so that its external beauty is at least equaled internally.

This is not the first chapel or cathedral on this site. Governor Macquarie laid the foundation stone for the first church in 1821, when the site was on the eastern fringe of Sydney Town, next to the convict barracks of Hyde Park, on a steep hill above the Woolloomooloo basin. This miserable site reflected the social position of the Irish Australian Catholics. However, even Vicar General Ullathorne, when he arrived in 1833, reported that Father Therry's still roofless church was "a solid noble building, the finest in the colony", which was completed for the arrival of the first bishop, John Bede Polding, in 1835.

Disaster struck on the night of June 29, 1865, when the first cathedral was burned down. We know from his letters that Archbishop Polding often waxed eloquent about his misfortunes. Already in a "sea of troubles", he explained that he was "prostrate, stunned at first by the blow". Eventually, however, he was "almost glad" that the "dreadful calamity" had occurred because of the widespread support outside the Catholic community that Catholics received and because of the new opportunities that now lay open.

Some months later, on October 6, 1865, he commissioned William Wardell, who had already designed Saint John's College at Sydney University and was the finest architect in New South Wales and Victoria, to design a Gothic cathedral in "any plan, any style, anything that is beautiful and grand, to the extent of our power". Wardell warned Polding that it would be "a comparatively costly work", a prophecy that remains true today, because he was building "not for today, but for all time", and "the supreme consideration is not what is cheapest, but what is best." God's house deserves no less.

Today, with modern technology and finance available through development funds or banks, we are used to completing huge building projects in some years. In the Middle Ages, cathedrals were usually only completed over many generations, sometimes across a century or more. Saint Mary's Cathedral falls between these two extremes. The work was substantially completed in three stages, with the official opening of the first stage, the northern section, by Archbishop Vaughan on September 8, 1882. Next, in 1902, Cardinal Moran provided a permanent roof, the stained glass windows, the central Cardinal's Tower, and one bay of the nave, while Archbishop Kelly erected the southern section with the façade and basis of the two towers in 1928. The beautiful spires on these towers were constructed in the Jubilee Year 2000. All in all, our cathedral was finished in one lifetime. Archbishop Redwood of Wellington, New Zealand, who even remembered the old Saint Mary's and preached at Archbishop Vaughan's ceremonies to mark the opening in 1882, was also present, aged ninety, at the 1928 completion ceremony.

Well might we say with the psalmist: "How lovely is your dwelling place, Lord, mighty God" and "Here God lives among his people." The duty of all of us who love this building and worship here is to ensure that this house of God our Father remains a house of regular prayer and does not degenerate simply into a museum visited by largely uncomprehending tourists.

I am pleased to claim, in truth and humility, that the cathedral is now used for worship more frequently than at any time in its history. We have a larger population than earlier generations, and transport is easier. Christ remains our only true foundation, and the physical stones in this building remain at the service of the Spirit and the many living stones, individuals of every age and race, who come here to pray.

Extravagant claims have been made for our cathedral. In 1928 the New South Wales premier Thomas Bavin, the son of a Methodist minister, described it as "the most beautiful cathedral that has been built in the world during the last two hundred years". I have friends in Melbourne and New York who would hear this claim with some skepticism! But Premier Bavin was completely correct in two other claims. First of all, that Saint Mary's is "the possession of all of us, no matter what class or creed we belong to" and that "it stands as a sermon in stone, silent but eloquent witness to the truth that men do not live by bread alone."

Archbishop Vaughan, more than anyone else, deserves praise as the founder of this cathedral. He personally wrote 1466 letters asking for money and one thousand personal "thank you" replies in raising the finance to complete the first phase. He claimed that this cathedral would speak to later generations of the faith of the generation that built it. He was correct.

Today, when many inside the Church, as well as a larger number outside her, can only muster a faith that is uncertain and weak, or even nonexistent, we need to ponder these stones, their beauty, and their order and strive to hear what they are saying.

September 23, 2007
Saint Mary's Cathedral, Sydney

THE CENTENARY OF THE
AUCKLAND CATHEDRAL

F IRST OF ALL, I should begin by congratulating the bishop, the dean, committee, and architect on the renovation of this Cathedral of Saint Patrick and Saint Joseph. It is a gem in your crown, a masterpiece of devotion and restraint, featuring local artists, craftsmanship, poetry, and history. It is a wonderful example of the best of Catholic tradition, developing certainly but respectful of the past, not rejecting it. The cathedral calls us to worship, prayer, and service. Its beauty sets a standard for all of us in this part of the world who are privileged to have the care of a cathedral.

Twenty years ago, I was a member of a joint-churches committee of enquiry into the jails in my home state of Victoria in Australia. When visiting a high security section of one of these jails, I was impressed by seeing an elderly Catholic nun chaplain surrounded by hardened criminals, one at least of whom was a murderer, who obviously admired her as a friend and helper.

On remarking about this to another priest who had worked for years with delinquents, he explained that those of us who regularly live and work with good people can get used to them and take them for granted. Others, however, who know evil well, and especially in the high security sections of jails that are often jungles, close to hell on earth, such unfortunates can be struck by the simplicity, by the aura of peace and benevolence around consistently good people. Undoubtedly, too, years of life experience and being a woman in a male prison strengthen the likelihood of this recognition.

In a similar way I suspect that society generally, including Catholics, can become insensitive to the contributions the Christian churches make to community life, to the vitalizing role Catholic teaching and practice play in the maintenance and increase of both social capital here and now in our civic society and spiritual or supernatural capital for life after death, which we shall only enter after personal judgment by our benign and all-seeing God.

If Ezekiel were writing today, he might have used the image of an electricity power station, but we still understand easily the symbolism of streams of living water coming from the Temple. I am sure that this is not a misleading symbol of Catholic community life here for the hundred years since the completion of the cathedral. Good Catholic communities, despite their faults and partly because they believe in personal repentance and God's forgiveness, do regularly bring health and teeming life to the wider society. As the years pass and the water continues to flow, new types of fruit emerge, perhaps not in every month as the Old Testament imagery claims, but regularly and in every generation, together with new medicines to heal new wounds.

Our first purpose in such an anniversary celebration is to thank God for the mighty efforts of those who labored before us. On this feast of Saint Polycarp of Smyrna, who was martyred around A.D. 156 and was an important link with Saint Irenaeus of Lyons in France, we remember in particular Bishop Pompallier, also from Lyons, who planted the apostolic succession of bishops in New Zealand, all the early missionaries and especially the Marists, then a recently founded congregation, who were given responsibility for the Western areas of the Pacific Ocean.

It was less than a year after the settlement of Auckland on September 18, 1840, that Bishop Pompallier received a grant of land for a church here. In 1848 the new Church of Saint Patrick and Saint Joseph, the first stone building in this city, became the cathedral of the new diocese of Auckland set up by Pope Pius IX, and there was a succession of changes and developments before the new cathedral of 1885 was dismantled, redeveloped, and completed in 1908.

I was pleasantly surprised but also pleased and honored when Bishop Pat Dunn invited me to celebrate this Centenary Mass, so following in the footsteps of my Sydney predecessor, Cardinal Patrick Francis Moran, who celebrated the inaugural Mass exactly one hundred years ago. Press reports spoke of "fine clear weather", a "grand line-up for the occasion" that included the Catholic Prime Minister, Sir Joseph Ward, members of parliament, and a packed church with representatives of the other Christian churches. Nearly £10,000 had been spent, and £586 was collected leaving a debt of nearly £5,000. The choir sang Millard's Mass in G.

You will be pleased to know that Cardinal Moran preached a rousing sermon of fifty minutes' duration on the text: "Pray for the peace of Jerusalem; and may abundance be unto them that love thee", and even more pleased to note that Bishop Patrick has written to me pointing out that it is not necessary to repeat his feat. I suppose only time will tell if his warning has been successful.

I am sure the cardinal was preaching to the converted, but he used Pius X's 1907 encyclical *Pascendi dominici gregis*, which condemned the errors of that age, summarized as Modernism, which was seen as a rationalist attack on revealed truth and an attempted revival of paganism. They were ancient heretical errors under new disguises, he explained. On a happier note, he rejoiced that there were then ninety thousand Catholics in New Zealand's four dioceses, fully equipped with churches, schools, and institutions of charity. This cathedral he described as a gem, "so fair in its proportions, so perfect in its architectural merit, and arranged in beauty even to the minutest details. Thus equipped in everything that was needed, Holy Church would be enabled in the fullest measure to carry on unfettered her glorious mission amongst them."

We would use different words today. Bitter experience has taught us not to be so triumphalist in tone, but my message would be similar. We have solid reasons for confidence about the future, as long as we continue to open all channels for the breath of the Spirit and continue to follow fully and happily the person and teachings of Jesus Christ as understood in the Catholic tradition. I mentioned that we began this centenary celebration by saying thanks, but equally important tasks are to ask the good God to bless our present activities and to give us hope and joy as we move into the future.

The Gospel reading for today about Jesus cleansing the Temple of the money changers and salesmen is a stiff reminder that we must strive to keep our faith, our motives, and our practice pure and not be poisoned by the world around us. We share much that is good with surrounding society, but the people of the Beatitudes must always experience intermittent tension with those who follow other ways. We know well that the old denominational rivalries between Christians are wrong in theory as well as practice and that one significant tension is with those of an aggressive secular agenda, which often wants to exclude the Judaeo-Christian tradition from all public influence.

New Zealand faces all the wonderful opportunities and challenges common to the peaceful, law-abiding English-speaking nations. But you have your particular opportunities and challenges with your own Maori peoples and the migrants from the Pacific Islands, who have done much to strengthen your Church in this city and my own archdiocese of Sydney.

We must always remember the Christian and Catholic capacity for new growth and rebirth. The new missionary orders that were born in nineteenth-century France after decades of revolutionary turmoil and anti-Christian violence were both unexpected and wonderfully fruitful. New Zealand benefited much from this.

I know that the journey of the World Youth Day Cross has been greeted enthusiastically by your young people and that more than four thousand young pilgrims are coming to Australia for World Youth Day in July. These are good signs. These are healthy fruits born as always from the streams of water coming from the throne of the Lamb, Jesus Christ Our Lord. These young people will be following the Cross.

May God continue to bless and reward the Catholic Church in Auckland, and may your Christian endeavors be blessed and go from strength to strength.

February 23, 2008
Cathedral of Saint Patrick and Saint Joseph
Auckland, New Zealand

THE DEDICATION OF THE
LATERAN BASILICA

Ezekiel 47:1−2, 8−9, 12;
1 Corinthians 3:9−11, 16−17; John 2:13−22

T HIS IS one of the strangest Catholic feasts to be celebrated on a
Sunday and probably on any other day: the Dedication of the
Lateran Basilica. Most people believe that the cathedral (a cathedral
is where the bishop has his "cathedra", the Greek word for teaching
chair) of the pope as bishop of Rome is Saint Peter's Basilica in the
Vatican. While the Holy Father lives in the Vatican City State and regularly celebrates Mass in Saint Peter's, that magnificent basilica is not
his cathedral. The pope's cathedral is the Basilica of Saint John Lateran
in Rome. The popes lived at the Lateran Palace until 1377.

In 313, the Emperor Constantine, after winning the Battle of the
Milvian Bridge on the Tiber River outside ancient Rome, issued the
Edict of Milan, which gave religious freedom to all Christians. Nearly
three hundred years of intermittent persecution came to an end, and
Constantine, and especially his mother the Empress Helena, began to
support the Christian community in many ways, although they were
only a minority, perhaps one-seventh of the population. Magnificent
churches, officially recognized as public places for Christian worship,
were built. We are used to church buildings dotted across our suburbs
and country towns, but before Constantine, there were almost no public church buildings, even small ones, to accompany the many pagan
temples.

The Lateran Basilica, the first Christian church in Rome, was built
on land originally owned by the Laterani family that had come into the
Emperor's possession. It was originally the Basilica of the Savior with
the dedication to John the Baptist dating only from the time of Pope

Gregory the Great, around A.D. 600. The land was given in 313 by Emperor Constantine to Pope Miltiades, who reigned for only three years, until A.D. 314, and the basilica has the imposing title of "mother and head of all the churches in the City and the world".

The church has been rebuilt and altered many times, with a major redesign in 1650, although the thirteenth-century cloister still survives. The last major redevelopment took place toward the end of the nineteenth century, under Pope Leo XIII. The main doors of the old Senate house from the Forum, the major legislative center for the ancient Roman Empire, still serve as the main doors of the basilica. It is one of the few remaining relics of those ancient times that are still working, although some aqueducts are carrying water today.

Before trying to explain the religious significance of this feast, we should acknowledge the tremendous gain to Christian people from Constantine's granting them religious freedom. In parts of today's world, Christians live under hostile pressure from governments or from extremist mobs. Religious freedom and what we know as the separation of Church and State are blessings to be vigilantly defended.

The religious importance of this feast is that it reminds us of the central role of the successor of Saint Peter, the papacy, in the worldwide unity and universality of the Catholic Church. Paul's letter to the Corinthians emphasizes that Jesus Christ is our only foundation, but in maintaining fidelity to His teachings and unity in faith, hope, and love around His person, the teaching and disciplinary role of the popes is vital. We must acknowledge that there is nothing automatic or easy about maintaining unity. We have only to look at the proliferation of Protestant groupings, often self-contained local units, to be reminded of the strength of Catholic unity.

The first reading describes one of the spectacular visions of the Old Testament prophet Ezekiel, perhaps my favorite prophet. With his vision of the streams of living water flowing from the Temple and bringing life to the countryside, we have a wonderful image of the contribution good Catholics make to the community. But the water has to be clean and pure so that the fish can increase and thrive and so that the trees by the rivers can produce fruit. When the water is polluted, it is not life producing but damaging.

In today's psalm, the imagery literally moves in the opposite direction to Ezekiel's vision, because in the psalm the waters of the river flow into the City of God. We could stretch this symbolism a bit and see there the contribution of lay people to the clergy, pope, bishops, and priests, through their hard work for Christian values in society, their loyalty and support for the Church leadership, and their requiring the Church's leaders to walk worthily in their vocations.

Let us conclude, then, by praying for the institution of the papacy and our present Holy Father, Pope Benedict, so that the popes will continue to play their divinely ordered role in maintaining unity and in ensuring a regular supply of living water flowing from all the different and local Catholic communities into society.

November 9, 2008
Saint Mary's Cathedral, Sydney

A GATEWAY TO HEAVEN IN CORK

I N THE SECOND-CENTURY "Teaching of the Twelve Apostles" (*Didache*), which is one of the readings in the official Prayer of the Church for last week, we find these beautiful words: "As this broken Bread was scattered upon the mountains and was gathered together and made one, so let your Church be gathered from the end of the earth into your Kingdom: for the glory and power are yours through Jesus Christ for ever and ever."

I am honored to begin the celebrations for 150 years of worship in your Church of Saint Peter and Saint Paul by celebrating this pontifical High Mass as a token gesture of gratitude from Australia, from the ends of the earth, especially from the Catholics in Australia for all the blessings the Irish brought to us Down Under. Undoubtedly the Catholic faith was the greatest of those blessings, but we thank God, too, for all the other human gifts you brought of family, hard work, a sense of justice, a love of freedom, and a sense of humor, which is almost as important.

Hundreds of thousands of Irish men, women, and children sailed from Cork Harbour for the New World of the Americas and Australia. Many of those departing did so unwillingly as guests of His Britannic Majesty, and many were unfortunate and broken. Others left freely, driven out by lack of opportunity for their children, and were scattered far beyond the mountains and across the oceans. But most of them and their successors have done well, built happy and productive lives, and in many cases they were strengthened and directed by their Catholic faith in Jesus Christ Our Lord, to whom the glory and power belong, now as certainly as they did when the *Didache* was first written.

A sesquicentenary is certainly a time to say thanks to Almighty God for all His blessings, but it should not be reduced to an exercise in nostalgia, a basking in the accomplishments of times past. A sesqui-centenary also looks forward confidently to the future and asks God's blessings on what we are doing today to meet our challenges and build constructively for the future.

Every age has its own difficulties, and sometimes these are steeper than at other times. But storms pass and pressures lessen eventually, and, if we have remained true to our Catholic fundamentals—faith, hope, and love expressed in service—then there will be leaders and believers to grasp the new opportunities and strengthen again the faith of our Fathers. And of course you should not forget that the level of religious practice here in Ireland is still higher than in any other part of the English-speaking world, with the possible exception of Malta.

I was born in the southeastern Australian city of Ballarat, famous for its gold in the second half of the nineteenth century and not far from Melbourne, which was led for forty-six years by one of Cork's most famous sons, Archbishop Daniel Mannix. The first ten years of my life were spent in the home that once belonged to my maternal grandparents, where a large portrait of Mannix hung on the wall. One of my aunts was Patricia Mannix Burke.

Mannix's tombstone describes him as "a father to his people". The faith strengthened in his time, and it was under his leadership that Catholics in Australia claimed their place in the sun and became an important part of the mainstream of Australian life through the self-confidence he inspired and the education he fostered. A first cousin of his, also from Cork, Bishop Daniel Foley, was bishop of my own diocese of Ballarat in the 1930s.

In this parish we owe an enormous debt to Archdeacon John James Murphy, who built this beautiful church, and to Edward Welby Pu-gin, the architect. The portrait of the Archdeacon in the Mass booklet portrays a formidable individual with an unusual personal biography, especially for a nineteenth-century priest. He exemplifies the powerful effects of a conversion, a change of direction as he approached midlife. At the age of fourteen, he was a midshipman on the Charles Grant for the British East India Company, returning home to leave again for Canada to work with the Hudson Bay Company. He lived for years with a native American tribe and was known as the "Black Eagle of the North". He was only ordained a priest at the age of forty-two after a conversion experience in Rome. We thank God for this turn of events, for his work here with the poor, especially during the Famine years, and we thank him for this church.

As the parish priest explained, this truly is a house of God and a gateway to heaven. Every church should lift our minds to heaven, remind us of the Transcendent, and lead us to the Mystery of the one true God. All church buildings should also remind us of the heavenly Jerusalem, and the symbols, decorations, and overall plan of neo-Gothic churches achieve this.

The center aisle recalls the glorified streets of heaven mentioned in the Book of Revelation leading to the altar, the banquet table for the heavenly wedding feast of the Lamb of God, a foretaste of heaven made possible by Christ's unique sacrifice on the Cross, which becomes present again every time Mass is celebrated. The beautiful columns that hold up the building with their decorated capitals, the pillars of this church, also remind us of all those hardworking people, the living stones, who keep a church community faithful to its vocation of service. They also echo the bronze columns believed to have been in the Temple at Jerusalem built by Solomon nearly one thousand years before Christ.

The tabernacle on the old High Altar contains the Blessed Sacrament, the abiding presence of Christ in the consecrated hosts, whose adoration is one of the characteristics and strengths of this parish today. Such a tabernacle is a development from and the culmination of the Ark of the Covenant in Solomon's Temple, where God's glory resided among the Jewish people. *The many statues of the saints that gaze down upon us in the central nave and in the sanctuary instruct us that the community of worship is the communion of saints, which embraces the past as well as the present and will continue into the future.*

I believe that one item missing is the foundation stone, a large block of limestone with names and date and blessed by Bishop Delaney, which has been mislaid and cannot be found. I cannot help but wonder whether the stone was laid in the Italian style, as happened in Rome last Monday for the new Australia House, the pilgrim center we will open there in eighteen months time. A hole had been dug, which contained a layer of cement on which I placed the signed stone. Workmen then covered this stone with cement and filled the hole with soil to remain there in perpetuity, or, as I remarked, to remain lost forever.

Certainly your accounts speak of the foundation stone being lowered into place.

I should conclude on a more serious note because the Gospel account from Mark about the feeding of the multitude from the seven loaves and a few fish is a spectacular and miraculous anticipation of all the human works of service that a genuine Catholic parish continues to offer. Certainly in a Catholic church the liturgy regularly reaches out to touch the Eternal as babies are baptized, couples are married, the people are nourished by the Eucharist, and sins are forgiven.

But grace works through nature, and we should not forget the everyday human help that this parish also continues to offer after 150 years —the sense of community, of common rejoicing in good times, of solidarity in distress, of the inner peace and reconciliation that are brought about by forgiveness, of the human structures forged by marriages and baptism, of the comforts given by visiting the sick and aiding the battlers, whether it be in famine times or when a pregnancy is unexpected. God's work is done in many ordinary and wonderful ways.

Let us thank God for the beauty of this church and for all the miracles of grace and acts of kindness that have been brought about in its 150 years of history. We also pray that God will continue to bless this parish community as it moves confidently and humbly into the future and continues to worship Christ Our Lord, who is always coming to meet us.

July 12, 2009
Pontifical High Mass in the Extraordinary Rite
Saint Peter & Saint Paul's Church, Cork, Eire

DOMUS AUSTRALIA IN ROME:
A BEGINNING

Ezekiel 37:21–8; John 11:45–56

A SHORT BUT BEAUTIFUL CHAPTER in the history of the Church will come to a close tomorrow, on Palm Sunday, when you as young pilgrims from Australia hand over the cross and the icon of Mary, which journeyed all around Australia and Oceania, to the young people of Madrid and Spain, where World Youth Day will be celebrated in 2011. For a brief period, we were at the center of the Catholic world. Like the other Australians here in Rome, I was moved by the tributes foreign delegates paid to the joyfulness, faith, and efficient organization of the Sydney gathering.

Catholics, unlike most other Christians, are instinctively universalist. Other Christians usually belong to self-governing local or national churches. We are very conscious of our unity across the centuries back to Christ and of our unity across the nations of the world, united through our bishops around the successor of Saint Peter, Pope Benedict XVI. Many or most Australians were struck by the variety of peoples, by the one hundred-plus nationalities in Sydney, and tomorrow in Saint Peter's Square, we shall be impressed once again by the unity of faith and the multiplicity of nationalities.

More than ten years ago, I was sent as an official Visitor (I think the Australian term would be "friendly inspector") of some seminaries outside Australia, and at the opening Masses I always read the long quotation I am about to read, without telling either staff or students the name of the author, or when and where he lived.

Although the Church is spread throughout the world to the ends of the earth, it received from the apostles and their disciples the faith which it professes. . . . The Church believes these truths as though it had but one soul and one heart, it preaches them and hands them on as though it had but one mouth. . . .

The Church founded in Germany believes exactly the same and hands on exactly the same as do the Spanish and Celtic Churches, and the ones in the East, those in Egypt, and Libya and Jerusalem, the center of the world. . . . Since faith is one and the same, the man who has much to say about it does not add to it and the man who has less does not subtract from it. (*Adversus Haereses*, bk 1.10:1–3)

This is a beautiful quotation. In about ten seminaries that I visited, only one staff member correctly identified the author. Suggestions varied widely, and one student even suggested the then-Cardinal Ratzinger as the writer.

In fact, the author was Saint Irenaeus, bishop of Lyons, in what we now know as southern France and which was then an important Roman town and fortress. The year was about A.D. 180, and indeed the Church in Lyons disappeared from history for many decades after Irenaeus, due to the pagan persecutions. Even then, Christians were conscious that they had inherited in a different and special way the promises the good God made to his people Israel in the prophecies of Ezekiel.

Ezekiel was the strangest of the prophets, who wrote when the northern tribes of Israel had disappeared from history and the southern tribes were in exile in Babylon. Things were bad; in fact, they could hardly have been worse! Yet God still spoke of the sons of Israel coming from everywhere to form one nation, no longer defiled but cleansed from their betrayals and sins. They will have an eternal covenant with the one true God, who will be their God, and they shall be His people. So too, gathered tonight from Australia here in Rome, eighteen hundred years after Irenaeus and more than twenty-five hundred years after Ezekiel, we see ourselves as the spiritual inheritors of the promises made to Ezekiel. Different one from the other, but united in faith.

The principal reason for the purchase and renovation of Domus Australia—Australia House—here in Rome is to strengthen the bonds of unity between the Church of Rome, the Church of Peter's successor, and the Catholic Church in Australia. We in Australia are almost as far away geographically from Rome as it is possible to be. Only New Zealand is a bit farther, but when we move past New Zealand, we begin to approach Rome from the West!

We follow in a long tradition of pilgrimage to Rome and of national communities building pilgrim centers here in the city. In A.D. 726, Ine, the king of Wessex in England, founded a church in Rome for Saxon pilgrims, which still exists but was rebuilt in 1540. English Catholics founded a pilgrim house in 1362, the Scots College began in 1600, and the Irish College in 1628. In other words, we are only breaking new ground for the Church in Australia.

This is the first Australian-sponsored Eucharist in this new center, and I ask you to pray that its work will be blessed in the years to come, so that the house becomes a home away from home for visiting Australians, a cultural and national as well as religious center, a place with daily Mass, which will encourage tourists to become pilgrims and will offer a variety of help to both those who stay and those who visit. May God bless our work.

April 4, 2009
Domus Australia, Rome

6

Jesus' Call to Follow

Mary, Mother of God

FATIMA—AFTER
SEVENTY-FIVE YEARS

THIS YEAR is the seventy-fifth anniversary of the apparitions of Our Lady in Fatima, Portugal, with October 13 being the anniversary of the "miracle of the sun". The apparitions began on May 13, 1917, when Lucia, aged ten, and her two cousins, Francisco, nine, and Jacinta, seven, were tending her parents' flock in a valley about a kilometer outside Fatima. All three were illiterate and not particularly pious; they recited the rosary each day, as they had been told, by reciting only the first two words of the Our Father and the Hail Mary!

Disturbed by lightning, they were running for shelter, when the two girls saw a "pretty little lady" standing above a tree. Only Lucia heard her say she was from heaven, telling them to come back on the thirteenth of the month for the next six months. Jacinta never spoke to Our Lady, and initially, Francisco could not see the vision. The apparitions were eventually approved by the Church, and both Pope Paul VI and Pope John Paul II visited Fatima on pilgrimage. However, some difficulties remain. It seems that Fatima is like so much of the rest of Catholicism, where we have confusion, if not error, mixed with truth, even in the Scriptures, with our treasures often found in earthen vessels or shoddy containers.

A couple of these difficulties should be mentioned. It was on May 13 that Lucia believed Our Lady to say, in answer to her question, that a local child who had died would be in purgatory until the end of the world. This seems excessive by any human standards. On October 13, Lucia believed Our Lady to say that the First World War would end that day and that the soldiers would soon return home; in fact, the War did not end for another thirteen months.

Crowds increased in number each month, without any encouragement from the government or the Church. In fact, this was a time of strong anticlericalism, and the secular government feared a religious revival. The local administrator was a violent atheist who imprisoned the children for a night on August 13, threatening to fry them in boiling oil! The children stuck to their story. The local priest was initially skeptical also, as was his duty, and he even wondered in June whether the apparitions were from the devil. With time, such opposition softened.

Our Lady was described as wearing a white dress with gold borders, tied at the neck with a golden cord. She also wore a white veil, carried a white rosary, and wore small gold earrings.

On October 13, an excited crowd of seventy thousand had gathered at the Cova in pouring rain for the expected miracle. Lucia's mother was frightened that there would be no miracle and the crowd would take revenge on the family; thousands were on their knees weeping and praying when Our Lady did appear, telling Lucia that she was the Lady of the Rosary. She then disappeared.

It was after this that Lucia cried out: "Look at the sun", and claimed she saw a succession of visions. The rain had now stopped, and tens of thousands saw the phenomena, which they described in various ways: the sun rotating, zigzagging from east to west, appearing to fall from the sky and then return. The "dance of the sun" was an extraordinary event by any calculations.

Church approval came slowly, after Francisco died of influenza in 1919 and Jacinta in 1920. A canonical inquiry was set up by the bishops in 1922, and in 1930 they declared the apparitions worthy of belief. Pope Pius XII was a great champion of Fatima. On the twenty-fifth anniversary, he consecrated the world to the Immaculate Heart of Mary, and in 1952 he consecrated Russia to Our Lady. Lucia claimed that if this were done by the pope and bishops, the conversion of Russia would follow.

Apparitions such as Lourdes or Fatima can never be at the center of our faith; only Christ, the Son of God, has this central role. Also, all apparitions fall under the authority of the Church, not just in the sense that the Church is forced to judge whether people can be prudently encouraged to visit a place and pray there, but, more importantly, whether the messages are in conformity with the gospel.

It was the messages of Fatima, despite the odd, difficult detail, much more than the October miracle, that gained Church approval. The threefold message of Fatima was the call to penance, to the recitation of the rosary, and to devotion to the Immaculate Heart of Mary. Lucia herself became a Carmelite nun and wrote two accounts of the visions.

Lenin had not staged his coup when the apparitions ended, and no one then foresaw the evil the Communists would unleash on the world. For many years, at the end of Mass, in response to the Fatima message, we prayed for the conversion of Russia.

The Communist collapse in Europe and Russia is a momentous event, mostly in its consequences, and never hinted at by the best opinion. Equally surprising was the visit of Mikhail Gorbachev to Pope John Paul II in December 1989, a visit that will rank with Leo the Great's bargaining with the barbarians in the fifth century or, more aptly, with the visit of the German Emperor Henry IV to submit to Pope Gregory VII at Canossa in 1077. "We need spiritual values, we need a revolution of the mind", Gorbachev told the pope. "All of them [the people of the USSR] have a right to satisfy their spiritual needs."

Whatever the subsequent history of Eastern Europe and the former USSR, the peaceful collapse of Communist atheism is a far greater miracle than the miracle of the sun. It is an amazing conclusion to the second Christian millennium.

September 4, 1992
AD2000

MARY—A SIGN
OF CONTRADICTION

I T WAS SAINT BERNARD who pointed out that just as God only came among us through the agency of Mary, so it is not improper for us to come to the Son of God and His Heavenly Father through this same Mary. Jesus was and is human and divine; a mystery that equals the mystery of the Trinity. Mary was only human, but she is the finest human embodiment of God's love and compassion, and her love takes us to her Son.

We Australians, even at a time of around 10 percent unemployment, live in a land of milk and honey, never dreamed of by our ancestors and that is still the envy of most people on this planet. But for many, this has not brought happiness, and there is much personal suffering. Why is this so? Alexander Solzhenitsyn, the great Russian novelist, pointed out many times that the terrible disasters of this century, two world wars, Nazism and Communism, occurred because people had forgotten God. Solzhenitsyn has claimed that for the Communists, the true Marxist-Leninists, hatred of God was their principal driving force.

In Eastern Europe and Russia, the Christian tradition survived in spite of "dungeon, fire, and sword," as the old hymn told us, and it is the Communists who have gone; and gone forever, we hope and pray. *But Solzhenitsyn has also pointed out with equal accuracy that we in the Western world have likewise "experienced a drying up of religious consciousness. The gradual sapping of strength from within is a threat to faith that is perhaps even more dangerous than any attempt to assault religion violently from without."* Only time will tell how we cope with these internal challenges, but I believe that Our Lady stands as an important sign of contradiction against one strand of the threats internal to Christianity.

Many supporters of the feminist cause in the secular media are either uninterested in or hostile to religion, although the media is always interested in conflict, and they will continue to combine with a small number of theologians who call themselves Christian to reject the notion that God might have become a man. Once the Divinity of Christ is rejected, the whole idea of redemption becomes impossible. In the Second Letter to the Corinthians, Paul tells us that "God in Christ was reconciling the world to himself." For extreme feminists, such language is a lie; evidence of patriarchy, which must be destroyed. Already one or two of these writers are speaking of devotion to Christ as "Christo-fascism".

It is a matter of record that few feminists have a strong devotion to Our Lady. I vividly remember hearing a lecture on women in the Scriptures where Our Lady was never mentioned! It seems to me that in the struggle, which has already begun, for the maintenance of Christian tradition, devotion to Mary, soundly biblical and minus superstition, will be one of the hallmarks of the truth.

In the past, Roman Catholics, Orthodox, Anglicans, and Protestants differed bitterly about what constituted the essential tradition of doctrine and practice; but all agreed that there was such a tradition, deriving from Christ and the apostles, which had to be maintained at every cost. In some way, today, in every great Christian denomination, it is this very notion of a central essential tradition that is under attack.

I do not want to overemphasize the spread of this poison here in Australia, but such ideas are in circulation. Not a few Christians reject the notion that Christ is divine; many more state that Christ could only teach from within the limitations of His period of history; many more will assert that Christianity needs to catch up with the times, "to get with it", as they say or used to say.

In the *Memorare*, the beautiful prayer of intercession traditionally ascribed to Saint Bernard but that more probably dates from the fifteenth century, we claim it was never known anywhere or in any age that any man or woman who prayed to Our Lady for help and protection was left unaided. It is for this reason that I mention these struggles, not to spread alarm or to exaggerate, but to ask you all to pray to Mary, our Mother, that here in Australia we shall continue to acknowledge the one great God and Christ His only Son and that the Catholic tradition of the Creed will always remain a vital public force in this country and in every one of the major Christian denominations.

As the Australian poet James McAuley wrote so beautifully:

> Dawn-wading ibis; desert pool
> Gold monstrance of our altars;
> Star of evening, shining calm
> On dark uneasy waters:
> Queen of Heaven, as we revere
> The Word that formed your story,
> So from our long distractions here
> Receive us into glory.

Fourth Sunday of Lent, 1992
"Walk With Mary" between Saint Patrick's and
Saint Paul's Cathedrals, Melbourne

OUR LADY HELP OF CHRISTIANS

Isaiah 9:1–6; Ephesians 1:3–6, 11–12; Luke 1:39–56

T ODAY IN ROME the Holy Father will consecrate the New Millennium to the protection of Our Lady. We are celebrating two thousand years since the birth of Jesus, although we are not entirely sure that we have the sums right, and some learned people say that Jesus was born in three, four, five, or six B.C. Whatever about that, it is a beautiful practice to count the years in our story from the birth of Christ.

It was not something that started immediately. It was not something that even started after the Roman Empire became Christian. It took some hundreds of years. In civil society, people counted from a variety of dates: the foundation of Rome, the coming of the Romans to Spain, or the recognition of Christianity in the Roman Empire. Then it was triggered by disputes about the date of Easter, and only gradually did this beautiful practice come to develop. So we speak of B.C. and A.D. —B.C., before Christ, and Anno Domini, from the Year of the Lord. I think it is worth battling to preserve these conventions, these styles, where quite a number today want to substitute B.C.E. or C.E.—before the Common Era or the Common Era for before Christ and A.D.

It makes sense for the Holy Father to ask Our Lady's protection in a special way because Mary took good care of Jesus, the Son of God, and if she did that, she can and will and does take good care of us. We are following along in a scriptural tradition because we are all aware that when Jesus was dying on the Cross, He said to John, "John, behold your Mother" and to His Mother "Behold your son." I think it is an entirely legitimate belief that on this occasion John was representing all of us.

In Australia we are under the patronage of Our Lady Help of Christians, a decision that was made by the Australian bishops early on, when they remembered more vividly than we do that Our Lady was invoked under that title at the time of Napoleon. Napoleon imprisoned Pius VI, who died in captivity, and then also imprisoned Pius VII. Thanks was given to Our Lady Help of Christians when the pope was liberated and Napoleon defeated.

We are also aware that Our Lady Help of Christians was invoked in the sixteenth century by Pope Pius V—a very austere Dominican who did a lot for the implementation—finally—of the Council of Trent and the reform of the Church when she needed reforming—much more, even, than today. Pius put together a coalition of Christian princes who defeated the Turks at the Battle of Lepanto in 1571. It was of enormous significance for the whole of Christian Europe, so that even Elizabeth I, the great Protestant Queen of England, who so ruthlessly and effectively persecuted Catholics, ordered that there be Christian celebrations of thanksgiving after that famous victory. And Pius V ordered thanks to be given to Mary, Help of Christians. Another interesting little detail is that when the news of the pope's death arrived at Istanbul, history records that the Turks he defeated danced in the streets.

Devotion to Our Lady is also an important bridge for us with our brothers and sisters in the Orthodox Churches, who are so close to us doctrinally and also in their ecclesiology. A recent document from Rome on *Jesus the Lord* reaffirms that we believe that the Orthodox Churches are genuine Churches with valid sacraments, valid orders, bishops, and priests. We have very good relations here in Australia, but it would be good to build on those and to take them forward.

The second reading today from Paul to the Ephesians speaks of Jesus and God's predetermined plan of the One who guides all things. In other words, we restate the Christian claim that there is such a thing as salvation history, the key to the whole history of the world and to the creation of the cosmos. And within that history, Mary played a crucial role. You might even say that the whole plan of salvation stood or fell on her decision to accept the will of God and to participate in the redemption.

It is wonderful that we believe—the gift of faith is an immense blessing. And as the number of people in our society who do not have any religion at all rises, the more we should thank God that, either through personal conversion or through the fact that we were born into Catholic families, we have the gift of faith.

It is such a strange and beautiful and startling belief that we have. Once upon a time, in ancient times, we believed that our little planet, the earth, was the center of the universe. We believed that the sun revolved around our earth and that the stars did, too. Now from science, we know much better. We know that there are probably as many stars in the universe as there are grains of sand on every beach in the world.

Our planet is very, very tiny in this immensity of space. In a parallel way, the birth of the Redeemer, a young, helpless baby in Bethlehem in the immensity of human history, among the billions of people who lived before and have lived since, is also a great cause for wonder. And that young girl, a most wonderful person, gave birth to our Savior. We do not know how old she was, twelve, thirteen, or fourteen, and we can be sure she was not highly educated.

It is such a miracle and such a startling belief. All the people who walked in darkness have seen a great light. It is the crucial and defining factor in history for us.

We know that Jesus had no human father. Therefore, all of Jesus' human heredity came through Mary and her ancestors. I am sure that Joseph had an important role in the development of the personality of Jesus, but that came through nurture, not through nature.

So just as we recognize what God is like through Jesus, so through Jesus we can also have a very good idea of what Mary was like with her faith, love, goodness, and strength. Because Jesus was a man, He was unable to reveal to us what we might describe as the feminine dimension of God our Father. But in a subordinate but very real way, Mary reveals something to us about God that Jesus could not reveal. And we thank God for that. It is one reason why so many people choose to approach God and Jesus through Mary. And it is connected, of course, with the human fact that in our families quite a number of children find it easier to talk to Mum than talk to Dad. That is certainly true in Australian society, but I suspect it runs right through human nature.

Mary is a model of faith and a model of love, and if we look at the Magnificat, that powerful prayer in Luke's Gospel, we can also gain some insight into the character of Our Lady. A number of people, even Catholics today, object to venerating Our Lady because they suggest that she was simply meek and a bit of a doormat and no appropriate model for anybody in the twentieth century. Yet every bit of evidence we have, from the Son she produced and especially from this Magnificat, even if it was not spoken by her exactly in this form, suggests otherwise. The Magnificat is an interesting and provocative prayer, which speaks of princes being pulled down from their thrones, of the Almighty showing the power of His arm, of the proud of heart being routed, and of the hungry being filled with good things.

It expresses a righteous anger, something that is sublimated. In the last week I was rereading again some of the poems of the Holy Father, which he wrote anonymously as a young priest when the Communists were still in control in Poland, and he speaks on quite a number of occasions explicitly about anger. He speaks about a righteous anger against caprice and cruelty and injustice, which were certainly some of the hallmarks of the society in which Jesus grew up.

So with every confidence in the evidence, we can appeal to Our Lady as a model of appropriate Christian strength, based on faith and hope and love. Mary is certainly an appropriate model for us in this day and age because Mary is a constant reproach to the modern cult of "self", to the modern ideal of pagan autonomy, that we can write our own rules, that we must construct our own future, despite tradition, despite moral truth, and, sometimes, despite the rights of others.

It is true that conversion to Christ, as Mary shows, always involves an act of submission, but saying Yes in freedom in no sense diminishes us. Salvation history would have either foundered or had to take a completely different course if Mary had not freely said Yes at the time of the Annunciation. Mary, therefore, reminds each of us of the vital importance of falling in with God's plan, of saying yes to our daily obligations, to what God wants us to do. Sometimes it is very hard to recognize what exactly that is, but there should be no doubt among us of our obligation to try to identify God's will and to follow it.

And finally, I would like to ask you to pray and invoke Our Lady's intercession for peace. It is a tragedy that in the Holy Land, the land where Mary and Jesus both lived, we now have renewed danger of the peace process collapsing and outright war breaking out again. This morning on the news, too, we heard again of violence in different parts of Indonesia and of continuing tension there between the small minority of beleaguered Christians and hostile Muslim fundamentalists.

So let us pray for peace throughout the world, peace in the Holy Land, peace close to our shores, and let us ask Our Lady's intercession and protection on us, that the flame of faith will continue to burn strongly in our hearts, in our families and society, and that we will be able to hand on the flame of faith, especially to the young people among us.

October 8, 2000
Mass for the Marian Congress
Saint Patrick's Cathedral, Melbourne

THE IMMACULATE CONCEPTION:
TEACHERS' GRADUATION

Genesis 3:9–15, 20; Ephesians 1:3–6, 11–12;
Luke 1:26–38

TODAY is the feast of the Immaculate Conception of Our Lady; a feast that is not widely understood by Catholics, although it was solemnly defined in Rome on December 8, 1854, by Pope Pius IX, less than a week after a small uprising had been put down in a rough mining town on the other side of the world called Ballarat; an incident we now recall as the Eureka Stockade. The bull declared that Mary, the Mother of God, from the first moment of conception had been free from original sin; in other words, that she was, and is, in a spiritual sense totally beautiful and perfect, full of innocence and holiness. She was worthy to be the mother not merely of a good man, not even of a great religious teacher, but of the Messiah, the Son of God. She accepted this, not in a burst of pride, but in wonderment and puzzle. "She was deeply disturbed by these words and asked herself what this greeting could mean."

I believe there are a number of messages in this feast for the two groups of graduates we have here in the cathedral; those who are about to commence work in the schools and those teachers who are furthering their education. This latter group knows well the consolations and rewards of teaching, as well as the humdrum, disappointments, and, especially, the need for persistence. All this lies before the preservice graduates. One or two of them might be tempted to think that the hard work is over. One or two, perhaps, having avoided overwork so far, will hope this tradition continues! All beginning teachers, however, are entering a noble profession that rewards richly those who work hard.

We might begin by reminding graduates, a reminder that would have been less necessary twenty or thirty years ago, of the important place devotion to Our Lady has in Catholic tradition. It is one of the boasts of Australian Catholicism, and we, as priests and teachers, must work to retain this tradition.

Secondly, this feast of the Mother of God, which emphasizes her perfection and holiness, also reminds us of the special claims and nature of Catholicism. Catholicism is a ferment of love, which works on people's minds and cleanses their hearts. It cannot be reduced to the common sense of the past or the wisdom of the present. The Church does not present a point of view, an option to be considered, but claims to teach truths: truths of faith and moral truths that explain a lot about God and life. These truths are sometimes difficult and often inconvenient. Our Lord said we were to answer these challenges—or pay the penalties from conscious rejection. This is not a modern perspective.

A word or two about the origins of the dogma might also be instructive. The development of this doctrine is not a story of triumphal progress or universal approval, but of difference and division for over a thousand years before 1854. Based on scriptural teaching, such as today's readings, our first evidence for the celebration of the feast is found in the Eastern Church in the seventh century. In the Middle Ages, most of the theological "heavies" opposed the doctrine, including Saint Albert the Great, Saint Bonaventure, and even Saint Thomas Aquinas in most of his writings. Strangely enough, the defense was led by a Scot, Duns Scotus (I think we derive the word "dunce" from him), who was, of course, an Oxford man.

Pope Pius IX, who defined the doctrine of the Immaculate Conception, was another man condemned to swim against the tide. Elected pope in 1846 as the movement for the unification of Italy was gaining strength and the currents of democracy and republicanism were coming into ascendancy, he was initially very popular. This changed dramatically. In 1849, he was besieged by revolutionaries in the Quirinale palace (now home of the Italian president) and forced to flee to Gaeta in southern Italy. At his funeral in 1878, the Roman mob tried to throw his coffin into the Tiber. He lost the Papal States but presided over a religious revival, especially in the English-speaking world, which included the Australian colonies. While his pontificate had many political and intellectual failures, these were more than balanced by spiritual and ecclesiastical achievements.

These examples are a long way from life in Victoria in 1984. Let me try to explain their significance. We do not want teachers who are slaves to the present moment, blind servants of today's trends, whether these are good, bad, or indifferent. We want teachers who know Christ, love Christ and the Church, who know their business, who know and love the world of today; but teachers who throttle the beasts that assail us, not once in a while, but day in and day out. The beasts I refer to are the consequences in our pupils of unemployment, family breakdown, religious indifference, and the coarsening of public taste.

Teachers must not leave to one side the many disturbed and difficult children, often victims of family breakdown and often alone and frightened behind their masks of indifference, rudeness, or aggression. These children need time and consistent, just discipline, sympathy, and much tact before they can be helped and consoled.

Teachers must not take refuge in the platitude, the false and misleading platitude, that schools can do nothing for the religious development of children from irreligious homes. Not every Catholic school, but good Catholic schools with good teachers can influence every type of student for the better. This work is hard and sometimes heartbreaking, but, as a minimum, every student should meet teachers who care passionately about Christ and His Church; every student should have experienced the warmth of Christian community in his school and at least know the basics of the religious tradition he might choose to ignore or reject.

Finally, teachers simply should not accept from students the vulgarity, abuse, and violence that are now a regular feature of some television shows and videos and that are tolerated in many circles. Such extremes are incompatible with a Christian community and we do children a disservice if they know no better and come to accept all this as normal.

I am sure you will often find these four beasts in rude health. They are far from being throttled, but the first reading speaks of the struggle between the seed of the woman and the followers of evil, of Satan the serpent. You are asked to join this struggle between good and evil, and I commend these causes to you. No battle was ever won without a fight.

Let me conclude with a pious story about an impious fellow, which I read in the *Southern Cross*, the Adelaide Catholic paper, some weeks ago. Frederick the Great was the ruler of Prussia from 1740–1786 who began the German rise to power, which was continued by Bismarck last century and which culminated in two World Wars this century. Described by one historian as a "barbarian of genius", he belonged to the Hohenzollern family, a group of ruthless military adventurers, who, the same historian claimed, "excelled in nothing but savagery and conquest". He also smelled a lot, washing rarely (even by the standards of the day), but was something of a patron of learning and the arts.

When he was to be crowned, his Prime Minister showed him the list of people to be invited to his coronation—princes, dukes, generals, and bankers, etc. "Where is Franz von Huegel?" he asked. "Von who?" came the reply. "He was my old teacher, and I owe him much more than any baroness or banker."

The minister still objected, claiming that the social status of teachers was too lowly for attendance at the coronation. Frederick insisted, and the story continues that in his kingdom teachers did have a place of honor, because "one good teacher makes many thousands of good citizens."

Pupil-teacher ratios are probably better now, but teachers live longer. I still think it possible for a teacher to be closely associated with a thousand children in a normal lifetime of teaching. Frederick might have been wrong on many things, but he was correct in being grateful to his teacher and in his estimate of the importance of teachers.

I wish all today's graduates, new and less new, my congratulations. I well remember my elation at the graduation of 1976 when we turned out our first Aquinas-trained teachers from a campus that was then embattled and whose future was parlous. As I leave the Institute, my feelings are more subdued, but my pride and confidence in the quality of our graduates has increased, and I have no fears for the future of the Institute.

Teaching is a noble profession. May Christ and His Mother bless all the graduates, and may you bring peace and learning to all your pupils.

December 8, 1984
Aquinas campus, Institute of
Catholic Education graduation, Ballarat

Christians in Public Life

THE RIGHT TO PUBLIC WORSHIP

T HIS BICENTENARY EUCHARIST to commemorate the first officially
permitted Mass in the young colony of New South Wales, celebrated by Father James Dixon on May 15, 1803, is a Catholic celebration of Christian faith, hope, and love. We have many reasons to
rejoice, to be grateful. Australian society has been good to the Catholic
community, and, in turn, the Catholics over more than two hundred
years have served well on the highways and many neglected byways
of Australian life. This tradition of public service has expanded and
flourished with the years.

Despite official requests, no Catholic chaplain was allowed to accompany the First Fleet. There was an Anglican chaplain, the Reverend Richard Johnson, a dedicated Evangelical, who struggled alone
against the drunkenness and licentiousness. A priest from the visiting
Spanish expedition of 1793 was astonished that there was not a single
church in the colony (an Anglican church was built later that year),
adding that the Spanish colonizers always built a house for God before
any human habitation and certainly before a jail. The NSW Governors
often fulfilled the role of chief chaplain, for example, decreeing days
of prayer in times of drought. Governor Bourke had the best record
as heavy rain fell nine days after his intercessions.

Father James Dixon was one of the three convict priests transported
from Ireland among the 560 Irishmen so punished after the 1798 Rebellion of the United Irishmen, a joint Protestant and Catholic uprising
led by the Ulsterman Wolfe Tone and inspired by the French Revolutionary principles of liberty, equality, and fraternity. Father Dixon was
described as a "kind and inoffensive man, rather wanting in energy and
decision". A priest of the Ferns diocese, he was not the stuff of rebels
and was friendly with the local Protestant gentry and clergy.

Protestant and Catholic friends attest that Dixon played no part in the insurrection. He was unlucky enough to belong to a family who were heavily involved, such as his cousin Father Thomas Dixon, who had been suspended by his bishop in 1794 for "drinking, dancing, and disorderly conduct". Captain Nicholas Dixon, a rebel leader, was his brother, and another brother or cousin, Captain Thomas Dixon, was accused of a leading role in a massacre of loyalist prisoners on Wexford Bridge. This was the background to his condemnation. He arrived in Australia on February 17, 1800.

The population then was about five thousand and a couple of thousand larger in 1803. About one-third were Catholics. Philip Gidley King was the Governor. He was a decent man of genuine faith, sometimes bad tempered and bibulous, capable of cruelty when his high hopes were disappointed. He had a difficult job running the colony as he battled Macarthur and the Rum Corps. He lamented their "credulous ignorance" and believed "no description of people are so bigoted to their religion and priests as the Irish."

Local Catholics had again petitioned for a priest in 1792 and 1796, and the Governor believed that a steady priest like Dixon would improve convict behavior and prevent another local rising like that of 1800. Permission to celebrate the Mass was proclaimed at Government House, Parramatta, on April 20, 1803, and Father Dixon was to receive five shillings a day as well as conditional emancipation.

The site of the first Mass is still disputed: open space, public institution, or private home. However, local tradition now favors James Dempsey's Kent Street home. James Dempsey and Father Dixon had been friends in Ireland, and the crucifix and candles on the altar today were those used at that first official Mass, passed down through five generations of the Dempsey family and now on a long-term loan to the cathedral. James Dempsey was the architect and head stonemason for the original Saint Mary's Cathedral, which burned down in 1865, and was a generous donor to the cathedral. Dempsey family tradition asserts that Father Dixon was forbidden to preach at his Masses and that much of his ministry was underground.

Governor King had hoped that the practice of their religion would do the Catholics "much good or, at least, no harm". He was to be disappointed. In January 1804, Dixon had been appointed "Prefect Apostolic of all Missions within the territory of New Holland" by the

Holy See, but on March 4,1804, 333 rebels at Castle Hill, under the Irishman William Johnston, began a wild bid for liberty by marching on Parramatta and Sydney. The next day, Monday, at Vinegar Hill, a detachment of twenty-five soldiers killed nine of the rebels and put the rest to flight. It was all over.

Only the leaders were tried. Some were hanged, others flogged, some reprieved. Although Father Dixon had ridden out with the New South Wales corps and unsuccessfully tried to persuade the rebels to surrender, permission to say Mass was withdrawn, and he eventually lost his salary. He had failed to prevent seditious talk among his Mass-goers.

We know little of his activity after this until he received his pardon on George III's birthday in 1809. He returned to Ireland that year, becoming parish priest of Crossabeg in 1819, after working as an assistant at New Ross in south Wexford. He died in 1840.

This is not a story of heroism played out in a grand setting. The first good shepherd to care for his flock in Australia was himself a convict supported by a minority of ordinary folk, convicts, ex-convicts, free men and women. From this small trickle, a mighty stream of living water has nourished Australian life.

Today, in remembering Father Dixon, we pay particular tribute to all those priests who have served God and their people during two hundred years in Australia. And also on this Mothers' Day, we should not forget the wives and mothers who passed on the faith in their families. We all continue in their debt.

Times have changed for the better since 1803. No longer do we have a small penal colony for convicts transported from the other side of the earth to a place where floggings and executions were regular events and the worst troublemakers sent on to Norfolk Island, where, Doctor Ullathorne later reported, those to be executed often welcomed their release. Relationships between the Christian churches in Australia are now excellent, despite occasional moments of strain about moral issues. Interfaith relations are also peaceful and sound, despite the rise of Islamic fundamentalism overseas. We therefore find it difficult to understand the depth of hatred and bitterness between Catholics and Protestants, English and Irish, convicts and jailers in those days. We are well rid of such hatreds and must always work to prevent their return.

The Catholic community is no longer a small, poor, almost persecuted minority, but is an active, energetic participant in the mainstream of Australian life; chastened by recent scandals, facing many challenges internally and externally, but basically confident, at ease, and, above all, at home in Australia. We thank God for all this. We pray that our lives may be worthy of the Christian doctrines we profess, and we pray that we will be able to pass on the treasures we have received to succeeding generations.

May 11, 2003
Bicentenary of the First Official Catholic Mass in Australia
Saint Mary's Cathedral, Sydney

REASON AND MORAL REALISM

Jeremiah 31:31–4; I Corinthians 3:1–6; John 14:15–21

B Y COINCIDENCE, as I was preparing this sermon, I read a speech Bishop Eusebius of Caesarea in Syria delivered in July 336, in the new city of Constantinople, to commemorate thirty years of rule by the Roman Emperor Constantine; he who stopped the persecutions and granted toleration to the Christians in 313 after nearly three hundred years of intermittent but increasingly vicious persecutions. Eusebius himself had been jailed in the persecution of Diocletian.

What surprised me was that Eusebius began this tribute by describing the one true God and the role of the Word or Reason of God (Logos), who is Jesus Christ. He follows this theme throughout, comparing God as Ruler of the cosmos with the emperor ruling his empire. Eusebius was not a democrat or republican, because just as there was one God, so there should be one ruler! The comparison is flattering, of course, for the emperor, but the Godly attributes and activities required of him are strict and demanding, very different from the antics of the ancient gods and the cruelty and hedonism of many earlier emperors.

Today we do not instinctively start with God and then systematically spell out the consequences for daily life of the Judaeo-Christian understanding of God. But if we are logical Christians, we do have a particular approach to history and life. There exists a Judaeo-Christian (and therefore monotheist) cast of mind, which follows from our understanding of God.

The God we follow is usefully delineated in today's readings. God is personal; indeed, He is more than a person, not merely because we speak of the three Persons of the Trinity, but because God is infinitely more capable of those activities which define a person, separating persons from animals and blind physical forces. The Creator God is rational and reasonable, who knows and decides and who loves. So the psalmist speaks of God as kind and merciful, full of compassion and love, who forgives our sins and redeems us from the grave.

God loves His children, refuses to let them become orphans, and sets up a covenant, a special relationship with a group He constitutes as especially His own. The Greek and Roman gods of mythology had no interest in human behavior, but the one true God is involved in our lives and keen that we follow His ways, that we love one another in community.

The Spirit of the Living God writes in our hearts, producing life and love, which need to be focused, channeled, and protected by laws and commandments. The link is quite explicit in today's passage from John's Gospel because the Spirit of Truth insists that if we love as we should, we must keep the commandments.

In other words, the traditional Christian understanding is that there is a natural moral law for human activities to be discerned by reason, which maximizes human flourishing when it is followed. Oddly, this is often rejected today by many of the same people who are most insistent that we respect the laws of physical nature, often paying such laws an exaggerated and even superstitious reverence in their ecological prognostications on the future. But that is another story.

Therefore an important divide today is between those who work to discern the moral truths in created reality—moral realists, often theists —and those who believe that our higher form of animal life is to be shaped and improved in any ways the majority or the more powerful forces in society see fit. This explains why there is no consensus on the foundations of human rights, why human rights arguments are used both to destroy and to defend human life. So, too, there are very different notions of conscience at work, even in the Christian communities, and different concepts of the person, as individual members of different collectives or individuals with sovereign powers, possessing a sphere of autonomy, where the aspirations for personal happiness compete with, and often prevail over, the rights of others. Struggles over the definition of the family are an example of these different contending forces.

In 2004, Professor Yves Lequette gave a provocative and pessimistic lecture at the Sorbonne celebrating the Bicentenary of the French Civil Code. Quoting Henri Battifol, he claimed that *"menageries will never*

make a society", because *"there can be no viable society in a meeting of egos."*
He grimly predicted that society will become more and more like a
procession of loners worshipping only two values, money and hedonism, profit and pleasure. "Without sufficiently robust family or political ties", he warned that society will become "a site of unending
confrontation between rival desires".

I believe similar forces are at work here in Australia. For me, the
question is how far we are down this track and what can be done to
explain and defend the traditional bases of community life, to defend
the consequences of Judaeo-Christian monotheism.

Lawyers have an extremely powerful position in Australia and not
merely because of your different roles in administering justice. Lawyers
also contribute mightily to public debate and the forming of public
opinion, in the framing of laws and in ensuring that a proper separation of powers continues. Lawyers are prominent in every level of
government. Your vocation is crucially important.

If we believe in God as Creator, Lawgiver, and Covenant Maker (and
His Son as our Redeemer), this has important consequences for public
life. I ask you to ponder these consequences, defend and develop them,
not because they are religious truths, but because they are rational, useful for persons, and beneficial for society.

The Spirit of the Living God will always continue to give life to
individuals and societies, when the Spirit can be found, identified, and
sometimes codified and protected.

January 29, 2007
Red Mass (for lawyers and judges)
Saint Mary's Cathedral, Sydney

THE PROPER ORDER OF THINGS

Romans 12:2; Psalm 67

W E ARE GATHERED here in Saint Stephen's to thank God for 150 years of self-government in NSW and for the progress this has brought, to ask God's continued blessing on our state and nation, and to acknowledge the indispensable contribution the Christian churches have made to the common good. We recommit ourselves, as approximately 70 percent of the population, to strengthening our contribution to what Saint Paul describes as "the good, acceptable, and perfect" in our society and maintaining the Christian voices in public discussion.

Recently, a retired senior figure publicly criticized the proposition that marriage between a man and a woman should be legally privileged. He objected that this was a Christian notion and therefore could safely be rejected in our pluralist society. The criticism was misconceived for a number of reasons. Men and women of every religion and of no religion marry one another, so there is nothing uniquely Christian or, indeed, Judaeo-Christian about marriage.

More importantly, Christian contributions to public debate espouse particular solutions, not because they are Christian, but because of the social benefits they confer or because they conform to the natural law, to the proper ordering of society. The marriage of a man to a woman brings immense benefits to society through the love and protection of parents for their children. In other words, there is an intergenerational dividend not equaled by any alternatives, and it is for this reason that marriage should be legally privileged. And there is much evidence that public opinion massively supports this and recognizes these benefits.

Christianity is one important source of public inspiration, and the different Christian churches might be described as mighty rivers watering our huge, dry continent. Governments and oppositions are the fruit of the society that elects them. They generally share more of the strengths and at least some of the weaknesses of their communities. We are in trouble when the percentages of good and evil are reversed! Societies where Judaeo-Christian truths and values are accepted and practiced are different. I suspect they are generally better. This is not inevitable, but they are certainly different. One does not need to think only of Communist states to realize this: one need only look at our neighbors.

The recognition of God to whom we shall answer for our conduct, the central position of love, the explicit rejection of hatred, the judicial curbing of the thirst for revenge, patience in suffering rather than eliminating the sufferer, compassion for those who weep and are persecuted, the exaltation of peace rather than war are marks of Christian Australia.

Not all these values are shared equally by explicitly secular societies or societies based on other religious or ethical codes. We are tempted to regard most of the values I listed as immemorial, plain common sense, and therefore beyond dispute. But the decency and fairness in our society are not inevitable or permanent; they need to be nurtured, explained, and defended to each new generation.

Christian churches today are major sources of harmony, even when they espouse views different from those of the secularist minority or even from the majority of Australians. A strong democracy accepts the rights of minorities and is tolerant of differences.

Tolerance does not mean indifference to differences; rather it means that genuine and important differences are discussed and debated within the bonds of civility. Democracy does not require moral relativism and is enriched by orderly public argument about contending truth claims. The Judaeo-Christian tradition has a vital public role in explaining and defending these perspectives.

In the past, the different Christian churches often followed different national boundaries and were sources of sectarian conflict. We thank God this era has passed and renew our commitment to preserving and developing a rich and varied polity.

With the psalm we pray, "the earth has yielded its increase; God, our

God, has blessed us." And so we conclude by asking that this continue. "May God be gracious and bless us and make his face shine on us", and we make this prayer through Christ Our Lord. Amen.

May 22, 2006
Ecumenical Service, Sesquicentenary of
Responsible Government in New South Wales
Saint Stephen's Uniting Church, Sydney

CATHOLIC CULTURE

Acts 5:27–33; John 3:31–36

T HE READING we have just heard from the Acts of the Apostles is slightly out of sequence because the Saint Peter who is confronting the Sanhedrin with courage and eloquence is not the man he was twelve days after the Resurrection but that same man transformed by the arrival of the Spirit of Pentecost and Jesus' post-Resurrection teaching. As a witness to the Passion and Resurrection, Peter can boldly proclaim that obedience to God comes before obedience to men, because God has raised up Jesus to be Lord and Savior.

On the other hand, the Gospel reading for this Easter feast comes from a much earlier period, when John the Baptist is explaining to his followers the difference between earthly and heavenly witnesses and the difference between himself, who is not the Messiah, and the Christ. John explains that he is only a friend of the Bridegroom, whereas the Bridegroom has the fullness of the Spirit and brings eternal life. Those who refuse to believe bring down the anger of God on themselves.

As we have come from all the continents around the world to discuss ways and means of strengthening the family, let me try to explain something of what being Catholic means in a world where we personally have not seen the Easter miracles and have not been fused into Christ's body of followers by personally following Him on the way to Calvary. That occurred nearly two thousand years ago. Most of us also are past our initial and often immature religious enthusiasms, which have developed into something stronger but quieter; faith and hope.

Like you all, I am first of all a follower of Christ, but very explicitly a Catholic follower of Christ, rather than an Evangelical or Protestant or Orthodox follower. Catholic comes from the Greek word for universal, which means that following Christ is open to people of every nation, class, and tribe. It also means that within the Catholic Church community and therefore linked to God's love, we have people of nearly every level of understanding and many levels of moral goodness. As I have often explained, sinfulness is one regular characteristic of Catholic communities. So are imperfect families. Few Catholics are living saints.

All of us act from mixed motives, and all of us are influenced by society, by the world around us, often in ways we do not recognize. Therefore, from the beginning, because following Christ is a communitarian exercise, underpinned by personal decisions, Catholic leaders have worked hard to develop a Catholic culture, a way of worshipping, interacting, and relating to the society around them. *I am not just talking about the world of high culture exemplified by Dante, Michelangelo, or Palestrina but about what the Anglo-American writer T. S. Eliot called "the total harvest of thinking and feeling", which is also expressed in a thousand ordinary ways in laws, rituals, folk stories, and habits of daily living.* This prevents us from being submerged by hostile forces and helps us pass on our treasures to the youngsters in our midst and to outsiders who are looking for meaning and healing. One reason for our present difficulties is that our Catholic culture, our way of looking at things and living our life, is being eroded and frequently misguided. Christians aid and abet these erosions.

Let me give two brief examples of how our Catholic culture began to develop to protect Christian faith. Originally in the Roman Empire, as there were no public church buildings, the sacraments were celebrated in private houses. It was metaphorically an underground Church. Initially, too, there were no specifically Christian symbols, as we took over pagan symbols such as the good shepherd, the fish and dove, an anchor or ship and gave them Christian meanings. Such understandings were invisible to pagan outsiders.

Only later, and especially with religious freedom under Emperor Constantine, did specifically Christian symbols develop, such as the cross and crucifix. Now we have magnificent cathedrals, beautiful churches, a splendid patrimony of Church music, art, and literature, which help sustain our faith.

From the earliest times, Christians celebrated Easter once a year and a special Eucharist every Sunday rather than the Jewish Sabbath. Pentecost and then Christmas or the Epiphany emerged as feasts to be celebrated at different times during the year. In 321, Emperor Constantine declared Sunday a public holiday, with immense long-term consequences. We should not be aiding and abetting those who want to make Sunday just another day.

A sixth-century monk, Dionysius Exiguus from Scythia, started to date history from the year of the Incarnation; which we now know as A.D., "anno Domini", and B.C., before Christ. Why on earth Catholic agencies should be enthusiastically supporting the use of C.E.—the common era—and B.C.E.—before the common era—is beyond me!

Christian faith has to be so preserved and defended in many public ways because we want to be able to offer Christ for acceptance to all sorts of religiously ordinary people, like many of us. It is also important to remember that the Catholic way of living is life-enhancing because it is based on the natural law and that one of the cornerstones of Catholic culture is the institution of marriage and the family. In our societies, where many do not share our faith, we defend Christian marriage, not because it is Christian, but because of its long-term benefits to spouses and children and because it is life enhancing. But we are also vitally aware that good, intact families make it easier to protect and hand on the flame of faith.

In some ways today, in the face of modern advertising and the press, it might be easier to protect Christian faith than to purify and preserve the ideal of lifelong marriage. Many people involved in matrimonial mishaps cling to their faith and find consolation there. Whatever of this, the struggles for faith and family are closely connected, and both are vital.

We must work to preserve our Catholic culture, perhaps as oases in hostile environments, interacting with them but not submerged by them, so that public opinion tolerates or supports strong marriages, personal Christian faith, and Catholic communities.

April 3, 2008
Second week of Easter, Mass for Members of
the Pontifical Council for the Family
Altar of the Chair, Saint Peter's Basilica, Rome

JUSTICE AND PEACE

2 John 4–9; Luke 17:26–37

THE LAST TIME we met in plenary session was during the war in
the Persian Gulf (1990–1991). I remember that when Cardinal
Etchegaray preached at that opening Mass, he reminded us that we all
carried the brand of Cain, our ancestor who killed his brother, Abel.
That war is now over, but there are new wars in Bosnia, in the former
Russian republics, in Liberia; once again in Angola and Somalia and
possibly even in Cambodia.

Good things have happened, too, as the Soviet republics followed
eastern and central Europe in rejecting Communism. Progress continues, with some hesitations, in the European Economic Community,
which Doctor Klein (France) has explained will not be a successor state
to the Holy Roman Empire, perhaps not even to the Roman Empire;
but time will tell! We have seen a peaceful transition of power in the
Philippines and democratic advances in South America and Africa.

But there is recession in many countries and real danger of a depression. In other words, it is difficult to assert in truth that there is now
more justice and a greater spread of peace than eighteen months ago.
To use the strange image employed by Our Lord in today's Gospel,
there are many places now where the vultures might justly gather (Lk
17:26–37).

Are we making progress in our justice and peace work? Is it worthwhile? Are our efforts only a drop in the ocean? Are we condemned
like Sisyphus of Greek mythology forever to roll the stone to the top
of the hill and then have it immediately return to where we started?
I was struck last night by Bishop de Almeida of Brazil's reference to
the millions of Indians and slaves who lived and died in suffering with
little, if any, human consolations.

Is our following of the new commandment of love always destined for disappointment? Are our hopes deceits? Is the anti-Christ, the deceiver, always to be the victor in this life? Three considerations might help us as we frame our answers to these questions.

First of all, we are constrained to remember always that we serve men and women, not humanity in the abstract. Because each person, no matter how poor or ignorant or evil, has a unique dignity, we do something precious when we help any one person. We learn from Matthew's Gospel that when we help such a person, we are helping Christ himself.

Secondly, we are called in faith always to remember that we do our work as followers of the crucified Christ, the Son of God and Son of Mary, who redeemed and saved us by His death as well as by His life and Resurrection. *We Christians believe that suffering, undergone in faith and love, builds up the Kingdom of God just as surely as our best efforts do.* This is not common sense, and, in fact, such a claim is offensive to those without faith. I remember vividly being lectured in Sri Lanka during the civil war there by a Catholic aid worker (not Sri Lankan) on the futility of believing in a good God when surrounded by such suffering. Sometimes our faith is sorely tested, but in faith we know two things: that we must always struggle to diminish suffering, and that no suffering however terrible, however resistant to our efforts, is beyond redemption, beyond being converted into fuel for the Kingdom.

Thirdly, in faith we are called to remember that all humans, good and evil, stand under the judgment of God. I was blessed with a marvelous Catholic mother and good Catholic schools, but there was a whiff of Jansenism about in my youth. I sometimes worried then whether the good God would be kind to me at judgment time. Perhaps as a bishop I should still worry about such things. However, the victims of violence and oppression look to judgment from another starting point; they look to God for vindication and for justice.

During the 1990 Synod and later in Romania, it was my privilege to meet Cardinal Todea, the Greek Catholic archbishop from the Transylvanian mountains. He was imprisoned for about fifteen years, five years of which were in solitary confinement, which might explain why he is now so unusually eloquent. At one time when he was free and Ceausescu was at the height of his power, Todea wrote to him saying that judgment was coming on him just as surely as judgment came to

Napoleon and to Hitler. A couple of senior officers of the secret police came to Todea to complain about this threat, but Todea answered that it had nothing to do with him as the judgment was God's. Todea lived to see the Ceausescus executed by their former Communist accomplices on Christmas Day, a feast day they had abolished.

Belief in the afterlife has waned in the Western world, although heaven has fared better than hell! However Christ is insistent on the final division of the good and the evil; two will be in bed, one will be taken, one will be left; two women will be grinding corn, one will be taken, one will be left. We do not know who exactly will suffer forever, but we do know there is a separation in the afterlife, and we must concede that it is appropriate for the victims of terrible violence, of terrible oppression, to expect that their persecutors will be punished or purified.

Our God of love has called the Church to work for peace and justice in faith, hope, and love. By God's grace the Church has accomplished much that is good, but even when we fail, our God of love will reconcile all things in Himself.

November 13, 1992
Final Concelebrated Mass of the Plenary Session
Pontifical Council for Justice and Peace, Vatican City

FEAST OF THE HOLY INNOCENTS

Matthew 2:13–18

TONIGHT WE CELEBRATE the Feast of the Holy Innocents with a renewed enthusiasm as we rededicate ourselves to the long-term task of explaining the culture of life more effectively to our fellow Australians. Years of experience tell us that this will be difficult, that we can expect no quick and radical change in public opinion. But the omens are better than they have been for some years, and the resurgence of Christian influence in public life in the United States has forced even some of our most secular commentators to notice and lament what is happening there. The question for us is whether something similar can occur here.

Tonight's Gospel highlights the struggle and recurrent violence that have accompanied Christ and His message from the beginning. The brutal tyranny of Herod, determined to erase even the slight prospect of some long-term threat to His rule by killing every young baby boy in Bethlehem, without any gesture toward justice, points out the contrast with our own age. We do have the rule of law, prosperity, quality education and health, a standard of living, travel, and communications never dreamed of by most other generations. We are truly blessed. Herod could never have attempted, much less succeeded, in executing those murders of the innocents in our society.

This is not to claim that there are no recurrent sores in Australian society. There is our inability to improve substantially the situation of our aborigines; the forgotten few hundred refugees still in that awful camp at Baxter. But the largest blot, the darkest shadow on Australian life (for many years) goes almost completely unmentioned. That is the tragedy of about one hundred thousand young Australians being aborted each year.

We do not stand in condemnation. We pray for all those involved in this drastic loss of life. One writer urged me before tonight's Mass to pray especially for the mothers involved and the fathers, because their dead children are certainly in God's care, in some way or other.

While we do need to remind ourselves of the importance of this struggle and of the need for more dedicated pro-life activists, the major focus of our work must be on public opinion; educating and illuminating, changing the mind-set of the large mass of people who refrain from thinking much about this problem, many of whom do not even want to think about abortion as the destruction of the human.

We know public opinion is uneasy about the huge number of Australian abortions. We need to offer options so that this number can be reduced progressively. As a contribution from the Catholic archdiocese of Sydney, I would like tonight to announce the creation of the Centacare Pregnancy Support Program. Some time ago I asked Centacare, our Catholic Welfare Agency, to develop this program to provide support to pregnant women who are contemplating abortion. It will be available not only to women but to their partners and families. A program of this kind can offer assistance to all women, including those who feel that they have no one to turn to for assistance; women of any religion and no religion.

As a Catholic community, we want to respond even more effectively to the needs of women facing an unexpected or difficult pregnancy by providing them with life affirming options. This will be a professional counseling and support service to women and their partners and families as well as a referral service for accommodation and appropriate ongoing support services. Obviously spiritual help will be offered if it is requested. Centacare's program will be available to women and their families in Sydney. Similar church-based programs exist in New Zealand and Scotland.

Of course the Feast of the Holy Innocents and the struggle for life involve much more than concern for the unborn. The Church's record over the centuries demonstrates this concern for the living at every stage of life. The fact today is that people are living longer and longer lives. When joined to the diminishing number of births, this has provoked a new worldwide situation, which is only now coming to the public's notice and will certainly provoke another reassessment, another change in public opinion, in the judgments of common sense. We are now facing the challenge of worldwide population decline.

For five or six years, scholarly articles have been warning of population decline in many parts of the Western world. This sounded strange, as we had been threatened for decades with overpopulation and a shortage of food and resources (which has not occurred).

Public awareness is now changing, coming to grips with the fact that no Western country, including Australia, is producing enough babies to keep the population stable. The American magazine *Newsweek*'s September cover read "Baby Bust: The problem is not having too many people but having too few." The penny has dropped; for some.

Fertility rates worldwide have halved since 1972 and are still falling faster than ever. Depopulation has already begun in some places and will get worse. Everything will be changed, most of it not for the better.

Russia is already down by 750,000 people each year. Western Europe could be losing three million a year in population by 2050, with Germany alone minus fifteen million in the next forty years, equal to the population of East Germany. For some time, we have known that Japan will lose thirty million of its 127 million in the next four decades.

What is new, to me at least, is that this decline will eventually be led by the developing nations even more than by the First World. China is a spectacular example, as its population will age in one generation as much as Europe's did in one hundred years. Countries that are not yet rich will also have to cope with depopulation.

Population collapse reverses the ratio of working taxpayers to elderly dependents. Already the Chinese one-child policy has provoked a dramatic imbalance in the sexes with 17 percent more men. By mid-century, China could lose 20 to 30 percent of population each generation. As only one-quarter are covered by old-age pensions, China will have the 1–2–4 problem, where the single child might be responsible for two parents and four grandparents.

In Australia, we might escape the worst of this if we can maintain or improve our birth rate. But the challenge remains.

I thank you for your presence and, more importantly, for your heroic work over the years in the defense of life. We need new ideas and extra people.

December 28, 2004
Saint Mary's Cathedral, Sydney

THE JAPANESE MARTYRS
OF NAGASAKI

I N FEBRUARY this year I traveled to Japan to commemorate the four
hundredth anniversary of the martyrdom of twenty-six Catholics
in Nagasaki. Their sad, moving story is lent special poignancy by the
countryside in which it took place, where the gardens and architecture
and even the very landscape speak at once of mystery and emptiness,
of transcendence and human insignificance.

In October 1596, a Spanish vessel bound for Mexico from Manila
was driven by storms and stranded on the coast of what is today the Kyoto prefecture. Japanese law at the time held that all stranded vessels became the property of the Crown. The emperor of the day, Hideyoshi,
although eager to maintain commercial relations with Spain, was in
need of the wealth of the ship's cargo to finance a military campaign in
Korea and was swayed to confiscate it by the advice of his courtiers.
The officers of the ship naturally protested the confiscation, invok-
ing the power and majesty of the Spanish King. At this, Masuda, the
anti-Christian emissary of the emperor sent to oversee the confiscation, asked to see a map of Spain's colonial possessions. These were
vast. In addition to the riches of the Philippines, Spain's empire in the
Americas extended from present-day California to present-day Chile,
Pope Alexander VI having divided the continent between Spain and
Portugal in 1493/1494. In enquiring how these possessions had been
obtained, Masuda asked if missionaries had paved the way, to which
an officer of the ship answered: Yes. Masuda promptly returned to the
emperor with this intelligence, offering it to him as confirmation of
his long-held suspicion that European missionaries were being sent in
order to prepare for the conquest of his country.

Emperor Hideyoshi acted immediately. Missionaries and their Japanese helpers in Kyoto and Osaka were arrested, and at the end of December they were condemned to be mutilated, exposed to public derision,

and then crucified in Nagasaki. Six Franciscans (one seized from the stranded Spanish vessel), three Jesuits, and seventeen lay people, from different nationalities and classes, the youngest being three teenagers of twelve, thirteen, and fourteen years of age respectively, had their left ears cut off and were marched from Kyoto to Nagasaki in the freezing cold, a journey of thirty days. The whole group of twenty-six was crucified on the Tateyama-hill in Nagasaki on February 5, 1597. The following month, all missionaries throughout the country were ordered to leave by imperial edict, and in the next year a great number of churches and the seminary at Arima were destroyed. Thus began 276 years of persecution of the Church in Japan. For two hundred of these years, the Japanese Church was entirely without priests, and when Western missionaries were finally allowed to return, the faithful asked three questions of them: Did they obey the pope, did they honor or worship the Virgin, and were they celibate? When the answer to each of these questions was Yes, they embraced them with the words: "Our hearts are with yours."

It is interesting to recall the point in history when these martyrdoms occurred. A little over one hundred hundred years earlier, Columbus had discovered America, and forty years before that Constantinople had fallen to the Turks. The rise of British power was over two centuries away. In 1610, the Church founded the first university in Asia, the University of Saint Thomas in the Philippines.

When I arrived in Nagasaki four hundred years after the martyrdoms, I found, not the ancient city in which the twenty-six were put to death, but the city rebuilt after the atomic blast of 1945. The ceremonies began in the morning with the Papal Legate, Cardinal Szoka, laying a wreath at the martyrs' shrine in the presence of the Papal Nuncio, Archbishop Carew, the archbishop of Tokyo, Cardinal Shirayanagi, and Bishop Shimamoto of Nagasaki. The small plaza before the shrine was filled with pilgrims and hundreds of secondary school children. After this, I visited the splendid museum of the martyrs, where I saw letters written by Francis Xavier and Francis Borgia to the King of Portugal, and *fumi*, small bronze images on which persecuted Catholics were required to step each year. Also among the museum's collection were statues of Our Lady disguised as the Buddhist goddess of mercy, usually with an unobtrusive cross.

The highlight of the commemoration was a long and beautiful Mass celebrated in Japanese by Cardinal Szoka in a stadium packed with six thousand people. The singing by the community was magnificent. The Japanese are a formal and reserved people, but beneath this demeanor are deep emotions. Many of the women attending the Mass wore white veils, and after the offertory, two huge arrangements of flowers were placed before the relics of the martyrs.

The cathedral in Nagasaki is large, with the front adorned by burned statues salvaged from the wreckage of the old cathedral after the atomic blast. There is a simple, eloquent monument in the Catholic kindergarten attached to the Catholic Centre in the city commemorating two hundred students and twelve teachers conscripted to work producing armaments in a nearby school building, who died a fiery death when the bomb was detonated. It is a monument raised in the hope and with the prayer that such an event will never happen again.

The next day I visited the Peace Park built at the epicenter of the explosion, where an ugly statue of a muscular sitting figure points skyward with its right hand and toward the cathedral with its left. In a peculiar and probably unintended way, the statue unites the two terrible but very different events that make Nagasaki known to the Westerner and the believer. The martyrdom of the twenty-six and the persecutions that followed four hundred years ago and the destruction of the city by nuclear blast fifty-two years ago remind us again of the fractured nature of this world, a world in which enormous evil is possible. But in the faith that sustained the martyrs in the midst of their tortures four centuries ago, and in the way this faith is remembered and kept alive by their fellow believers today in this devastated city, we are also reminded of the hope that the Resurrection of Our Lord yields for all, the promise of Life in all its fullness.

April 7, 1997
Melbourne

SAINT THOMAS MORE

T HIS YEAR we are celebrating 150 years of responsible government
in New South Wales, one of the oldest democracies anywhere in
the world. This is a reason for pride and quiet celebration.

It is my privilege today as archbishop of Sydney to present to the
New South Wales parliament, on behalf of the Catholic community, a
beautiful bronze statue of Sir Thomas More, who was born in England
in either 1477 or 1478 and was beheaded on Tower Hill in London
on July 6, 1535, on the orders of King Henry VIII.

This gift is a recognition of how much all of us owe to our Australian
democratic practices and traditions, to the Westminster system of government that we have inherited, and to our politicians. I congratulate
the sculptor Louis Laumen on capturing More's spirit. I believe that
this beautiful piece will always be a silent but powerful reminder in
this place of the need for high principles, service to the truth, and,
above all, moral courage.

More has been canonized as a saint and martyr and is the patron saint
of statesmen and politicians. Robert Bolt's play and film called him *A
Man for All Seasons*, and More contributed significantly in many different areas. More was a writer and religious controversialist, a lawyer,
lecturer, and envoy abroad, and with the coronation of Henry VIII
he began a brilliant public career. At the age of twenty-six, he entered
parliament and held a succession of offices, becoming Privy Council-
lor, Knight, Speaker of the House of Commons, high steward both
of Oxford University, his alma mater, and Cambridge University, and
eventually succeeding Cardinal Wolsey as Lord Chancellor in 1529. But
we do not commemorate and honor him today for those considerable
achievements.

Catholics in particular and many others remember Henry VIII as a
tyrant who executed many of those closest to him, including some of

his wives, and split the Christian Church in England from the Catholic Church. But when he ascended the throne, he was seen very differently. He was young, vigorous, genuinely religious, a good linguist and musician, and a friend of the "new learning". In fact, the English rise to power began with the Tudors, especially under his daughter Elizabeth. Perhaps the best modern parallel to understand the enthusiasm he generated was the election of J. F. Kennedy as president of the United States in 1960.

The first half of the sixteenth century in Europe was an exciting time. Columbus had not long before discovered the Americas, and in Italy the Renaissance had produced Da Vinci, Raphael, Michelangelo, and many others as well as the Renaissance popes, often worldlings or worse, but great patrons of the arts and of the return of the classics.

More helped bring the Renaissance to England. He was the friend of scholars such as Grocyn, Colet, and especially Erasmus. "You must be Thomas More or nobody", Erasmus began at their first meeting, with More replying, "And you must be Erasmus or the devil." He worked hard to have the study of Greek introduced into Oxford.

It was More who invited Holbein to England, warning him that he might struggle for commissions, and it is through Holbein's magnificent portraits and sketches that we understand Henry's England so much better. This sculpture is based on Holbein's portrait of More now in the Frick Gallery in New York. There it hangs not far from the flat, evil face of Thomas Cromwell, Earl of Essex, also painted by Holbein, who consolidated Henry's power through the suppression of the monasteries and was also executed by this same king for his pains.

More was undone by "the King's great matter". Henry's wife, Catherine of Aragon, was unable to produce a son, and Henry wanted to marry Anne Boleyn. For various reasons, Pope Clement VII refused to allow the matter to be decided in England and refused to nullify Henry's first marriage.

More was a cautious lawyer, who mistrusted his own ability to stand by his principles and took refuge in silence, although refusing to attend Anne and Henry's marriage. Henry was probably inclined to compromise, at least at the beginning, but Anne was relentless, and the stakes were raised to assert Henry's religious supremacy in England as head of the Church. On this Thomas would not budge.

Ironically, More had originally believed that the popes were a human development and had warned the young Henry against too close an alliance with the papacy. Ten years of study brought him to the conclusion that the position of the pope as the successor of Peter was divinely ordained. But once again that particular Catholic conviction is not the reason we honor Sir Thomas More in this place.

We are paying tribute to More's courage, to his adherence to principle, to his opposition to tyranny. He did this with few companions and little support. Only one bishop, John Fisher of Rochester, shared his view about the importance of the pope, while most Catholics thought he had exaggerated things badly. His favorite daughter, Meg Roper, together with all his family, believed his sacrifices were unnecessary. Even more poignantly, during his entire lifetime, there were only a couple of popes who aspired to religious respectability and the papacy became ruthlessly secularized. It was these excesses that provoked Luther and the Protestant Reformation.

More was a man of his times, and the title of saint does not imply lifelong perfection. He regarded heretics as small "l" liberals today regard racists, while going farther, so that during his time as chancellor, six Protestants were executed. We thank God that we have moved past such excesses.

More was a serious follower of Christ throughout his life, a clear example of an outstanding citizen nourished and inspired by religious principle. His *Dialogue of Comfort against Tribulation*, written during his fifteen months in the Tower, is a beautiful expression of faith and a support and comfort for all who are suffering.

More was a loyal friend and had many friends. He was a good family man with an unusual sense of humor. He had style to go with his substance. In his own final words at the scaffold, "I die the King's good servant, but God's first." And he had lived as he died.

June 8, 2006
Parliament House, Sydney

CENTENARY MASS FOR
BLESSED MARY MACKILLOP

Colossians 3:12−17; Matthew 6:25−34

TODAY WE CELEBRATE the one hundredth anniversary of the death of Mother Mary of the Cross. We are gathered to thank God for her wonderful contribution and ask His continued blessing on the Josephite sisters.

We know her better as Blessed Mary MacKillop, because Pope John Paul II declared her "blessed" in 1995, which is one stage short of being officially proclaimed a saint. It is almost certain that she will become our first publicly recognized Australian saint, and we hope Pope Benedict will make this declaration soon. We should remember that the Catholic Church celebrates the feast of her saints on the day they die rather than on the day they are born, to emphasize the reality of life after death and the importance of God, who is the main cause of our happiness in heaven.

It is not easy to become a saint, (or so they tell me), not merely because it takes hard work to follow Christ's teachings heroically across a lifetime, but because the Vatican conducts a detailed examination of the evidence over many years. To help him in this task, the pope has a Vatican department, the Congregation for the Saints, which decides not merely that the person proposed has done wonderful good works but also that he was a person of exemplary faith and prayer, hope and love. The term "devil's advocate" comes from the older canonization processes, where an official argued against such claims. A saint, therefore, is an outstanding follower of Jesus Christ, a model for everyone of how to live a full Catholic life.

Often Catholics have a devotion to a particular saint, because they admire the way that saint lived or because they feel that particular saint in heaven would understand them, listen to their prayers, and intercede for them with Jesus Christ. *I went to pray at the tomb of Mary MacKillop immediately before my installation as archbishop of Sydney.*

Naturally, Catholics do not worship the saints, because only the one true God, Father, Son, and Spirit, is worthy of our deepest reverence and highest love. Like all Christians, Catholics worship the one true God alone, but they admire the saints, respect their example, and ask for their prayers. Mary, the Mother of Jesus, is the greatest saint, but there is an infinity of difference between the majesty of God and even the most wonderful of Christ's followers.

A saint has to live the Christian virtues in a heroic way, but often they live ordinary lives, doing their small daily tasks extraordinarily well. Mary was not a fantastic eccentric like the stigmatic Francis of Assisi, did not perform the miracles attributed to Joseph of Cupertino, and did not travel and baptize like Francis Xavier (although she traveled a lot visiting her convents), but she was a great and good woman, who was determined that young Australians would come to know Christ and the Catholic tradition and receive enough education to prepare them for life. She knew this would mean trouble and that she would encounter difficulties, because she took the name "Mother Mary of the Cross".

Saints need not be persons who come from other countries and from distant ages, because every community needs its homegrown heroes, local models to encourage it in the right direction. We Australians need Blessed Mary as a guide and encouragement. Australians, too, can be good and, indeed, very good.

Mary was born in Melbourne on January 15, 1842, in Brunswick Street, Fitzroy, the eldest of eight children of Alexander MacKillop and Flora MacDonald, who had emigrated—separately—from the western highlands of Scotland a few years earlier. By happy choice, in the year 2000 the archdiocese of Melbourne opened the Mary of the Cross Centre at her birthplace for the support of families suffering from the effects of drug and alcohol abuse.

Mary was baptized at Saint Francis' Church, Lonsdale Street, and grew up in the then-fledgling settlement of Melbourne, where local legend has it that she and her brothers and sisters played under the gum tree outside Saint Francis' after Mass on Sundays. That gum was used to construct the bishop's chair in Saint Patrick's Cathedral. Originally prosperous, the family soon fell into financial difficulties.

Working as a governess in Penola, South Australia, she came under the influence of the local priest, an unusual English geologist, Father Julian Tenison Woods, and together they founded the Sisters of Saint Joseph of the Sacred Heart. She started her first school in 1866, when Australian education was something of a shambles before the "free, compulsory, and secular" reforms of the 1870s. Many children did not go to school or want to go to school. In eighteen months, she gained ten followers, and a year later there were thirty-nine sisters. By the time of her death in 1909, she had established 109 houses, staffed by 650 sisters, teaching 12,400 pupils in 117 schools across Australia and New Zealand.

Within the Catholic Church, the fundamentals remain unchanged over the centuries, but popular understandings of these essentials, styles of prayer and personal devotion, and the range of church activities and agencies do change across the generations. We must be careful to recognize Mary MacKillop in her own terms first of all, not reshaping her according to our present religious or even secular insights. It says something that we pray to her as Blessed Mary MacKillop, not Blessed Mary of the Cross.

Mary was not just a fine educator and philanthropist, although she was that. She was a saint, and it was her love of God and His only Son Jesus Christ that drove her on and prevented her from lapsing into bitterness at her mistreatment. She was not an agnostic like a number of worthy Australian heroes, but a woman of faith and daily personal prayer. She remained totally loyal to the Church leaders even when they treated her disgracefully.

Scotland is still a rather anti-Catholic country, and her Scottish background helps older Australians recognize that she was one of us. She lived here in North Sydney, and is now buried here among us. She worshipped in the North Sydney chapel and in the half-completed Saint Mary's Cathedral. She crossed the harbor in the ferry before there was a harbor bridge and traveled slowly by horse and train to visit her convents and works of mercy.

Mary had many problems during her life, not only with bishops (one excommunicated her, and another expelled her from Adelaide), but with her own sisters, who divided into the "Brown Joeys" and the "Black Joeys" under the control of the local bishop, and with a shortage of money and with bad health. She spent the last eight years of her life as an invalid after a stroke, although her mental faculties were unimpaired.

Despite all this, she put God's work first. She wanted to do what God wanted and succeeded brilliantly, which explains why God blessed her efforts with so much fruit. Her strong faith gave her the strength and tenacity to stick to her purposes, to refuse to abandon her principles.

She was not just looking out for herself. She practiced the virtues Paul preached to the Colossians, kindness, humility, gentleness, and patience. She practiced love by following the Beatitudes and the commandments.

She was a wise adviser to her sisters because she accepted Christ's message into her heart. She was grateful for the blessings she received, and this enabled her to inspire confidence and transmit peace of heart to her sisters.

I hope that many of our young will be like Blessed Mary and do great things for the Church and our country of Australia, and I hope and pray that all of us will be inspired by her example and pray to her that our faith and goodness will be strengthened and that Australia will remain decent, safe, and prosperous.

August 8, 2009
Saint Mary's Church, North Sydney

THE JESUIT TRADITION—
SAINT IGNATIUS OF LOYOLA

I AM DELIGHTED to celebrate my first Mass as archbishop of Melbourne for the Xavier College community on the feast of Saint Ignatius. I am especially pleased to celebrate Mass here in our cathedral, completed one hundred years ago, that is, fifty years after the creation of the diocese, and now beautifully restored. It is your cathedral. I hope you are proud of it, because many of your parents would have contributed to the $9.5 million we collected for this purpose. It is a worthy house of God; as good as we can do.

I suspect, and hope, that nearly all of you are proud to belong to the Xavier community. You certainly are blessed educationally. You belong to a proud intellectual and educational tradition; not by any means the oldest in the Catholic Church (the Benedictines predate the Jesuits by about a thousand years, and the Dominicans by more than three hundred years); but arguably the most influential and distinguished.

I hope that at Xavier you learn to value tradition, the many good things that our generations have received from the past that enable us to build for the future. The Jesuit educational tradition will give many marvelous advantages if you use your opportunities. Christ Our Lord told us that it is not of first importance whether we are rich or clever or good athletes or the products of good, bad, or indifferent families. Christianity is not like the rest of society, which rewards the champions. In the parable of the talents, Our Lord told us that some people have ten units of ability, others five or six, others one or two. What is important in God's eyes is that we use whatever talents we have to the best of our ability. Learn what you can; take the opportunities offered to you.

This applies to your religion and your faith also. I am not going to speak much about Saint Ignatius himself, anticipating that you all know the basics of his story well. Do not forget what a great man he was; burning with love and zeal, strong, a leader who was able to inspire complete devotion among some of the finest men of his generation. He was tough, too. I am not sure that every one of us would have liked him, but every one of us would have admired him. He played a major role in saving the Church at the time of the Protestant Reformation, when Northern Europe was lost. He knew that religious decline cannot be reversed without prayer and penance, that interior renewal and interior reform are essential when we get too comfortable! I like the story attributed to an old Jesuit who said that he was not afraid to die and meet Christ Our Lord, but he was apprehensive about having to give an account of himself to Saint Ignatius!

In the "Spiritual Exercises", Ignatius spelled out what he saw as the main reason why God created us; what he called the "fundamental principle" for our existence. He saw it as the first or basic principle for our lives. "Man has been created", he wrote, "to praise, reverence and serve our Lord God, thereby saving his soul." Ignatius did not discover or invent this teaching, which comes from the first of Our Lord's two basic commandments, to love God first and love our neighbor as ourselves.

This idea is taken up in the Xavier Mission statement in the first paragraph, where we read that "the Jesuit tradition . . . seeks to enable students to find God in all things." This fundamental principle of Ignatius is also taken up in today's first reading from the Old Testament Book of Deuteronomy. Moses told the people to obey the voice of the Lord your God. Keep His commandments; because it is not beyond your strength or out of reach.

Therefore, one characteristic of all Xavier men should be that they know in their heart of hearts about the love of the one true God and that they have answered Yes to God. Most Australians do not deny God; fewer still will insult God. But you will be tempted to ignore God; or to acknowledge His existence but downplay His importance. The Australian temptation is to believe that you can have a good time, or even live the good life, without God.

Most Australians are still Christians. But the most significant religious change in the last thirty to thirty-five years has been the rise in the number of people without religion from about 2 percent to about 16.5 percent. It is higher in Victoria, 18.9 percent.

We Catholics are now the largest religious group in Australia. Our numbers have increased by 43 percent. We are nearly 29 percent in Victoria. Victoria seems to be a good place for Catholics and unbelievers! In other words, there are too many "RCs"; not Roman Catholics, but "retired Christians". And unfortunately too many Catholics, including some young Catholics, who are a different type of RC: resting or relaxed Catholics!

You, too, as young adults are going to be forced to choose for God or against him, either through ignoring or rejecting God. This was another central teaching of Ignatius, that each person must choose one standard or the other; the standard of the one true God carried by Jesus Christ His only Son or the standard of evil and selfishness, of Lucifer, the enemy of mankind. I hope and pray that you will always choose God.

Once again Ignatius is building on and explaining the basic New Testament teaching of Our Lord and Saint Paul. For Paul, to know and accept Christ the Lord is worth any sacrifice. It brings a supreme advantage. Paul claimed that, in comparison with this, everything else is like rubbish.

Paul speaks of running, trying to capture a prize. I hope and pray that all of you, too, are runners in the religious handicap race. Many of you come from families that are blessed with a deep religious faith that they have passed on to you. Some of you might come from families that do not understand too much about God, or even have much sympathy for things religious.

Whatever of this, each and every one of you must be an honest searcher, racing for the finish, at whatever pace you are capable of mustering. Do not be frightened men, of little faith, like those in the boat with Our Lord, who thought they could not cope, who thought they were sinking. Christ, as Son of God, shows us what God is like; loving, forgiving, interesting, and unpredictable, but reasonable and good and kind.

Take a minute to try to imagine the one good God, that whirling mystery of love and intelligence, who is found not just in the immensity of the universe or the complexity of the atom; not just in wonderful music or the beauties of nature or the activities of the saints; but, as the Book of Deuteronomy reminds us again, the one true God who is in our hearts and in our mouths, not just up in the heavens or beyond the seas.

If there are any among you (and please God there are not many) who are unable to accept that Christ is the Son of God or unsure whether God exists, I ask you to pray in honesty and openness: "Dear God, if you exist, bring me to your truth and love." And to those students who are blessed with the gift of faith, I ask you to pray for any of your fellow students who are unable to believe or who, while believing, are reluctant to choose God, to say Yes to goodness and faith.

There is a wonderful Jesuit motto, used by one of your sister schools north of the Murray River: *Quantum potes, tantum audes*. Dare to do as much as you are able. In simpler Australian terms, we would probably say, "Go for it—to the best of your strength and ability", so that you truly say Yes to the one true God and Christ His Son.

May that one true God bless you all, your teachers, parents, family, and friends. And may you all, in every human and spiritual sense, go from strength to strength.

July 31, 1997
Mass for Xavier College at
Saint Patrick's Cathedral, Melbourne

Universities, Hospitals, and Schools

THE CHURCH AND
SCIENTIFIC RESEARCH

Recently, I heard of a senior official from mainland China who was traveling in the Western world and trying to work out what was the principal factor that led to Western supremacy, not just in medicine, science, technology, but also in economics, self-government, and even in literature, art, and music. Certainly some of our music and art is corrupting and decadent, but there is no art or music in other cultures to match the range of emotion and the depths of spirituality that can be found in some Western music and art. Why did the scientific revolution begin and develop so spectacularly in the Western world? Why did Western economies, the free market, first produce such extraordinary wealth; certainly not for everyone, but for many or even most people in a country like Australia? His answer would surprise and even shock many educated people in our country, because he concluded that the catalyst, not just for the basic decency, but for the spectacular intellectual development that lies behind Western achievement, was to be found in the core of Christian beliefs.

We are not accustomed to think like this. One devout Catholic university student asked me recently why it was that she had been taught to respect every religion but her own, which she had been encouraged to criticize. This is not a bad question.

We have been taught to recognize and praise the Enlightenment with its rejection of religion and authority. We have heard how Galileo was put under house arrest by the Catholic Church; of the debate over evolution between T. H. Huxley and "Slippery Sam" Wilberforce, the Anglican bishop of Oxford and then Winchester.

And even if we do not know too much of these stories, many Australians are tempted to see scientific research and the Christian religion in a necessary relationship of tension and perhaps even hostility.

Within this mistaken framework, Catholic participation in a Research and Biotechnology Precinct would be seen at best as an anachronism and marriage of convenience, if it was not something of a contradiction in terms.

Saint Paul writing to the people of Corinth pointed out our debt and his debt to the master builders who went before us, and every educated person must be grateful for the traditions of learning and civility we have each inherited. Paul goes farther and names Jesus Christ and His teaching as the central foundation, the indispensable basis. I happen to believe that Paul was right and that the Chinese official, an agnostic contemporary of ours, an outsider to our society, was also correct in recognizing Christianity as the most important catalyst for our achievement.

You will be relieved that I am not going to attempt to explain this claim now, although a politically incorrect American sociologist, an agnostic professor called Rodney Stark, has written three interesting books on the theme. The most recent, published in 2005, was *The Victory of Reason: How Christianity Led to Freedom, Capitalism, and Western Success*. He provides ample food for thought.

Christians believe the one transcendent God is rational, not capricious, and that His creation does not revolve in an everlasting cycle of return. Such presuppositions prompted the search to discover the rational laws of physics and mathematics and led to the notion of progress.

Christians do not believe that the universe is a bleak combination of deterministic physical laws and wholly random biological events, where our existence is totally a product of chance and totally without purpose or meaning. We do not worship nature and do not see natural forces as forms or abodes of divine beings. We do not see God as a remote, impersonal divinity explained largely by Newtonian mechanics. Such things as self-replication, cellular development and splitting, and the metabolism and striving of organisms are not foreshadowed in this world of the inorganic.

Indeed, I believe it quite proper for a Christian to claim that the one true God is not revealed "so much in the regularity of the universe as in its irregularities which permit the emergence of new and unsuspected levels of action and reaction" (A. O'Hear, *Plato's Children: The State We Are In*). Nature sustains us, and we have our rightful and unique place in nature's creative process. This is doubly true of a research institute.

All of us, and especially institutes of biological research, have to practice a genuine respect for nature—or pay the price. Last night I could not find the origin of the saying that "God always forgives, man sometimes forgives, but nature never forgives." The bit about nature is certainly true because nature remorselessly punishes violations. We recognize this in thousands of examples, ranging from soil degradation to industrial pollution to the side effects of drugs such as thalidomide. Perhaps this principle is also at work in today's powerful and pervasive myth of global warming. I wish Godspeed to the Victor Chang Cardiac Research Institute and the whole Saint Vincent's Research and Biotechnology Precinct. Your work should be extraordinarily significant in many ways. I pray that you will always respect what is uniquely human, that research funds will be your servant and not your master. May your work inspire great generosity in the community to complete the $67 million already donated by state and federal governments and private funding. And as God's coworkers, may you only enhance and develop nature as you serve the men, women, and children of Australia and beyond.

August 2, 2006
Groundbreaking ceremony,
Saint Vincent's Research and Biotechnology Precinct,
Victor Chang Institute, Sydney

150 YEARS OF HEALTH CARE

I N THIS MASS we gather to thank God for the many blessings received and the wonderful works accomplished during the 150 years of Saint Vincent's Hospital, Darlinghurst. While we draw inspiration from the past, we see this, not as an exercise in nostalgia, but as an encouragement to even greater works in the future. Therefore, we pray for wisdom and perseverance and call on God's support for all our future endeavors.

At Catholic Sunday Masses, regulations stipulate that scriptural readings are to be proclaimed. Sometimes these readings fit the situation perfectly; and on other occasions they provide a context for our deliberations.

Certainly I suspect that the Old Testament prophet Isaiah was not even hinting at our continent of Australia when he spoke of nations of every language and distant islands who had never even heard of God coming to witness His glory. In our celebration, we are explicitly acknowledging in faith the one true God of Isaiah.

The Gospel today wonders about how many will be saved at the end of time and speaks of the final division between the good and caring, who will be rewarded, and the evil ones—the goats, hardhearted, closed in on themselves, and unheeding of the suffering around them —who are destined for punishment downstairs. Today is not the occasion to pursue this theme, but very early in your professional lives, much earlier than in other professions, doctors and all nursing staff are forced to confront the mysteries of human suffering and death. These experiences force you to choose as you define, at least in practice, the nature of your personal contributions to health care. We hope and pray that many of you, indeed all you, will continue to have an explicit and developed Christian and Catholic understanding of your obligations.

A friend of mine wrote recently that *a fundamental struggle is beginning in educated circles throughout the Western world between those who believe God created us and those who believe we create God*. Generally, theists believe in natural law and human nature, and they respect the natural law and work to help humans and enhance human nature.

Atheists and militant agnostics, on the other hand, see religion as a private therapeutic exercise and fundamentally irrational, an outdated social construct, while traditional notions like natural law and even human nature are there to be used, improved, or discarded according to changing human imperatives, often financial imperatives.

Few divides are as fundamental as this one. Under the leadership of the Sisters of Charity, Saint Vincent's Hospital has always placed itself with God, and we hope and pray that the overwhelming majority of the leadership and staff, all those who choose to work in the tradition of Catholic health care, will continue to choose God and compassion.

There is no dispute that it was deep Christian faith that inspired the five Irish Sisters of Charity who migrated to Sydney in 1838. The Sisters' mission was clear: to assist the poor and disadvantaged. Their early work included helping convict women and children at Parramatta, at what was then known as the Female Factory; assisting families during the 1844 influenza epidemic and caring for prisoners and their families at inner-city Darlinghurst Gaol.

In 1857, the Sisters of Charity established Saint Vincent's at Potts Point as a free hospital for all people, but especially for the poor. Three of the hospital's founding Sisters were professional nurses, having trained in France, and they brought their knowledge to the colony. From its humble origin of twenty-two beds, the demand for Saint Vincent's services led it to move to its current site at Victoria Street Darlinghurst in 1870, where we now have a vast complex of buildings and departments.

The challenges facing Catholic hospitals today are considerable. Recent times have brought a huge growth in the scale and activities of all hospitals, a parallel growth in public expectations, escalating health care costs, greater competition from for-profit hospitals, and changes from the influence of the market upon health care relationships.

Once health care was understood as a form of compassionate service between a professional and a patient. Today, society increasingly understands health care as a commodity supplied by "health care providers" to "health care consumers" under the direction of "health care managers". I hope the Sisters of Charity and Saint Vincent's continue to resist this language. Consumers are always human beings, who represent Christ Himself for believers.

Generally, this explicit personal care will not require inefficiencies, although some pagan options will be cheaper. For example, euthanasia would be cheaper than long-term care of the sick. But that is also another story. Other challenges facing our great Catholic hospitals include less support from a weakened Catholic subculture and declining vocations among founding congregations.

Catholic hospitals have to balance a necessary concern for economic stability, professional reputation, and cultural acceptability with a concern to maintain the Catholic identity and mission of the hospital and, especially, the dimension of genuine Christian service. Saint Vincent's has found this balance. The hospital has grown into a leading medical, surgical, and research facility and has been at the forefront of innovation in areas including cardiac, lung, and bone-marrow transplantation. You provide a full range of adult diagnostic and clinical services and are a principal teaching hospital of the University of New South Wales, with close affiliations with a number of other universities, including the Australian Catholic University and Notre Dame University.

Saint Vincent's has maintained its Catholic identity and mission. You continue to be a community of service to those in need and to maintain your own Catholic identity, mission, and conscience. You continue the healing mission of Jesus, mediating the compassion of God to a suffering world and serving a suffering Christ in your patients. You witness to the presence of Christ and to Catholic teachings about the value of human life and the dignity and destiny of the human person. And you make special provision for the most disadvantaged or those most vulnerable to neglect.

In all this, Saint Vincent's shows that health care ministry is an expression of the broadly sacramental character of the Catholic Church. Catholic hospitals are signs and instruments of union with God, brought about by service of the sick, by the witness given to gospel truth, especially that every person is made in the image of God, and by worship offered in prayer and pastoral care.

Many of us here have personal reasons for gratitude to Saint Vincent's. Only a month ago I was a patient, or guest or consumer and client, dependent on the professional competence and kindness of nurses and doctors. And so as one of many, many patients, I express my personal thanks.

Let me conclude by reading the message I received a few days ago from the Vatican, which I will consign to Sister Elizabeth for the archives:

> The Holy Father was pleased to be informed of the One Hundred and Fiftieth Anniversary of Saint Vincent's Hospital in Darlinghurst, and he sends cordial greetings to the Sisters of Charity, members of the hospital staff and all present for the Eucharistic celebration. His Holiness is confident that this occasion will be an opportunity for the Sisters and their collaborators to reaffirm their love for Christ in the poor, the sick and the lowly (Mt 25:40) and to renew the moral obligations they have assumed in the apostolate of Catholic health care. Commending all those gathered for the celebration to the protection of Mary, Salus Infirmorum (Health of the Sick), the Holy Father willingly extends his Apostolic Blessing as a pledge of peace and joy in our Lord Jesus Christ.
>
> Cardinal Tarcisio Bertone,
> Secretary of State, from the Vatican, August 20

August 26, 2007
Saint Vincent's Hospital, Darlinghurst
150th Anniversary Mass, Saint Mary's Cathedral, Sydney

CATHOLIC UNIVERSITIES
AT THE HEART OF THE CHURCH

Isaiah 11:1–4; 1 Corinthians 12:4–13; Luke 8:4–15

THIS EVENING we gather in prayer and worship at this Eucharist to invoke God's continued blessing on the University of Notre Dame, Australia, as we celebrate a changing of the guard, the inauguration of a new chief executive, Celia Hammond, as Vice-Chancellor. We thank God for what has been achieved under the retiring Vice-Chancellor, Professor Peter Tannock. God has blessed this university, and we pray that it may continue.

It seems appropriate within the framework of the Mass readings to reflect on the role of a Catholic university in our contemporary Australian life. We often remark on the increasing Americanization of Australian life, but Catholic Australia has not followed Catholic United States in its enthusiasm for founding universities. This commitment to tertiary education is one of the sources of American greatness, and the Australian equivalent of the American ratio means that we would have about twenty Catholic colleges or universities in Australia. We only have two, although both have multiple campuses across states.

Saint Paul writing to the Corinthians speaks of the one Spirit giving a variety of gifts to different individuals, just as the body has many different parts. So, too, a large religious community like the Catholic Church has a bewildering variety of religious and service institutions as well as the equally bewildering variety of religious orders. It is sometimes alleged that not even the Holy Spirit knows how many women's religious orders exist! In Australia we have parishes, hospitals, homes for the elderly, research institutions, social welfare agencies, missionary and development groups as well as a wide range of educational agencies from kindergarten to tertiary level.

So the lecturers at Notre Dame do not teach like priests in a pulpit; do not give religious instruction like that received in a primary or even a senior secondary school. They do not offer personal formation like a seminary, and Notre Dame is not primarily or exclusively a research institute. Neither is Notre Dame a technical school imparting particular skills in our technological age.

Sometimes it is easier to spell out what a university should not be than to win general agreement about what makes a university. One American university president quipped that a university was a community where everyone was united in a common concern about car parking!

Pope John Paul II's 1990 apostolic constitution *Ex Corde Ecclesiae* spoke of the Catholic university as an academic community that protects and advances human dignity and culture through teaching, research, and services offered to the local, national, and international communities. It has an institutional autonomy and guarantees academic freedom within the confines of truth and the common good.

More particularly, Notre Dame is at this moment largely an undergraduate university, offering a range of first-rate professional courses. Students are encouraged to struggle to discover truth and meaning, to respect and love the culture within which we live and are equipped to think, to analyze and synthesize; to solve problems, to build on and improve what they have received, and to conserve all the good they have inherited. They are encouraged to scrutinize reality as they struggle to put together a personal synthesis of higher truths.

Notre Dame is also a lay-led Catholic university. We rejoice in this, although the university acknowledges gratefully the support it continues to receive from other sections of the Church. *Ex Corde Ecclesiae* recognizes that, today, Catholic universities depend "to a great extent on the competent and dedicated service of lay Catholics". For Pope John Paul II, this was "a sign of hope" and "a confirmation of the irreplaceable lay vocation in the Church and in the world".

I remember hearing a few times of academics claiming that a Catholic university should have good relations with the Church. I always objected to that claim because it is an error, somewhat like the error of those Catholics who contrast their own community with "the official Church". While this is not repeated as often as it used to be (at least in my part of the world), we must always remember that there is only one

Church. Certainly there are officials in the Church, and it is generally beneficial to have good relations with them (although we never find a pearl in an oyster where there is no grit)!

So, too, a Catholic university does not have a good relationship with the Church, because it is an institution, a community within the Church. Pope John Paul's document is entitled *Ex Corde Ecclesiae* —from the heart of the Church—precisely to make this point. The Church is not coterminous with the clergy. All communities of the baptized live and work within the Church. Notre Dame is at the heart of the Catholic Church community in Perth, Broome, and Sydney.

The Australian Government today is encouraging each university to develop its particular strengths, to find its niche. If we go to Isaiah's list from the first reading, I suppose all universities are committed to searching for wisdom and insight, for counsel and knowledge, and preparing young people for the proper exercise of power. But only a religious university, or perhaps a theology faculty in a secular university, would search out the proper meaning of "the fear of the Lord".

Certainly a Catholic university has to be committed to a systematic exploration of the God question, of the relationship between faith and reason, of the interaction of Catholicism and culture today as well as in the past. Significant twentieth-century thinkers like Christopher Dawson and T. S. Eliot insisted that religion stands at the heart of every thriving culture and civilization. Certainly Nazism and Communism showed us two examples of life without God, cruel and disastrous experiments. A contemporary British philosopher, Roger Scruton, has explained one dimension of this beautifully. He writes that the loss of religion means that knowledge is lost, and this brings, not liberation, but a fall.

One essential dimension of human life is how we confront suffering, diminishment, and loss. Christianity enables us to bear our losses by setting them in a transcendental perspective, not as meaningless afflictions, but as sacrifices, consecrated suffering. Scruton also claims that a relentless pursuit of pleasure rather than penitence produces a contagious hardness of heart: "Those brought up in our post-religious society do not seek forgiveness", he claims, "since they are by and large free from the belief that they need it. This does not mean they are happy. But it does mean that they put pleasure before commitment and can neglect their duties without being crippled by guilt."

This is a grim picture of a godless public opinion. Our common-sense notions have been heavily influenced by two thousand years of Christianity and a post-Christian common sense would be radically different. A Catholic university encourages its members to examine and evaluate such claims and counter claims. A small minority today is working hard to make our society deaf to God's call to faith and love. This is a struggle in every age, but it is being waged more intensely now in the Western world.

Stan James' poem points out the danger:

> Sometimes we're at our lives
> The same way dogs are at a concert
> —We hear all the sounds
> And none of the music.

The Gospel today tells us of the seed falling in different places to produce widely different harvests. Let us pray that Notre Dame University will go from strength to strength and produce a hundredfold harvest, educating people who are not only interested in God, but believers and doers, people who recognize good Christian music and love it.

August 4, 2008
University of Notre Dame Australia, Fremantle

A CATHOLIC FIRST
IN THE BRITISH EMPIRE

John 10:1–10

THE GOSPEL according to John presents us at this Mass with the image of the sheepfold, and the gate to the sheepfold is Jesus Christ himself. "Anyone who enters through me", Jesus says, "will be safe: he will go freely in and out and be sure of finding pasture" (Jn 10:9).

And we hear in this Gospel another word from Jesus: "I have come that they may have life and have it to the full" (Jn 10:10). It is especially fitting that we should hear a passage from Saint John's Gospel at this Mass to celebrate the 150th anniversary of the foundation of the College of Saint John the Evangelist within the University of Sydney. It is fitting, too, that this passage speaks of a flock gathered together in a sheepfold from where, provided they pass in and out of it through Christ, they will be sure of finding "good pasture".

For why does Saint John's College exist if not in order to help its members to find the sweetest and most satisfying of pastures, or, as Jesus described it, "to have life to the full"? People come to a university to pursue knowledge—at least we hope they do, and we hope that gaining knowledge will not only be a good thing in itself, good for the student's own personal and spiritual growth, but that it will be a benefit to human society, that it will contribute to advancement and progress.

Back in 1850's Sydney, the complex interplay of religious tribal loyalties, politics, and the "Irish Question" might have obscured some of the higher motives behind encouraging young Catholics to pursue an education at the newly founded University of Sydney. Knowledge for its own sake is all very well, but Saint John's College was to be a place where Catholics could receive the education needed to exercise influence on the public affairs of the emerging colony of New South Wales, now the jewel in the crown that is the Commonwealth of Australia.

The founding archbishop, Dr. Polding, wrote in these terms in 1857 to the faithful of the archdiocese about the potential benefits of Catholics attending the university: "It may be the means of incalculable benefit. If any one indulges in visions of worldly ambition and is smitten with what are in truth the marvelous capacities and prospects of this country; let him reflect, that those capacities can be wielded, and those prospects realized, only then, when by means of such training as Universities can give, the land shall supply its native race of priests and statesmen, of lawyers and physicians, of soldiers, and sailors, and artists."

Polding's language is cast in the idiom of the Victorian era, but there is a wisdom there and a sense of vision that readily speaks to us today. Higher education is still the key to actualize the potential within our young people, our nation, our society and culture. Knowledge, enlightened by faith in Christ, who is Wisdom Incarnate, ennobles the men and women who strive for it. This was and is a high ideal, a soaring, inspiring prospect for Saint John's College to make real.

At the same time that we extol the virtues of higher learning, however, we need to recognize that those who seek knowledge, those who study at university, are only human, usually in the younger and less experienced part of life, and as such are subject to all kinds of pressures, influences, and emotions as they live their student lives. These hostile pressures from drugs, alcohol, and pan-sexualism have increased, and the confusion about self-imposed limits, and where they should be placed, is probably deeper than it ever was.

Not only are undergraduates subject to the pressures of academic timetables, but they are often a long way from home, separated from previous support systems of family, friends, and mentors and encountering new ideas, new people, new problems, new choices. As a Catholic college, a significant part of the reason why Saint John's was founded and continues to exist is to help protect and, indeed, enhance the spiritual and moral dimension of life. The second Rector of Saint John's, the Reverend Doctor John Forrest, sent a notice to the Catholic clergy and laity around the colony, assuring them that Saint John's would provide for their sons a suitable residence in which religious education would have its proper place, a place where "their morals would be protected from the corruption and vice inseparable from a large city".

I do not know that Doctor Forrest or his successors down to the present time could claim 100 percent success in that endeavor, but surely it would be a breach of trust between the college and its students, and, indeed, between the college and the wider Catholic community, if we were to give up trying to help our bright young students grow and blossom as women and men who are intellectually, spiritually, and humanly mature.

The venerable denominational colleges that guard the university campus on three sides are testimony to a similar conviction by their diverse founders that the pursuit of knowledge will be a richer and more rewarding experience when supported by a framework of collegial life, with its elements of faith, friendship, sportsmanship, and mentorship.

Like most other institutions, it has to be admitted that our Saint John's College does not always achieve the heights and loftiness it should. The original soaring tower above the main doors, "the gate to the sheepfold", planned by William Wardell as a clear statement of the college's orientation to the source of all wisdom, was in practice reduced to the abbreviated form that we know as the "Freehill Tower". That tower is grand and is a fine monument to the generosity of Countess Eileen Freehill in memory of one of the college's early students and Fellows, but it is not the elevated upward-reaching noble pile that was first envisaged. One would not want the reduced height of that tower to be in any way emblematic of a reduced faith and commitment by those who live in its shadow—any more than one would want the reduced height of the central tower of this cathedral, also designed by William Wardell and also a victim of thrift—to be emblematic of a reduced faith and commitment by those who live in Cathedral House.

But the curtailed tower of the college may certainly be considered emblematic of the fact that there are things that sometimes do not go as planned, that we do not in fact live in an ideal world, and that the foundation of Saint John's was an audacious enterprise that struggled for a long time to prove itself viable. The number of students was only in the twenties and thirties for many years, and while Lindhurst was something of a rival, the basic problem was that most Australians then were not interested in higher education. The challenge of viability in the changed reality of universities today remains, but the new facilities being planned for the college have, we all hope and pray, the capacity to enhance that viability and, indeed, to enable Saint John's to be even more effective in achieving its goals. The challenge is for Saint John's to be not only a bigger "sheepfold", but also one that has Christ ever more integrally as its "gate".

If the consciously secular nature of the University of Sydney, present since its foundation, should be allowed to have the effect of "quarantining" the academy from religious faith and the search for truth, then all of us, not least the academics, would be diminished. As Pope Benedict XVI wrote recently in the address he was scheduled to deliver in January at the University of Rome "La Sapienza":

> If reason, out of concern for its alleged purity, becomes deaf to the great message that comes to it from Christian faith and wisdom, then it withers like a tree whose roots can no longer reach the waters that give it life. It loses the courage for truth and thus becomes not greater but smaller.

The presence of the Catholic colleges within the University of Sydney and the mutually respectful way in which the bodies corporate of university and college are able to cooperate in fact help make the university more truly a university, whose roots can still draw water from the faith and wisdom that enabled it to be planted. That Saint John's College, through its members, has been helping to water those roots for 150 years is something for which to be very grateful.

Across those 150 years, members of Saint John's—including many of you here this afternoon—have made valuable contributions to the life of our nation, our culture, our community. I thank in particular all members of the Council over those years, the long succession of rectors, especially the present rector, Doctor David Daintree, a true university man, strong in the faith, who has done a fine job. All the friends of Saint John's College need to work to provide foundations adequate for the next 150 years so the college continues to nurture those who seek knowledge and wisdom, giving them the capacity to contribute more and more to the community.

The college's heraldic motto—*Nisi Dominus frustra*—reminds us that without the Lord all our efforts will be in vain; without him, we might gain knowledge, but we cannot find wisdom; we can have life but not have it "to the full". Jesus Christ is the "gate" to the "sheepfold". If, in the search for knowledge and truth, we pass through Him, we will indeed be sure of finding pasture. May all who go in and out of Saint John's College in its next 150 years be blessed by Christ, the Gate, through whom is found freedom and the fullness of life.

April 13, 2008
150th Anniversary of the Foundation of the College of
Saint John the Evangelist within the University of Sydney
Saint Mary's Cathedral, Sydney

A NEW CHRISTENDOM

Acts 13:26–33; John 14:1–6

A s GRADUATES of Christendom College, followers of Jesus Christ, and therefore children of Abraham (like those mentioned in the first reading), you have many reasons for gratitude. I would suspect that few graduates anywhere have been encouraged as effectively as yourselves in the search for wisdom, that lifelong quest for the truth, the good, and the beautiful which Christendom College espouses. You have not studied at a college whose Catholic identity has been damaged or weakened, but in a community that explicitly acknowledges the supremacy of faith and reason and that Our Lord and Savior, Jesus Christ, is "the way, the truth, and the life". I repeat that you have many reasons to be grateful.

As you know, there are different levels or stages of faith. In the first of these stages, we pray to God when we are in trouble or when we need something, just as a young child appeals to his parents. I explain regularly to teenagers that if they do not even pray to God when they are in trouble, then their faith is weak indeed.

A higher form of faith is represented in our prayer to God for forgiveness, especially when we ask to be forgiven for death-bearing sins, which drive God's love from our hearts. Sometimes this prayer expresses a very deep faith indeed, for example, when we ask God's forgiveness for terrible sins and crimes. *I regularly tell youngsters that God would forgive Stalin, Hitler, and Mao if they repented. This is an enormous faith claim.*

Yet another higher level of faith is expressed when we thank God for the many blessings we have received. Sometimes we do this more easily in extremities, after a narrow escape or a recovery from illness, but we also need to thank God for the wonderful everyday blessings that we can take for granted.

Jesus' Call to Follow

Parents are always imperfect—like their children. Quite remarkably, many parents improve dramatically during those ten years when their children grow from fifteen to twenty-five years of age, but good and loving parents give their children an irreplaceable advantage. Children should always thank God for their parents, just as they thank God for the gift of faith, for health, and for the prosperity and intelligence that make a tertiary education possible. Christians, and especially Catholics, should be people who are grateful and who also express their gratitude to all who help them—to parents, family, teachers, and friends; to those who have developed the immense Catholic network of communities and institutions that over two thousand years have constituted what we call "Christendom" and of course to those who founded Christendom College.

The story of Our Lord's curing the ten lepers and of the one who returned to give thanks is not just a story about some Jews. It tells us a lot about human nature, because I am sure that all those cured of leprosy were grateful to Jesus. It was simply that nine of them were too busy, or too excited, tied up with the family, to say thanks. Please God no one in this class of graduates will make a similar mistake.

Today is the feast of the martyrs Nereus and Achilleus, Roman soldiers who converted and refused to serve any longer in the pagan Roman army. They were probably executed around the year A.D. 300 under the Emperor Diocletian, who was the last great Roman persecutor. He retired early back home to an immense palace he had built on the seashore at Split in Croatia, to cultivate his gardens and grow cabbages. The mausoleum built to hold his remains is now the small Catholic cathedral, because the Christians when they came to power threw his body into the sea and installed the remains of the local Bishop Domnius of Salona, whom he had executed. I have often wondered whether his early retirement was connected with his failure to crush and eliminate Christianity.

However, we are celebrating today Nereus and Achilleus, not Diocletian, and their example reminds us of the personal integrity and sacrifice over the centuries that have fueled the growth of the Church. It is sobering to be reminded that during the twentieth century more people gave their lives for Christ than in any other century, and all of you, like all of us who are older, will be called to struggle and sacrifice in order to remain faithful.

Just as there are many different rooms in the Father's house, so I am sure that you will follow many different paths as you enter the next stage of your life's journey. *But none of you, not one of you, will be able to escape the great culture wars convulsing our societies, which struggle for the survival of Christian values in the public life of Western society.* Especially here in the United States, I believe there are solid grounds for optimism, despite all the losses and the scandals, because the fight-back is well under way. And Christendom College is part of this new growth.

Let me conclude by returning to one basic truth, which, no doubt, has been repeated to you many times during your years in college. As Catholic Christians, we are children of God, brothers and sisters of Christ. This means that we are free, not slaves, not even servants, but free children. However, if we are to continue to exercise our freedom wisely, our faith will need to be nourished through regular prayer. It is the pure in heart who continue to see God in faith and a high promise in our early adult years is no guarantee that our faith cannot weaken, that our hearts will not be hardened by the fascination of evil as the years pass.

To be grounded in Thomistic wisdom, to love our Western culture, to be taught to go to the primary sources, all of these are considerable advantages, but only regular prayer can fuel our faith, hope, and love; only prayer will keep us in the struggle. It is not impossible to slide into becoming sympathizers rather than participants, Christian agnostics rather than prayerful believers, aesthetes and dilettantes rather than warriors and builders of the new heaven and the new earth. Prayer and perseverance will keep us on track.

May you all continue to take refuge in the Lord and go on to do great things for the Kingdom of God in Christ Jesus Our Lord.

May 12, 2006
Baccalaureate Mass, Christendom College
Front Royal, Virginia, United States

LOVE AND REASON

Isaiah 32:15−18; I John 4:7−11; Mark 12:28−34

OUR FIRST READING from the prophet Isaiah could be applied, without too much exaggeration, to the Australian story in this Great South Land of the Holy Spirit. Despite the brutal origins of the convict system, despite the injustices heaped upon our indigenous brothers and sisters—which we still battle today, often ineffectively—millions of Australians have lived peaceful lives in quiet dwellings, turned the countryside into fertile land, and established security and a fair measure of peace.

Despite all our imperfections, the Spirit has been poured on us from above, and one of these channels of grace for Australian society has been the Catholic Church here and, more particularly, the Catholic schools. We should thank God for what we have received from our predecessors in Catholic education, especially those who labored for ninety years with no government aid; we should rejoice in the service that we presently offer and ask God for wisdom, courage, and perseverance as we confidently move into the future.

All Catholic communities, and especially Catholic schools, have to be communities of faith and love—or they are neither Catholic nor communitarian. This is the import of the two New Testament readings tonight. God Himself is love, and it was this love within the Godhead which inspired the Father to send His Son to live and die among us and then send His Spirit to give us the capacity to believe and to follow Jesus' teachings in our daily lives.

The Lord Jesus did not come with a set of questions or comfortable affirmations. He came to us with a set of answers, with the requirements that we repent and believe, and with the commandments that, first of all, we must love the Lord our God with all our heart, all our soul, all our mind, and all our strength and the equally difficult second commandment that we love our neighbors as ourselves.

A few of our students might be unclear about how we should love God, and some, like a quarter of their peers, might wonder whether there is a God to be loved. But all of them should know that we teach, as Jesus taught, that God loves each one of us and that we should love one another. By and large, our students understand the Christian commandment that they love one another, as I dare to believe that, overwhelmingly, our schools are happy communities, generally well geared to helping the less fortunate here and overseas.

However, we need to go farther—and we do. We must show in our lives and make explicit in our teaching that Christ's is a tough love; not sentimentality, not the soft tolerance of anything goes without any principles, but clearheaded compassion and sympathy. Christian love does not allow us to love and then do anything we feel like doing (as a saying of Saint Augustine is alleged to suggest). We are stuck with Christ's warning that if we love Him we shall keep His commandments. It is possible to keep the commandments without love, although I suspect this rarely lasts long. Such formalism is always empty and often poisonous. Love is essential, but we cannot love one another without keeping the commandments.

Pope John Paul wrote magnificently on faith and reason and on the essential relationship of truth and freedom, and I want to say a few words on the equally essential link between love and reason, or rationality.

Recently, Pope Benedict has been in the news for his academic address at Regensburg, his old university, once the seat of the Holy Roman Emperors. His passing references to Islam dominated the media, but most of the speech was about the importance of God for every society, and especially Western societies like ours, emphasizing that rationality is an attribute of God. God is not cranky or capricious. God is truthful.

The pope quoted the beginning of John's Gospel: "In the beginning was the Word and the Word was with God and the Word was God", pointing out that the Greek word "Logos" means both word and reason. The Holy Father acknowledges that this reverence for reason was taken into Revelation, into John's Gospel from Greek philosophy, and this was a providential conjunction. Here lies one of the secrets of

European and Western civilization. Here lies the reason for our Catholic schools, for our reverence for education, why Catholics should never be fundamentalists and can never be postmodernists who reject the idea of truth. More practically, it means that whatever measure of success or failure we might have religiously with our students, we must labor mightily to convince them that they stand under the truth; that they can no more ignore the search for truth than they can turn their back on goodness or love.

It is a tragedy that so many young Catholics feel they are free to pick and choose their beliefs, that so many of them believe all morality is relative to time and place, to particular circumstances. Are they free to pick and then choose to reject the two great commandments of love? Of course not. A Christian is not someone who follows his conscience in a loving way. Every human being is obliged to do that. A Christian is a person who elects to follow the person of Jesus Christ, who returns Christ's love, who believes that Christ explained the reasons for living and how we should live. A Christian accepts the two great commandments of love or he is not a Christian.

A Christian acknowledges his failure to love and requests forgiveness. A Christian does not define his sins out of existence and is not free to reject the central Christian mysteries after a little mature consideration. A Christian is someone who accepts Christ's answer. Here lives the secret of the survival of the Catholic Church for two thousand years and two hundred years in Australia. To stem the exodus, we need to hang on to the children of Catholic parents; but to reverse the trend, we need to inspire many to conversion, to a change of life, to a new acceptance of Christ and of the Church.

By a happy coincidence I was shown recently the speech Father Paul Stenhouse, a Sydney MSC, gave at the relaunch of Peter Coleman's biography of the great Australian poet James McAuley. McAuley was a cultural warrior, a politician, the first editor of the magazine *Quadrant*, immersed in the struggle for truth and love. An unbeliever at first, then much impressed by a missionary bishop and nun in New Guinea, he became a Catholic in 1950.

This was how he saw what became for him "the supreme question: Whether the Catholic Church is not in fact the sole mistress, guardian and nurse of the infinite spiritual wealth of the Christian tradition, the only full and authentic source of that living water for which my soul is enflamed with an increasing thirst". That is the question for us, too.

At the very least, our students should know what the Catholic Church claims. We are not offering one holiday package from a set of equally valid alternatives; nor are we offering a philosophy, another way of life. We are calling our students to faith in the Son of God, a faith lived out in the Catholic Church.

Faith and love reinforce one another in truth. When faith and love are strong, we seek the truth and are not searching for shortcuts, not fudging the challenges. I believe a few lines from McAuley sum up our situation:

> I know that faith is like a root
> That's tough, inert and cold;
> Yet it can send up its green shoot
> and flower against the cold.
> I know that there is a grace that flows
> When all the springs run dry.
> It wells up to renew the rose
> and lifts the cedar high.

September 28, 2006
National Catholic Education Conference Mass
Saint Mary's Cathedral, Sydney

LORETO KIRRIBILLI CENTENARY MASS

Isaiah 56:1, 6−7; Romans 11:13−15, 29−32;
Matthew 15:21−28

O NE HUNDRED YEARS is a long time. Perhaps not so long in the two-thousand-year history of the Catholic Church, but still a long time by Australian standards and by the standard of any personal lifetime. So it is appropriate that the Loreto College community comes to your beautiful cathedral to thank God for one hundred years of educational achievement at the present site on Milson's Point, although Loreto had been nearby in rented houses since 1901. We do not come just to thank God, although this is our primary duty because we should not take our blessings for granted (least of all a Loreto education), but to ask God's continued blessings on the Loreto Kirribilli community today and for the many years ahead. We can see few clouds on the horizon at the moment, but no one can tell what is around the corner, and it is always good to ask God to continue to look after us personally and spiritually.

In the introduction to your college's official history, the author has written that if we wish to understand the educational vision of Kirribilli, we should "go first to Ballarat, and listen to an ageing, deaf, compulsively communicative Irish Mother Provincial", Mother Gonzaga Barry, who made the initial Australian foundation in my hometown of Ballarat in Victoria in 1875.

In the briefing notes I received for this Mass, I learned that I shared the privilege of a Loreto education with Pope Benedict XVI, who has just been with us, and Pope Gregory XVI, a stern pope from around the middle of the nineteenth century. Certainly I remember the nuns who taught me with affection and gratitude.

Today's Gospel is not a politically correct story, because Our Lord is brusque toward the Canaanite woman pleading for her daughter. *The*

Sydney Morning Herald could have waxed very self-righteously about the bluntness of Our Lord's initial replies. It is useful to remember that Jews then generally did not mix with foreigners because they regarded such contact as defiling; just as some Muslims today will not mix with non-Muslims. Jesus' disciples were not as high-minded in any sense, because they wanted Our Lord to do something to stop the woman shouting, to get her off their back.

But Jesus pointed out that He had come only for the Jews, the lost sheep of Israel, and then that He was not about to give the children's food to the house dogs. The Canaanite woman was a match for him, replying that "even the house dogs can eat the scraps that fall from their master's table." This was the breakthrough, the turning point in her struggle for her daughter. "Woman, you have great faith. Let your wish be granted." And from that moment, her daughter was well again.

The woman's story demonstrates faith and perseverance. The second reading makes the same point, theologically, as Paul insists that while the Jewish people generally have not accepted Christ, they remain God's chosen people and "will enjoy mercy eventually"; an enigmatic claim that is often interpreted as predicting a Jewish turning to Christian faith.

So, too, the Loreto story is a history of faith and perseverance. Mary Ward's innovations in the seventeenth century were resisted by many in the Church leadership, and the sisters could only work on the Continent, not in England. Her order, which was based on the Jesuit model of education and an active apostolate, was suppressed in 1630, and she was briefly imprisoned in 1631. On her release, Pope Urban VIII approved the order after some small changes to the rules. Indeed, her role as the true founder of the Institute of the Blessed Virgin Mary was a matter of considerable dispute, even among the sisters in Australia. The fact that she was English might have been a factor among some of the Irish sisters who founded Loreto in Australia, but Kirribilli seems to have been solid for Mary Ward from the beginning.

So, too, the Ballarat foundation struggled, especially in the financial collapse of the 1890s, when "Marvelous Melbourne" bit the dust. Victoria (with Argentina) had been the richest country in the world around 1890, but the collapse was extreme, and many thousands emigrated elsewhere looking for work. Three hundred Victorian state schools had to close. So I well remember as a child hearing how the

Loreto sisters were able to resume the construction of the beautiful Children's Chapel by Lake Wendouree only through the generosity of Countess Elizabeth Wolff-Metternich, who had gone back to Europe to organize her affairs and died there. She had hoped to join the sisters.

We should also remember that there was no government support for Catholic education for most of Kirribilli's history. A symbolic breakthrough occurred in 1963, but significant amounts of money only started to flow in the 1970s.

Therefore, Kirribilli existed for a long time on the generosity of the sisters, then most of the staff, who did not take a salary, on parents' fees, and the generosity of many local families like the Heatons. We have pressures and challenges today, but they are nothing like the financial challenges of the past.

Loreto schools in Australia follow a number of themes in their Mission Statement. The integrity that is sought is based firmly on the Christian faith; not a vague religious yearning, not a diffuse spirituality or sense of awe, but an explicit faith in the one true God and Christ His Son.

I acknowledge this faith, this willingness to cooperate with other agencies in the Church, with gratitude, as do the local parish clergy today and from years past. One hundred and sixty Kirribilli students took part in the World Youth Day school group, a wonderful achievement and an excellent spiritual investment for the future. Kirribilli, too, has long acknowledged that privilege brings with it responsibility, that duties accompany all rights. Social justice activities continue to thrive, supported by lay staff and sisters through the Saint Vincent de Paul group and the visits to the women's refuge and many other activities.

Loreto schools have always been recognized as centers of beauty, music, and Catholic culture. Originally, even at Kirribilli, there was not too much emphasis on external exams or the sciences. Those times are long past, and your academic results are among the best in the Catholic schools. While this must not be done at the expense of other values we share, academic excellence must continue to be among the highest priorities at Kirribilli. I am sure it will be. I hope and pray, too, that Kirribilli will continue to be a happy place, a school with "good spirit". While this does not guarantee excellence in other areas, it is a wonderful foundation for every accomplishment, religious and secular.

Originally the Loreto schools in Australia were very Irish, but this changed as Australian patriotism developed, especially with the push toward Federation. There was always a strong vein of practicality and common sense, as institutions do not survive for one hundred years without it. Mother Gonzaga Barry used to look on God as "her banker"! She was committed, not just to the three Rs, but also to the three "Hs"—"the cultivation of head, heart, and hand". She wanted to cut across the usual categories of "State School" and "Church School" to a kind of university for the education of women. And this was around 1890.

Times have changed. The cohesiveness of the Catholic community has been changed by migration and prosperity, and the pressures on regular practice of the faith and on family life have increased. New opportunities abound for ex-students, but these bring new challenges, not the least of which is balancing marriage, family, and a career.

I will conclude with a passage from one of Mother Gonzaga Barry's letters of 1887 to her "dearest children". The language and imagery are a bit overblown by our standards, but the message that calls us to remember the world of the Spirit remains as true as when the words were written.

> I compared you to a "goodly row of pearls"—our Lady's pearls— and as such I still regard you; but you must, besides, be God's little coral workers, building up with your tiny supernatural acts a solid foundation hidden in your own pure and loving hearts—a foundation so firm that all the waves of the world's sea cannot shake it, and on which God can raise a superstructure to last for all eternity.

August 17, 2008
Saint Mary's Cathedral, Sydney

MASS FOR BROTHER J. D. HEALY

Wisdom 3:1–69; Romans 6; Matthew 5:1–12

THE BEATITUDES express for us many of the values that will be important, and therefore heavily rewarded, in the next life. Those people will be specially blessed who are gentle, merciful, pure in heart; those who are peacemakers.

Those of us who were privileged to know Brother J. D. Healy, who died in Sydney on November 6 at the age of eighty-eight (then the oldest living Christian Brother), will realize that many of the qualities listed by Our Lord in the Beatitudes belonged to him and were practiced by him with an ease and a courtesy unusual even among good men. Brother Jack, as he was known in Ballarat, was born in Ballarat East on April 19, 1899. He left home to join the brothers at Strathfield when he as fourteen; his younger brother Bernie joined some years later. He was teaching primary classes by the age of seventeen in Balmain, and he spent most of his working life and retirement in Sydney, except for his time in Ballarat and on the Melbourne provincial council. He was provincial of the Sydney province of Saint Mary's from 1959 to 1966.

He lived through two World Wars and a major depression. He saw the years of struggle for educational funding; he was a local and regional leader in education and among the brothers at that unique time in the 1940s and 1950s, which was such a high time of faith and practice. He lived through the Second Vatican Council, the coming of television, and the arrival of successive waves of new migrants, which have brought us to our present new and radically different religious situation.

In all this time, he remained courteous, optimistic, and fully human; light years away from the unsympathetic caricature and distortion that some would lead us to believe were the Christian Brothers of that era. Brother Healy was certainly a product of the preconciliar Church, but the struggles of his life enriched and purified him. He was not sour or wounded.

I am privileged to be asked to preach this homily, but I am less than fully equipped to pay him adequate tribute because I was only in primary school when he was principal. I belonged to his choir but was never taught by him. However, I do have two qualities that emboldened me to accept this task. Through my mother, I belong to the same tribe of Irish-Australians from Ballarat East from which Brother sprang and to whom he returned nearly every year; and I certainly and proudly belong to the community of Saint Patrick's College, Ballarat, where he gave such distinguished religious and educational leadership.

The Ballarat East Catholic community was centered around the Church of Saint Alipius. It was in the Saint Alipius presbytery that Peter Lalor's arm was amputated after the Eureka uprising and massacre. The community was Irish-Australian; they were not rich, but they were proud, conscious of their traditions, politically interested, and involved. They were talkers and charmers, capable of quarrels and grudges among themselves, but equally able to close ranks against external threats, real or imagined. The extended family was available and influential. It was a world of school, parish, and Labor politics; of missions and sodalities and South Street Choral competitions; of Aussie Rules football and cold winters.

Saint Patrick's College in Ballarat transposed many of these qualities, and its old boys took them into a wider world of farming, the professions, and the priesthood. The college's priorities and achievements probably seem clearer in the mists of the past and when compared with our indifferent present performance; but even then they left no doubt about what they were about. Brother Healy was a religious, a teacher, and he was interested in sport and competition. He explained things in those terms and lived it that way. What you saw was what you got!

The college annual of 1950 said that the college was located in "that invigorating and salubrious climate which renders Ballarat so popular". It was this climate which developed "the fine physique and healthy appearance for which the children of Ballarat were so much admired". Ballarat also had the advantage of convenient distance "from the distracting and dissipating life of the metropolis"!

Boarding fees were £40 a term for those over twelve years, and boarders had to bring the usual clothes plus a cap, one pair of rosary beads, and two coat hangers! The college won most local sporting events, except in the rowing, although the crew were "nearly up to concert pitch", after an early disappointment, and "will give a good account of themselves"!

In 1950, Father Frank Little, later archbishop of Melbourne, was one of five old boys ordained that year, and eleven boys left the school to commence training for the priesthood or the brothers. In the diamond jubilee year of the college, 1953, there were 216 ex-student priests, thirty-one ex-student brothers, and sixty-six ex-student seminarians.

Brother Healy was a religious and then a teacher, and Saint Patrick's College under his leadership reflected these priorities, as in fact it does now. I could not honestly make this claim of every Catholic school, then or now.

The completion of the magnificent college chapel was one high point of Brother Healy's principalship. He told me he was criticized then because it was supposed to be too big. He expressed his delight to me some years ago that now it was not big enough for all the Saint Patrick's College students.

He wanted the chapel to be "a symbol of the main purpose of Catholic education, to make religion, in accord with Church tradition, the center and inspiration of college life". This was his ambition. It is also a fine epitaph for Brother Healy and his generation of Christian Brothers.

To say this was his first priority is not to denigrate in any way the human, educational, or sporting achievements of those times. The social mobility, especially into the professions, that the Brothers encouraged in their students then has few equals in the English-speaking world. Those of us who benefited from this must be eternally grateful. Such progress does not come easily or automatically, and one of our tasks is to do as well with more recent arrivals.

Brother Healy gave his life for Christ and lived it out in practical cooperation with the bishops, priests, religious, and laity of his time. He was particularly unusual then in the breadth and variety of his friendships. At the chapel opening, Bishop O'Collins, then bishop of Ballarat, said Brother Jack was "a big man, with a breadth of vision and an artistic sense". Cardinal Freeman, one of his ex-pupils and a lifelong friend, said that "he radiated both authority and sympathy in such fine proportions that [his pupils] were led to respect the one without pre-suming the other; to admire him as a master and revere him as a friend." It is one of the sad ironies of history that such a distinguished man has no memorial to him at Saint Pat's, while his great friend and ally Brother Bill O'Malley has a couple of magnificent monuments.

We pray, then, for the soul of Brother John Dominic Healy, that he may be loosed from his sins. We are confident that he is at peace, in God's hands, no longer needing his Catholic hope, rich with the promise of immortality. We thank God we came under his influence and thank God for his human and religious achievement.

December 16, 1987
Saint Carthage's Church, Parkville, Melbourne

On Life and Love

IS FAITH WITHOUT WORKS DEAD?

The Two Great Commandments

"I came that they may have life, and have it abundantly"

John 10:10

JESUS GAVE US a great commandment: to love God with all our heart and strength and to love our neighbors as we love ourselves. We think of this imperative sometimes as two commandments, but Jesus made it clear that the two are really one (Mk 12:30–31). Love of God must include love of others, but love of others sometimes ignores or rejects God.

Sometimes we can just fail to see Him, like the disciples on the road to Emmaus, who only recognized Jesus when He broke the bread (Lk 24:13–32). For Catholics, faith and service are bound up with the Eucharist. The Body and Blood of Christ sustain us and inspire us, and we bring its reality to others when we serve them. It is part of what gives Catholics an edge, a capacity for perseverance and renewal, for avoiding burnout when serving those who are in greatest need.

Helping those in need shows our respect for the dignity and equality of all human beings and returns to God something of what He has given us. This is the message of the Gospels. It is a message we need to learn and relearn, to grasp and take more and more deeply into our hearts.

Good Works Are Good

Good works are always good. We can be sure of this. Jesus tells us in Matthew's Gospel (25:31–46) that whenever you do something for those in need, you do it for Him. By showing love for others, we are loving Christ. As Jesus will separate the sheep from the goats as the King on Judgment Day, it is clear that genuinely good works will bring us to salvation, even when we do not recognize Christ in those we serve.

Are good works enough? Where does faith—and prayer and worship—come in? Are these optional extras?

Some of the young people who gathered before Easter to help me prepare this pastoral letter argued that good works alone are sufficient for life in this world and the next. But others suggested that works done without faith in Jesus are meaningless. Good might still be done, but what will help us know that doing good is what we should prefer? How do we know that goodness will endure? This is where faith comes in.

Christians are people of faith and people of service. Why are these two aspects of our life connected? Saint James tells us that "just as the body without the spirit is dead, so faith without works is also dead" (Jas 2:26). We know that faith should bear fruit in good works.

God Has No Hands But Ours

"The poor have good news brought to them"

Luke 7:22

Jesus told his disciples that he came "to bring good news to the poor" (Lk 4:18). What is the good news that Christians bring to the poor today? Let me give one example. Welfare workers estimate that 107,000 people are homeless in Australia, and that 90 percent of them have suffered some sort of trauma. In Sydney alone, five hundred people sleep out each night. The Saint Vincent de Paul Society's night patrol helps 150 of these people per night, forty-four thousand a year. Part of bringing Jesus' good news to them is giving them food and a blanket. But it is not just the food and blanket that are the good news.

Jesus came for all of us, but especially for people on the margins. He brings love and life. Out of love, Christ laid down his life for us, and Christians are called to imitate this. This means we use our lives to help others, and especially those who are unwanted (1 Jn 3:16–17). Like

Jesus, we have to give the homeless food and shelter, but we also have to heal their hearts. This can only be done through love, which means through relationships. The poor are not just people we "do good" to: they must also become our friends.

This is the good news Jesus brings: God loves us, unconditionally and forever. But God has no hands but ours. It may not sound like much when compared to the prizes and the glamour that the world offers to the lucky few. But for those who have nothing, kindness is everything. To love and be loved is the source of life itself, the reason to hope and the reason to continue living. This reminds us that it is not just those who are materially poor whom we have to serve, but also those who are spiritually poor. Some of these are not short of money or resources. They are not starving or homeless. But they can be without love, without faith, oppressed by a sense that they are not wanted. Loneliness is one form of poverty that is growing rapidly, outpacing material poverty. "Who needs me?" "Who cares if I live or die?"

Too often these questions go unanswered. The answer is love. We must always be ready to give friendship and a helping hand.

Christians believe in love. Those who believe in God's love must love others (1 Jn 4:7–21). This is our faith, a faith that makes everyone who has it wealthy—full of abundance, full of life. Money cannot give us this sort of abundance. Possessions cannot return our love.

Love lives through action. It is not just a nice feeling. It inspires outreach, takes us out of our comfort zone, to personal inconvenience, difficulty, and sometimes to embarrassment and even danger. Love can be hard work, especially when the people we seek to serve are not particularly lovable. There is always a cost to discipleship.

Having faith does not mean having all the answers, so that we can solve everyone's problems once and for all. This is the mentality of a "do-gooder", not of someone who wants to serve others. The good works of people of faith are based on the recognition that we can never do it alone. We need God's help, and we need the help of others just as they need our help. Today others are in need, and we help them. Tomorrow things may change, and it will be our turn to accept help. This is part of the cost of discipleship, too: learning that if we want to make a difference, we have to learn humility—and gratitude.

Faith and Love: Which Comes First?

"That we might serve him without fear"

Luke 1:74

If we do not love, we are not really Catholic. We are Catholic when we love and believe, and we practice love because we are Catholics. Our faith generates compassion, especially when we contemplate the life, death, and teaching of Jesus. And through the example of Jesus, we are led to service without fear.

The Catholic Church holds together many diverse groups committed to the service of others. In the Church, lay people, priests, religious, and bishops are all called to serve in different ways. Most of us, most of the time, have to start in a small way. The opportunities the Church provides for service—through parishes, schools, religious communities, youth groups, and welfare and charity organizations—are one of her greatest strengths and contributions.

Service requires work and effort. It also requires prayer. Often people say they are too busy to be doing what they should be doing. Too busy to pray, too busy to exercise, too busy to spend time with other people, too busy to talk. If this is the case, we are too busy for relationships—which means we are really too busy to live.

Relationships start at home. Our first neighbors are our parents, sisters, and brothers. The seeds of Catholic faith are planted in our families, to flower into service and great deeds for others. We start in our families, in our parishes and schools, and with our friends. But Christians end up going much wider than this. *Charity begins at home but should not remain there. Faith is a verb. It means love through action. Prayer is critical—for getting us started, keeping us moving, showing us the way, and giving us strength and courage. But it is important to make a start. Like a bicycle, we fall over if we are not mo ving. We need God to help us so that we can help others.*

Faith and works are a gracious circle—the opposite of a vicious circle. They come together, not as a coincidence, but as providence. A living faith is not about looking after number 1, or an attitude of "I'm OK, you're OK." It is about someone to follow, the need for meaning, a God to worship. It touches on self-esteem, believing in oneself, and loving oneself, but if it stops there it dies. Dying to self disperses the darkness—not just for ourselves, but for others. Even shining one little light into the great darkness does help. There are many ways of doing this, even in hard times for faith like our own, but we need to begin.

Do Christian Principles Have a Place in Public Life?

*"Blessed are those who hunger and thirst for righteousness,
  for they will be filled"*
Matthew 5:6

Some young people are strongly committed to social justice. Social justice is a broad area of activity involving people of all beliefs and no beliefs. What sets Catholic social justice work apart is that it is inspired by Christian faith. Like Saint Francis of Assisi, we believe that our love for others is crucial in bringing people to faith in Jesus. Christian service must always be bound up with faith in some way, if only by the example and inspiration we give. It is our actions that must speak our love. Then people will know we are Christians. Our actions speak loudest. We have to show people that we mean it when we say that we believe in love. Christian social justice work is one central way of doing this. But it can also test us. We will only keep at it and will only continue to do Christian social justice work if we cling to the Lord and do not depart from him (Sir 2:1–6).

When we serve others, we are often confronted by the flaws in our society. Where do these come from? From social and political structures? Or from the fault lines of the human heart? In reality, it is not easy to divide these things. Our personal failings influence the systems around us, even systems that are established to correct our shortcomings or to counterbalance them. Concern with these questions leads some people into public life and to involvement in the institutions that shape our society and values. Catholics need to be active in public life, right across the range of opportunities that a modern democracy like Australia puts before us.

A few claim that Christians should not be involved in public life, and specifically in politics, unless they put their Christian values to one side. This is a form of intolerance. It also misunderstands the relationship of faith and democracy. Christians have a democratic right to express their beliefs and argue for them. *Political action is a special form of service that belongs to lay people.* Committed Christians bring valuable gifts to democracy, such as an ethic based on serving others out of love—of treating people as an end in themselves, not as a means to the ends of others. Without these values, politics—and social life— quickly become zero-sum games. Those with the most votes or the most power take all. This is why democracy needs religion, people of faith who build community, encourage solidarity and service.

Pentecost Pastoral Letter 2004
Catholic Archdiocese of Sydney

LOVE NOT LUST

Proverbs 31:10–13, 19–20, 30–31;
1 Thessalonians 5:1–6; Matthew 25:14–30

I T IS SOMETIMES, perhaps even regularly, asserted that Catholics rarely hear a Sunday sermon these days on sexual morality. I probably would have to plead guilty to that charge, although in many other places I have tried to present Christian teaching on this vital topic. In my distant youth, many serious Christians, not just Catholics, were tempted to think that sexual failings were the worst sins, perhaps the only sins worth mentioning. We know that this is not the case, as there are many sins worse than sexual weakness, although sexual sins are regularly prompted by selfishness, which can sometimes be brutal, aggressive, and even violent, bringing great harm to others.

Most Sunday congregations are very mixed, with people from every age group, including the very young, and this mix is not ideal for sermons on sexuality. But it is unusual in our sex-obsessed society, where all of us and especially the young are bombarded relentlessly in the media with vulgarity and soft porn, that we have a silence from the pulpit.

In this youth Mass on Sunday evening with a cathedral full of young people, mostly university students, I decided to say a few words on the topic beginning from the excerpt from Proverbs about a perfect wife and concluding with the parable about the talents. As I follow the discipline of the Latin rite in the Roman Catholic Church, I am a celibate priest, without a wife, and therefore less qualified than any husband to speak about the blessing of a good wife. But everyone is the son or daughter of a mother, and as most mothers are wives, I am more than happy to agree with the author of the Book of Proverbs that a good wife is priceless, although I would leave it to the husbands to decide how many wives are perfect! Good marriages purify the couple both as spouses and parents, where their mutual duties radically diminish natural selfishness. But a lot depends on the qualities spouses bring to a marriage; so they need to train and prepare.

Lust is still one of the seven deadly sins and not because Christians are spoilsports. A disordered sexual appetite causes damage. This rudimentary self-knowledge is essential, together with a realization of our limitations.

Healthy sexual desire is a blessing, but like every desire it needs to be trained, well directed, and restrained. We now recognize that sexual addiction is as much a disease as addiction to drugs or alcohol, because habits feed on themselves for good or ill.

I chose this topic because of the sad news last week that New South Wales is suffering from an epidemic of sexually transmitted diseases among teenagers, where the rate of diagnosed chlamydia among girls and young women is more than double the rate found among teenage boys and young men. The sixteen- to twenty-four-year-olds had the largest percentage infected, and southeast Sydney and the Hunter regions were the worst affected areas. Lust is more of a problem among older age groups than it is among teenagers, but it is sad to see some of them making trouble for themselves in the future with the threat of infertility, as they are encouraged to drift into disordered patterns of life while still at school.

Across Australia fifty thousand youngsters tested positive for chlamydia last year, more than twelve thousand of them in New South Wales. Disturbingly high rates were found among fifteen-year-olds. Doctors estimate the real rate of annual infections at a quarter of a million a year, because many are too embarrassed to seek medical help or persist in thinking they are invincible, that such diseases only strike others.

Too many of our young people are sold short on sex because nobody is telling them the whole truth, and many have to learn only from their mistakes. I once had an eighteen-year-old Catholic from a Catholic school claim he did not know sexual intercourse before marriage was sinful. Many are relentlessly encouraged to reject the traditional Christian teachings on sexuality, usually without any sort of examination or comparative assessment. And even churchgoing young Catholics can be tempted to think that Christian teaching is too negative or impossibly high minded.

It is evidence of a very low estimate of young people's altruism to tell fifteen- and sixteen-year-olds that the best answer to sexually transmitted diseases is a condom, as was implied in last week's press reports. No one is perfect, and our instincts are partially disordered, but human beings are more than a mass of uncontrollable desires. Self-control is possible and necessary.

Sexual activity is lit by a fire, sacred or profane, that in the long term either purifies or corrupts. It is not as morally neutral as other physical activities, not a recreational right, because sexual activity should be linked to love. And love comes from our hearts and changes the core of our being. Lust is selfish and uses the partner as an object. Love is unselfish and acts with the good of the loved one always in mind.

In the Christian scheme, love, openness to children, and sexual activity are all linked together as a worthy ideal, a trinity preparing for marriage and family. True love is urged to wait. Truly human teaching on sexuality recognizes the need for ideals as well as human weakness. Lust is damaging, an easy option, but true love is precious and different.

A final word about the parable of the talents. While the commandments are for everyone, more is expected of those brought up in loving households where Christian teaching is respected. The good God expects you to live by the principles you learned at home and not succumb to the lowest standards of those around you. Society needs this, too, if we are to avoid sinking into an ever deeper morass of sexual irresponsibility, with ever-worsening consequences for children and parents.

November 16, 2008
Young adults' evening Mass
Saint Mary's Cathedral, Sydney

HUMANAE VITAE

M ANY CATHOLICS honestly believe that Pope Paul VI in his letter *Humanae Vitae* of 1968 was wrong to reaffirm the traditional Christian teaching against artificial contraception, common to all Christian churches until early in the twentieth century. However this may be argued, the Holy Father was right on two scores: on the dignity and beauty of married love and on the dire practical consequences of the contraceptive mentality, of selfishness at work.

The widespread use of the pill unlocked the sexual revolution in Australia and the Western world, which brought an increase in abortions, marriage breakdowns, the number of single mothers and of homeless children. These dark consequences of casual sex are hidden from view, while sexuality itself is constantly debased in films, magazines, and advertising. Young men and women, their relations often troubled by a lurking mistrust, are more reluctant than ever to commit themselves to each other unconditionally for life. Individuals are asking the Church to legitimize homosexual activity, to bless single-sex unions. We have the tragic AIDS epidemic. In the area of sexuality, the signs of the times have validated Paul VI's pessimism about the future, and like the true prophets of the Old Testament, he was derided and denounced for his predictions.

His letter on human life, *Humanae Vitae*, published thirty years ago this month, is probably the most famous and least understood encyclical in history. Its publication provoked a whirlwind of dissent, academic and popular, and in the following decades the pill was to become one of the most widely accepted medical developments in human history. Despite our increased scientific knowledge about the side effects of chemicals, despite our greater sensitivity on ecological issues, this is still the situation.

Paul VI promoted responsible parenthood. He taught that couples must decide how many children they should have and how they should be spaced, taking into account their own physical, economic, psychological, and social circumstances and their duties to God, themselves, their family, and society. But he rejected methods of family planning that involve interventions upon the body or the marriage act, radically separating love-making from life-making. Paul VI also foresaw that popular pressure and government authority might be brought to pressure people into contraception, sterilization, and even abortion: this is very publicly the case in some countries such as China, but even in our own country, couples tell me they are constantly pressured by friends, family, and work circumstances to keep their family size small.

Since 1968, with the encouragement of the pope's teaching about the sacredness of married love, medical scientists have developed the knowledge for couples to manage their fertility without the use of harmful drugs, surgery, or artificial devices. In the past thirty years, great advances have been made in the area of natural family planning. Sadly, many of our people are unaware of them and still talk dismissively of what are, in fact, very effective techniques.

The World Health Organization has demonstrated that couples can easily be taught fertility awareness. This information assists them in seeking help for infertility or to avoid pregnancy. Women are taught to recognize when they are fertile and infertile, and they can then choose when it is appropriate for them to have sexual intercourse. They can predict the onset of ovulation and monitor their fertility and infertility even during irregular cycles, while breast-feeding, after oral contraceptive use, and approaching menopause. Advances in natural methods of family planning have not only helped preserve respect for marital love and for the ecology of the human body: they have also empowered women to take a greater role in decisions about their reproductive health, enhancing self-confidence and self-esteem. We owe much to Melbourne doctors John and Evelyn Billings, whose discoveries in this area achieved worldwide recognition.

Many Catholics will know of *Humanae Vitae* only by its reputation as the encyclical that banned Catholics from using contraception. Therefore, it is appropriate to consider Pope Paul's arguments, but it is equally important to examine the neopagan alternatives on sexuality, marriage, and family that commercial interests are thrusting upon society. Are families better off? Are more young people happy? Are we content to allow the sexual revolution to continue unimpeded, damaging more and more of both young and old? How can we enlist more young Australians in the struggle to defend loving, responsible sexuality? When shall we decide enough is enough?

On the occasion of this anniversary, with the lessons of thirty years of sexual "freedom" now available to us, I urge you to read (or reread) *Humanae Vitae* in a spirit of openness. Prayerful reconsideration will not hurt any of us, because doing God's will, whatever the difficulties in identifying it, should be our basic aim.

July 25, 1998
Pastoral Letter for the
Thirtieth Anniversary of Humanae Vitae
Melbourne

MANY MARTYRS

Acts 13:14, 43–52; Revelation 7:9, 14–17;
John 10:27–30

OVER THE YEARS in different countries, I have been privileged to meet great men and women who have suffered much for their faith in Christ and in the Catholic Church. Early in the 1990s, I visited the diocese of Grodno in Belorussia (or White Russia), now known as Belarus, a country caught between Russia and Poland, where I was invited by the bishop to address the clergy. They were all old, buried in immense black suits and overcoats, priests who had survived up to forty-five years of Communist persecution. Generally, their faces were inscrutable, gnarled, and chiseled; they seemed a formidable lot, until they smiled.

On another occasion, in the countryside of southern Cambodia, I met a Vietnamese nun, who had been the only religious—there were then no other bishops, priests, or nuns—working in Cambodia secretly in the time of Pol Pot, who killed at least a million people, one-eighth of the Cambodian population. All the local priests and bishops died in prison, and all missionaries were expelled.

In Ukraine, there was Bishop Vasylyk, a Greek Catholic, one of the heroes of the underground Church, whose exploits celebrating Mass (which was forbidden for years) were famous, as he escaped over rooftops and in various disguises. In the last days of Communism, he and a group camped out in the Red Square, Moscow, demanding religious freedom in Ukraine. And I have not mentioned Cardinal van Thuan of Vietnam and Cardinal Todea of Romania, both of whom spent fifteen or more years in Communist jails, some of those years in solitary confinement.

On many occasions, I have pointed out that more martyrs died for their faith and more confessors suffered imprisonment in the twentieth century than in any other century in history. That is one record we do not want to break in this the twenty-first Christian century!

All of this is a rather long-winded introduction to a reflection on today's reading from the Book of the Apocalypse, which will continue to be the centerpiece of my Easter sermons during the next few weeks.

Our generation has therefore produced an above average percentage of that "huge number, impossible to count, of people from every nation, race, tribe, and language" who stand before the throne of God and of the Lamb dressed in white and holding the palms of victory and martyrdom. They are witnesses who were either martyred during some persecution or who suffered severe penalties or imprisonment. It is reliably estimated that 130,000 Vietnamese have died for the Catholic faith in persecutions over about three hundred years. With this background, it is probably not surprising that of the four priests ordained here yesterday morning, two were born in Vietnam and chose to study for the priesthood, despite the hostile pressures of the Vietnamese Communist government.

The heroes of today's second reading are described as enjoying the happiness of heaven, where their tears have been wiped away and the Lamb of God Himself is leading them to streams of living water. For them there will be no drought, no hunger, and no thirsting. In fact, they are sharing God's divine life, and we are reminded that we, too, here on earth, are united mystically with these heavenly witnesses. We follow Christ in the obscurity of faith, but they are in God's presence. They no longer have to struggle to preserve and refine their faith and their hope, because these virtues are not needed in God's warm love.

These verses from the seventh chapter represent the second part of the sixth seal, the second-to-the-last of the seven seals. The scroll that Christ receives from the right hand of God represents God's plan of salvation for the whole of humanity. Only Christ can open this scroll, and He brings God's plan to fruition through His life, death, and Resurrection. The seals are the positive and negative forces controlled by Christ that take His plan forward, as the awful struggle between good and evil regularly flares up and then recedes over all ages.

The first four seals are negative and feature the terrible horsemen of the Apocalypse, while the fifth and sixth are more positive. The first part of the sixth seal recounts the Day of God's wrath, the coming of

God for judgment, described in Technicolor with a variety of cosmic upheavals, before we come to the beauty and tranquility described in today's reading.

I mentioned last week that we should not try to tie these graphic and exaggerated images to any one historical event, and the experts claim that the seven seals or forces should not be seen as acting in sequence. War, injustice, and death are unfortunate constants in human history, but these evils can only go so far, because they are under the control of the Risen Christ and the final victory of the Lamb of God is assured.

That is why we pray to the Lamb of God, who takes away our sins, just before Communion in every Mass. With confidence, we ask Christ Our Lord whom we address as the Sacrificial Lamb, to have mercy on us and, finally, to give us peace.

This is our prayer, and our faith tells us our prayer will be answered.

April 29, 2007
Fourth Sunday of Easter
Saint Mary's Cathedral, Sydney

BABYLON VERSUS
THE NEW JERUSALEM

Acts 15:1–2, 22–29; Revelation 21:10–14, 22–23;
John 14:23–29

I N THIS EASTER SEASON, which is now approaching its conclusion with
the feasts of the Ascension and Pentecost, we celebrate not only the
fact that Christ has risen but also that He has redeemed and saved us.
What does that mean? How can the Christian claims to salvation and
victory be reconciled with the struggles in our own hearts against selfishness and sin and the long catalogue of extreme evils throughout history? Last Sunday, Archbishop Pius Ncube of Bulawayo, Zimbabwe,
preached in this cathedral. He was also active here in Australia with
the media and speaking to the Prime Minister to denounce the violence and disorder in his homeland. The tragedy there is not unique,
unfortunately.

While the Kingdom of God has its roots among us, it is always far
from perfect, and sometimes its fruits are smothered or destroyed by
the spirit of evil. That is why we pray not to be put to the test, not to
be placed in extreme circumstances.

The second reading at the Sunday Masses of this third Easter cycle
from the Apocalypse uses a wide range of exotic symbols from the
Old Testament to explain the struggle between good and evil, which
will continue until the end of time; to explain the fuels that drive
the contending forces of good and evil and then the final triumph of
Christ's forces of faith, hope, and love. In other words, the images often move between the present and the future. Incidentally, it is useful
for understanding the final chapters of the Apocalypse to refer back to
chapters 55–66 of the Old Testament prophet Isaiah and chapters 40–
45 from Ezekiel. Nearly all the spectacular and difficult passages about

Michael's battles with Satan, for example, the sea of fire, the rule of the Beast and Armageddon, and the final confrontation between good and evil, are not included in the Sunday readings.

Today we have a vision of the New Jerusalem, the holy city coming down from heaven. It is full of God's radiant glory, decorated with magnificent jewels. Once again the symbolism of twelve is used with the twelve gates to symbolize the twelve Jewish tribes of God's chosen people from the Old Testament and the foundation for the new people of God gathered around the twelve apostles and their successors the bishops. The New Jerusalem is beautiful, coming like a bride adorned for her husband about to participate in the heavenly banquet, when there will be a final symbolic marriage between Christ and His Christian followers; or, to use a couple of crucial Apocalypse symbols, a symbolic marriage between the Lamb of God and the bride.

This overlapping of images and symbols is not the way we usually write and think in the English-speaking world. I remember being told as a child not to mix my metaphors, not to make the images manifold, much less contradictory, but the author of the Apocalypse comes from a different culture of two thousand years ago.

We must remember that this symbol of the New Jerusalem, like the other symbols in this book, is not pointing to only one reality but is a complicated symbol of heavenly realities, which intrude into history, even into our daily lives, in an imperfect way. Obviously the New Jerusalem points to God and His mysterious work, which is in progress, brought about in history. God's victory is completed only at the end of time, but it is being brought about now to the extent that good people are battling effectively against evil in its many forms.

The New Jerusalem is a community of people, because we cannot live simply as individuals, and we are saved because we are good community people, people who live by truth and justice and live in love. The evil opposition to the New Jerusalem is symbolized by Babylon, the Middle Eastern kingdom that destroyed the Jerusalem Temple in the seventh century B.C. and drove the Jews into exile. It epitomizes evil, like Sodom, Gomorrah, Egypt, and the Roman Empire of the time of writing, which could not be mentioned explicitly. The memory of Nero's persecution of the Christians in Rome was vivid and alive in Christian circles, even in the East at Patmos, where Saint John was writing.

Babylon is evil, a harlot, rooted in the things of this world, with no heavenly dimension. It is a kingdom driven by lies, violence, and lust, bitterly hostile to love. Babylon has a pact with the dragon and is served by the two beasts, which come out of the sea, which is a symbol of chaos separating God from His people.

At different stages in history, the Holy City, which will become the New Jerusalem, is trampled by the nations, suffers much, but the Temple, the altar, and a number of faithful worshippers are protected (11:1). The dangers for Christians are real, extreme in some periods, but the followers of Jesus will never be completely destroyed, never obliterated by satanic deceit and lapsing into the worship of false gods.

Gog and Magog, two mythological figures representing evil, marked with the sign of the beast, have grisly fates. Gog and Magog are consumed by fire as they attack the city of the saints, while the devil, the beast, and the false prophet are thrown into a lake of fire and brimstone! The author of the Apocalypse takes evil seriously as it brings terrible and eternal consequences. But this strange book is ultimately a hymn to the victory of love, where the New Jerusalem is suffused with peace and light and the streams of living water flow from the throne of God and the Lamb.

May 13, 2007
Sixth Sunday of Easter
Saint Mary's Cathedral, Sydney

MASS FOR PREGNANT WOMEN

1 Kings 19:4–8; Ephesians 4:30 — 5:2;
John 6:41–51

T HIS MORNING we are celebrating the second annual Mass and Blessing for expectant mothers here at Saint Mary's Cathedral. Like all
of you present, I came here to pray for these mothers and the fathers
of the children as well as praying for your personal intentions.

For most of her history, the Church probably did not feel the need
for such a Mass, but in these changing times, we need to reaffirm the ·
basics of our understanding of human nature as well as the fundamentals of our Christian understanding of what is important in life. In the
old days, Catholics were tempted to believe that having children was
not only the main reason for marriage, but its only important rationale.
At the time of the Second Vatican Council in the 1960s, and especially
after Pope Paul VI's encyclical on natural family planning in 1968, a
broader understanding of marriage developed that saw the mutual development of the spouses, husband and wife, as an equally important
reason for marriage. These two important goals remain the mainstay
of the Catholic theology of marriage today.

In secular life, the popular understanding of yesterday has been stood
on its head, and some have even abandoned part of the story. In the
radically secular theory of the good life, the marriage of a man and
a woman, or the partnership of two individuals, sexual activity and
the procreation of children are separated totally, three separate factors.
In this alternative theory, sexual activity does not have to be "making love", with love set aside cynically, while adults are seen to be
autonomous, which means everyone can decide his own standards of
right and wrong.

Elements of this package are offered to our young people, who are generally sympathetic to the idea that we must preserve our planet for the future, that we must respect our physical environment. But human beings are the crown and summit of creation, masters but also guardians and servants of our world of nature, and each generation also has an obligation to provide children for the future, to continue the human race. This is a sacred duty, which most adults understand instinctively and are happy to accept. But an increasing minority are unaware of these fundamental perspectives that shape the Christian way of living.

In these weeks, the Gospels recount Jesus talking about the "bread of life", a term that has different layers of meaning. But the bread that comes from heaven and brings its rewards in the next life as well as this life can mean correct teaching, the teaching of Christ, which presupposes an accurate understanding of the purposes of life. Theologians say that grace builds on nature, takes human life to new heights of goodness and happiness. We saw wonderful glimpses of this in the hundreds of thousands of happy pilgrims at last year's World Youth Day. Many Australian non-Catholics were amazed that so many young people could be as happy and life-giving as well as good and well behaved. Following Christ's teaching has this effect. Accepting the bread of life or following Catholic teaching also gives us strength in times of trial so that we can persevere through difficulties.

Elijah, the great Old Testament prophet and defender of the one true God, had fled into the desert to save his life. He was frightened and depressed, unsure he could continue. Twice he was strengthened miraculously by bread and water, so that he recovered his strength, took heart, and marched for forty days until he reached Horeb, the mountain of God. This incident has a symbolic meaning for us, exemplified in the many instances where adults have said to me that they do not know how they could have coped in their difficulties without their Christian faith.

Motherhood is a central fact of life, perhaps the central fact, and a respect for motherhood is essential to the Christian understanding of life. We thank God that in Australia the annual number of births is slowly increasing so that in 2008, 296,610 babies were born, the highest ever number of births. Like every other country in the Western world, Australia is not producing a sufficient number of babies to keep the population stable without migration, but with a fertility rate of 1.94, we are close to the 2.1 figure required.

Generation is an eternal mystery, whereby the father and especially the mother share in God's creative power. It is the woman who pays directly for this shared generation. No matter how the child was conceived, no matter how many problems remain, her child is precious because she knows that she or he is loved by God, and she rejoices as she sees the hope of eternal life shine within her child.

Every child is a gift, ultimately a gift from God, a mystery that inspires awe, even in outsiders, so that the blessings are reckoned to outweigh the burdens by far. Children, lovemaking, and marriage are an eternal triangle; a sustaining ideal that sometime comes unstuck, but it remains an ideal whatever the particular different circumstances.

Mary, the Mother of Jesus, experienced more than her share of difficulties in her life with Joseph as she brought up Jesus. May she pray for and protect all the mothers here today with their beautiful children.

August 9, 2009
Mass for pregnant women
Saint Mary's Cathedral, Sydney

7

Saint Paul, Missionary Trailblazer

CONVERSION OF SAINT PAUL

Isaiah 6:1–8; 1 Corinthians 15:1–11; Luke 5:1–11

T ODAY I want to reflect on the conversion of Saint Paul, one of the three reluctant teachers in today's readings. The prophet Isaiah proclaimed his unworthiness very eloquently, and he was equally explicit about the unworthiness of his contemporaries: "What a wretched state I am in! I am lost, for I am a man of unclean lips and I live among people of unclean lips." He eventually complied with God's invitation: "Here I am, send me." Just before Peter and James and John were called to be "fishers of men", Simon Peter said to Jesus, "Leave me, Lord; I am a sinful man", but, hearing the call, they left everything and followed Him. Writing to the Corinthian Christians, Paul summed up his story: "Since I persecuted the Church of God, I hardly deserve the name apostle; but by God's grace that is what I am", that is, the greatest missionary teacher of the first millennium, perhaps of all Christian history.

In Australian parlance, none of these teachers fancied themselves for the position; none of them thought they were up to the job. To continue the idiom: that type of unworthiness would be true of us in spades; or at least true of some of us, as I cannot speak accurately of the unworthiness of others!

All of us have some idea of what Paul became as a Christian, but what type of Jew was he? In the first chapter of his Letter to the Galatians (1:13–14), Paul explains that in his earlier life he had "ravaged the Church of Christ and tried to destroy it", as he was "exceedingly zealous for the tradition of (his) fathers".

Paul was the best educated of all the New Testament writers, with Saint John as his only rival (and we know nothing of John's theological education). Paul tells us (Acts 22:3) that he was a pupil of Gamaliel, but he was not a typical follower, because Gamaliel belonged to the school of the scholar Hillel, the more liberal of the two dominant Jewish theological trends. When the collection of laws known as the Mishnah was drawn up about A.D. 200, Hillel's school clearly predominated, but in Paul's time there was a fierce struggle between the liberals (comparatively speaking) and the hard-line Pharisees, the Shammaites, militant right wingers and men of violence.

Paul's anti-Christian history shows that he was a Shammaite. The argument was not simply about lenient or strict interpretations of the law, but about what were the most appropriate aims and agendas for Israel.

The Hillelites believed in letting Herod and Pilate and even Caiaphas rule Israel politically as long as they could faithfully follow the Law, but the Shammaites believed that this was not enough and that Israel should be freed from the tyranny of the gentiles and by violence if necessary. In first-century Judaism, "zeal for the traditions of the fathers" meant using knife, sword, or stones. Paul's presence at the martyrdom of Stephen demonstrated that he was practicing what he believed and taught.

The majority of the Pharisees were then Shammaites, not merely political revolutionaries, but religious *sicarii* (dagger men), like those who died at Masada, deeply pious Jews. Their heroes were Elijah and the Maccabean soldiers. We know that one of the twelve apostles was Simon the Zealot, previously part of this wider group.

Paul believed God would redeem Israel by acting on the nation's behalf and so save the entire world through His chosen people. Abraham was to undo the sin of Adam, and this was sometimes described as a mighty court case where Israel would be vindicated. Although they used end-of-the-world language to describe this, they were waiting for earth-shattering events within history, a great turning point or climax. Paul believed this great day would come when people followed the Law properly and that it was legitimate to force people by violence to do the right thing.

This complex of views changed while Paul was on his way to Damascus, "breathing threats to slaughter the Lord's disciples" (Acts 9:1). He was knocked down and blinded, so profoundly shocked he could not eat or drink for three days. He believed that he had seen Jesus and that this was not merely a spiritual experience.

In his conversion, Paul accepted Jesus' bodily Resurrection and that God had acted through Jesus in a way that he had previously believed God would act through Israel at the end time. The age to come and the present age had coalesced in Jesus the Messiah, the Son of God.

Paul's theological world was turned upside down, but so was his moral world, where forgiveness and love replaced killing and violent coercion. No wonder he was in shock. The message is clear. If a man like Paul can become a convert to Christ, then conversion is a possibility for us as well as our pupils. But we have to do our part.

Saint John Chrysostom was archbishop of Constantinople from 398–404 and, we are told, preached 250 sermons on Paul's Epistles. He was one of the most famous preachers in history, known as "the Golden Mouth", but he was also outspoken and tactless, dying in exile after he called the Empress Eudoxia a Jezebel. Chrysostom pointed out that Paul was greatly blessed by God's grace but also had to struggle fiercely himself to do God's will, to curb his wayward instincts.

Paul explained his difficulties at some length, Chrysostom told his people, so that they would not "leave everything to God and sit there sleeping and belching".

That is good advice for us, too.

Sunday, February 4, 2007
Saint Mary's Cathedral, Sydney

PAUL AND THE ONE TRUE GOD

Acts 22:3−16; Mark 16:15−18

T ODAY is the feast of the conversion of Saint Paul, which we heard about in the first reading from the Acts of the Apostles. On the way to Damascus, Paul is thrown down and rebuked by Jesus because of his persecutions of the Christians, even if at that very early stage followers of Jesus were not yet called Christians. That occurred later for the first time at Antioch. In a break from the usual practice where feasts of saints do not replace the Sunday readings, the Church this year allows us, because it is the year of Saint Paul, to celebrate the feast and meditate on Saint Paul's contribution.

Paul became the apostle to the gentiles, the non-Jewish peoples, although he did not know Jesus during His lifetime and therefore was not one of the original twelve apostles chosen by the Lord. He traveled widely around the Mediterranean as a Christian missionary; only Francis Xavier would rival him centuries later. Paul was also a theological genius, who explained Jesus' role in the terms of classical Jewish theology.

When talking about Paul, I rely a lot on Bishop N. T. Wright, the Anglican bishop of Durham in England, who regards Paul as the intellectual equal of Plato, Aristotle, and Seneca. I was surprised by this, but Wright himself is for me the best Scripture scholar in the English-speaking world, and I take his verdicts seriously. For those of you who like to read good theology, which is clear even when it is deep, I recommend Wright highly. Most of what he writes is fully acceptable to Catholics.

The Jews believed in the one true God (monotheism) and that they were His chosen people (election). The Jews also believed that history was taking them forward to the last days. In other words, for them there was one God, one people of God, and one future for God's world. Paul never abandoned this framework, but developed and redefined it around the Messiah and the Spirit. Paul reread Israel's Scriptures so that the death and Resurrection of the Messiah formed the unexpected but always intended climax of God's lengthy plan, which extended across the ages and led to a new Exodus.

I often recall a sophisticated reporter who was interviewing me (not all reporters are knowledgeable about religion), who was surprised when I said that Christians regard God as the Creator of the universe. I never dreamed of it otherwise, because if God is not Creator of the cosmos, then He is not God! We take this understanding from the Jews, for whom the Creator and Sustainer of the universe is the God of Israel, who chose them and will judge them and the world at the final judgment.

However Paul's principal opponents were not the Jews. His opponents were pagans, those who believed in the many false gods of the ancient world, fictions that led them through idolatry into immorality and degradation of communal life. We must never forget that daily life for most ancients was brutal and awful, untouched by Christian ideals of compassion, which was regarded as a weakness. By accepting the teachings of Christ and following Paul's preaching, the new followers of Jesus founded new types of small communities according to different values, where women were to be treated by the men as they would respect themselves; where marriages were to be lifelong, sexual activity linked to love and self-control, children loved, forgiveness practiced, slaves and foreigners welcomed into the community, the sick cared for, abortion and infanticide (especially the killing of unwanted baby girls) rejected.

For Paul and the Christians, paganism embodied human failure; it was the wrong way to go in the search for decency and long-term happiness. While there were substantial difficulties and changes in popular understanding, Christ could be explained as the Messiah who was being waited for by the Jews, but the Jews also understood that the one God acted through his "Shekinah", the tabernacle presence of God as the Jews traveled to the Promised Land. For them God had also acted through Wisdom, as we read in the Old Testament wisdom literature, and of course God had revealed His will and wisdom through the "Torah", the Law. For Paul, Jesus became the new leader into the

Exodus, and we could claim that Paul made Jesus the embodiment of the Law, with superior teachings that built on the Law and did not reject it completely.

"Son of God" was also a term used by the Jews in a variety of senses to describe the angels, the people of Israel itself, and even the Messiah. Paul developed this meaning so that Wright sees Philippians 2:6–11, with its high Christology, as also being deeply Jewish, where Paul understands the human being Jesus as identical with the One who from all eternity was equal with the Creator God. That equality was founded in Incarnation, suffering, and death as well as the final Resurrection. Paul struggled successfully to find ways of thinking the unthinkable and saying the unsayable about Jesus and the Spirit for Jews and pagans.

We can understand something, or even much, of the skepticism of the pagan Athenians when they heard Paul claim there was only a single Creator God, not many divinities, and that this one true God was made known through a crucified Jew! For many nonbelievers today, these remain two extraordinary claims.

Sometimes we Christians forget our Jewish roots and links, but the Jews were and are God's chosen people. They are part of our history. To win converts from Judaism, Christ Our Lord had to be explained theologically in terms that a religious Jew could understand. Paul especially did this.

We thank God for Paul's achievement, which continues to enrich our religious living and understanding and gives us deep and beautiful insights into the heart of the Triune God of love.

January 25, 2009
Feast of Saint Paul
Saint Mary's Cathedral, Sydney

PAUL ON JUSTIFICATION

2 Samuel 12:7–10, 13;
Galatians 2:16, 19–20; Luke 7:36—8:3

THE EXCERPT from Saint Paul's letter to the Christians in Galatia about what makes a person righteous, or justified, is sandwiched between two stories of forgiveness. The first features King David, who was forgiven for arranging the murder in battle of Uriah the Hittite so that he could marry Uriah's wife. But the penalties were to continue across the generations for David's family, so that now "the sword will never be far from your house." And so it proved to be with Solomon and the tragedy of his sons.

The second relates to Jesus' treatment of the notorious public sinner, a prostitute, who washed His feet while He was at dinner with Simon the Pharisee, dried them with her hair, kissed, and finally anointed them with oil. The host was scandalized by the entire procedure; the unseemly behavior of this social outcast, Jesus' courteous reception of her ministrations, and His even more provocative teaching on forgiveness, where He links the woman's faith and love to the forgiveness He grants. His fellow guests had some realization of the significance of His claiming to forgive sinners and sins and murmured, "Who is that man, that he even forgives sins?"

This is spelled out in another equally provocative way by Our Lord, where He explains that the debtor who has a large debt remitted is likely to love the creditor more than someone freed from a much smaller debt. Applying these lessons to His host, Simon, who had received Jesus politely but without the usual courtesies of a kiss of greeting and the washing and anointing of His feet, Our Lord claimed that "It is the man who is forgiven little who shows little love."

We must never take the reality of God's forgiveness for granted, because it is one of Christ's most wonderful teachings and gifts to us,

even in an age like our own where a large range of sins, but not all of
them, are often defined out of existence by appeals to the primacy of
conscience. Every person is obliged to follow the truth by exercising
his conscience, judging what is true and good. Christians are believers
who accept Christ's answers.

In our society, where up to 20 percent of people do not believe in
God, this minority cannot access God's forgiveness and are badly limited in how they cope with their guilt. Often this is displaced, renamed
to surface as anger, while its deep roots are unrecognized and ignored.

Christ's emphasis on a new brand of forgiveness helps explain Paul's
claim that it is faith in Jesus Christ that makes a person righteous, not
obedience to the law. Paul does not oppose faith to good works or
keeping the commandments, although it is obvious that we can obey
for the wrong reasons. Paul wants us to obey, to follow the law, which
is now refocused by Our Lord's teachings.

Paul was answering an almost modern misunderstanding that reduces
religion to morality. He was insisting that following the law is not of
first importance, although it is also vital, because the person of Jesus
is at the center. Our faith in Him as Son of God is the essential ingre-
dient, and our good actions follow as we imitate Him and follow His
teachings.

Paul is also emphasizing that no human being can make himself worthy to be in God's presence simply by his own efforts. We cannot, so
to speak, pull ourselves up by our own bootstraps, but do so through
the life of Christ that courses through us.

Justification is a difficult concept for us to grasp. One reason for this
is that in the aftermath of the Reformation, some strands of Protes-
tantism mistook the concept of justification to mean that having faith
was all that one needed to be assured of salvation. Seeking salvation
through good works was thought to suggest that it was something we
could earn, when the point the Reformers were trying to make was
that salvation comes from God and is entirely His gift to us.

But when Paul wrote about salvation in the Letter to the Galatians,
he had other ideas in mind. Paul was, of course, immensely learned in
the Scriptures and the Jewish Law. In the Jewish tradition, the idea of
justification was bound up, not with how to know whether someone
is saved, but how to know if they are part of the covenant community. As Anglican Bishop Tom Wright has written, for Paul, justification is "not so much about salvation as about the Church". This issue

arose among the early Christian communities from discussions about whether the non-Jewish members of the Church must undergo Jewish ritual practices, such as male circumcision, to become a member of the Church. Paul answered this question in his Letter to the Galatians by saying that it is sharing Christian faith, not ritual practices such as circumcision, that makes people members of the Church. Having faith is what authenticates our claim to be Christian and to be part of the Church, and, Paul claims, such believers are thereby justified.

We are called to be a light to the world, and it should be possible to recognize Christians through the many good things they do for other people. But we do not need to have a proven record of goodness to be accepted as a member of the Church. Given our weaknesses and our many failings, this is just as well. The Church is a hospital for sinners, not a club for saints, and it is our faith that gains us admission and calls us to repentance. Through the sacraments and through the healing power of His love, God can then help us to do the rest and receive the blessing of Godly forgiveness.

Sunday, June 17, 2007
Saint Mary's Cathedral, Sydney

PAUL ON SEXUALITY

Ephesians 5:21–32

I HAVE DECIDED to speak about the beautiful passage we have from Paul's Letter to the Ephesians on the central topic of marriage and love. By way of introduction, I want to mention two unrelated pieces of my recent reading. Within the last week or so, Pope Benedict gave an extensive interview to a Bavarian journalist. The Holy Father was asked why he did not speak against homosexual marriages, abortion, and contraception on his recent visit to Valencia for the World Meeting of Families, especially as Zapatero's government there is very anti-Catholic and actively legislating on such issues.

Pope Benedict replied that Catholic teaching does not begin with a series of negatives. The Christian package is positive, before we set out the limits. Men and women are made for one another, while love has a set of grades or ascending stages—sexuality, erotic love, and then agape, or charity—so that marriage is the union of a man and woman in love and happiness, constituting a family with children and so ensuring the continuity of the human race. None of this is a Catholic invention but follows from the laws of nature. Some nonbelievers are hostile to any such concept of natural law, because the need for a Creator follows closely on the acknowledgment of ordered creation, and they know this.

All of this is quite uncontroversial for churchgoers, but in the wider world it is politically incorrect and fiercely contested in the media and among those who try to influence young people.

Recently, the results of a three-year study on Generation Y in Australia, thirteen- to twenty-nine-year-olds, have been published. Not all the news is bad, but more than a quarter of the young Christians are moving away from their Christian origins. Prominent among the reasons given by those who no longer identify with the Catholic Church were our teachings on homosexuality, sex before marriage, and abortion and Church attitudes to women. Most of these ex-Catholics want us to change our views on such issues. Important Church teachings cannot be reversed, but they are open to better understanding and more appropriate explanation and teaching, and Pope Benedict was speaking good sense on this issue—and of course on many others. He is a marvelous teacher.

So today I want to say a few words about Pope John Paul's theology of the body, a happy by-product of the sexual revolution of the sixties. This theology is based in large part on today's excerpts from Ephesians. Sexuality has to be linked to love and life, and orthodox Christians over two thousand years have always taught that sexual activity is good and holy within marriage.

Genesis is the first book of the Old Testament, and the Apocalypse, or Revelation, is the last in the New Testament, constituting the book ends of the Bible. The first tells the story of Adam and Eve, and the last compares the union of Christ with His Church to the union of a man and woman in marriage, where Christ is the bridegroom and the Church is the bride. There is an important symbolism here.

I regularly ask young people, whose life choices, to a large extent, still lie before them, to examine closely the alternatives to the Catholic package as they move into adult life. They should test the spirits and see whether the non-Christians, and especially the anti-Christians, are leading happy and productive lives. What package works better?

The validity of Christian teaching on sexuality and marriage is demonstrated in the wounds of those who do not practice it. Infidelity and irresponsibility do not bring freedom; they bring slavery, imprisonment to bad habits, and even addiction. Pagan life today is like driving a car with flat tires. Men and women are gifts to one another, because sexual activity is an offering of love to the other rather than a search for self-satisfaction.

Christ Himself was compassionate toward sexual sin, which is usually a misdirected search for love, but sexual fidelity is a struggle. And we know that cut-price Christianity does not work, does not attract joiners, although it can stir up some nostalgia and distant sympathy. There is of course no such thing as cost-free Christianity, which is a poisonous myth.

The human body is also a spiritual mystery, a sign of what is hidden in

God from all eternity. *We can even see sexual intercourse, crowning the deep, loving relationship of a man and woman, as an intimation, initial evidence of the exchanges within the Trinitarian God, Father, Son, and Spirit.* We never heard this sort of talk when I was growing up.

We should all be committed to working for a civilization of love, which is founded on sex, marriage, and family, on the essential linking of love, sex, and new life. Let us pray for young people that they will choose well and wisely.

Sunday, August 27, 2006
Saint Mary's Cathedral, Sydney

PAUL ON SIN AND DEATH

Jeremiah 20:10−13; Romans 5:12−15;
Matthew 10:26−33

As a starting point I will bounce off from the last section of today's Gospel, which, I must confess, gives me some personal consolation. In these few lines we hear Our Lord promise that if we declare ourselves for Him in front of others, He will declare His support for us before God our Father. He does not require that we do this wisely or cleverly; He does not require us to do it successfully, so that others are convinced. His protection is assured if we have a go; if we speak up publicly for Christ before our family or friends or Christ's enemies or the general public.

Paul is the witness to Christ above all other witnesses; a greater teacher than Saint Peter, the rock man or foundation of the Church, and even than Saint John, the author of the fourth Gospel, the Epistles, and probably of the Book of Revelation. Paul was a trained theologian, an extreme Shammaite Pharisee, who believed violence was justified in God's cause. We know he was present at the stoning of Stephen, the first martyr, and approved of the killing, and in this brief passage we hear him talking about sin and death and the role of the law before Christ came to turn the Jewish world upside down.

Paul shared the conviction of his people that the Jews were the chosen people of the Creator God, the one true God. Only God's love explained the unlikely choice of this small difficult collection of tribes, squeezed between Egypt and a succession of powerful kingdoms to the East: Assyria, Babylon, and then Persia. Sin had come into the world with Adam and Eve, and human rebellion had led to regular strife, fed by arrogance and pride.

Even before the Law of Moses, there was evil and humanly caused suffering, because the calling of the Jewish people through Abraham was the beginning of God's particular answer to the problem of evil and the challenge of correctly focused worship. *Israel was to be the light of the world, showing what it meant to be truly human. There, among them, true meaning was to be found.*

We should remain clear on this connection today also, the connection between sin and death, between evil and lies, violence, exploitation, and injustice. Pope John Paul was right to speak about the culture of death as he opposed abortion, euthanasia, and hostility to children as the birthrate dwindles through the spread of a contraceptive mentality. Truly knowing God improves society, increases peace and harmony as well as personal wellbeing.

Sin is inherently expansionist, which is why we need to oppose evildoing. And the Law given to Moses was part of God's plan through Israel to combat wrong, to restrain evil people, and, as we would now say, to respect people's rights.

The Law came from God and does in human life what the sun does in creation. It brings light and life into the human heart. The hidden rules of the universe that bring peace of heart and harmony to society and reveal the answers to the riddle of existence are found in the Law, while the pagan nations blunder in the darkness.

Tolerance and respect for others should not distract us today, and especially today, from recognizing that when people do not follow God's teaching, their lives become a mess; or at least the lives of their victims become a mess. Abraham and then Moses with his Law were called to undo the sin of Adam. We are even better equipped to battle against sin because we have Christ and His teaching, which completely outweighs the sin of Adam; Christ's redemptive love conquers hatred and violence; His amazing grace saves us even at our wretched worst. Like the Law, Christ's coming is a free gift from God, which we have not earned and is not due to us from the nature of things.

God worked in stages through Adam, Abraham, Moses, and then Our Lord, the Christ, the long-awaited Jewish Messiah. It is not as though the good God made a number of attempts to help solve the human problem and improved with each attempt. In His wisdom, the good God geared His interventions to the human capacity to receive and the capacity of the Jewish people to deliver the goods, to demonstrate His love.

God's spirit was not entirely absent before Abraham and Moses, nor was the Spirit inactive in the other great civilizations and the other wilder groupings outside Judaism, any more than the Spirit is absent outside Christianity today. But in all those societies, the farther they are from the truth, the stronger the reign of death.

All the ancient societies were cruel and oppressive, with life organized to support the ruling minority. I do not know of any pagan society without slavery.

Christ called us to universal love, not just respect for our own people. He urged us to forgive, rather than urging an eye for an eye and a tooth for a tooth. And Our Lord showed us that salvation does not come from the power of force and violence, but in some mysterious way it was achieved through His suffering and death. This transformed the status of the majority of the people, the losers and underdogs. No longer were they individuals who had lost out in this life and the next, but in some way, they were a privileged group. Blessed are the poor; blessed are those who mourn. It is the pure in heart who will see God, not the men of violence.

The gifts from Christ's coming still outweigh the price paid for the fall of Adam.

June 22, 2008
Saint Mary's Cathedral, Sydney

8

Hold Fast to What Is Good

HOLD FAST TO WHAT IS GOOD

Ezekiel 37:1–14; Psalm 23;
Galatians 5:16–17, 22–25; Luke 8:4–15

W E ALL KNOW that Christ Our Lord is often described as the Good Shepherd of today's responsorial psalm. We are told that He leads us near restful waters, revives our flagging spirits, enables us to rest peacefully. In developing this image on one occasion, Jesus explained that such a shepherd was prepared to leave the ninety-nine sheep to search out the one who was lost.

Few countries today have a shepherd who cares for only twenty or thirty sheep, and in Australia with large farms and huge flocks, Our Lord's advice is not very practical. If the lost sheep was valuable and probably healthy, it might make sense to take the time to search for it. More usually it would be left behind or its absence not even noticed. Jesus was saying that both He and His Father are not like this, because He knows each one of His sheep, and like a good father He goes searching for the lost one He loves, particularly if he is sick or in trouble or unable to help himself.

Earlier in this Mass, I welcomed you all to this World Youth Day week, and I repeat that welcome now. But I do not begin with the ninety-nine healthy sheep, those of you already open to the Spirit, perhaps already steady witnesses to faith and love. I begin by welcoming and encouraging anyone, anywhere, who regards himself as lost, in deep distress, with hope diminished or even exhausted.

Young or old, woman or man, Christ is still calling those who are suffering to come to Him for healing, as He has for two thousand years. The causes of the wounds are quite secondary, whether they are drugs or alcohol, family breakups, the lusts of the flesh, loneliness, or a death. Perhaps even the emptiness of success. Christ's call is to all who

333

are suffering, not just to Catholics or other Christians, but especially to those without religion. Christ is calling you home; to love, healing, and community.

Dry Bones

Our first reading today was from Ezekiel, with Isaiah and Jeremiah one of the three greatest Jewish prophets. From droughts, all Australians understand a valley of dry bones and fleshless skeletons. But this grim vision is offered first of all to any and all of you who are even tempted to say "our hope is gone, we are as good as dead."

This is never true while we can still choose. While there is life, there is always the option of hope, and with Christian hope come faith and love. Until the end we are always able to choose and act.

This vision of the valley of the dry bones, the most spectacular in the whole of the Bible, was given when the hand of God came upon Ezekiel while the Jews were in captivity in Babylon, probably earlier rather than later in the sixth century B.C. For about 150 years, the political fortunes of the Jewish people had been in decline, first of all at the hands of the Assyrians. Later in 587 B.C. came the final catastrophic defeat and their transportation into exile. The Jewish people were in despair, powerless to change their situation.

This is the historical background to Ezekiel's dramatic vision where the dead were well dead, whitened skeletons as the birds of prey had long finished their ghastly business of stripping off the flesh. It was an immense battlefield of the unburied.

A hesitant and reluctant Ezekiel was urged by God to prophesy to these bones, and as he did so, the bones rushed together noisily, accompanied by an earthquake. Sinews knitted them together, flesh and then skin clothed the corpses. Another stage was needed, and the breath, or Spirit, came from the four corners of the earth as the bodies came "to life again and stood up on their feet, a great and immense army".

While we now see this vision as a prefiguration of the resurrection of the dead, the Jews of Ezekiel's time did not believe in such a conception of the afterlife. For them the immense resurrected army represented all the Jewish people, those from the Northern Kingdom taken off to Assyria, those at home, and those in Babylon. They were to be reconstituted as a people in their own land, and they would know that the one true God alone had done this. And all this came to pass.

Over the centuries, we Christians have used this passage liturgically at Easter, especially for the baptism of catechumens on Holy Saturday night, and it is, of course, a powerful image of the one true God's regenerative power for this life and eternity. Secular wisdom claims that leopards do not change their spots, but we Christians believe in the power of the Spirit to convert and change persons away from evil to good; from fear and uncertainty to faith and hope. Believers are heartened by Ezekiel's vision, because we know the power of God's forgiveness, the capacity of Christ and the Catholic tradition to cause new life to flourish, even in unlikely circumstances.

The Sower and the Seed

That same power glimpsed in Ezekiel's vision is offered to us today, to all of us without exception. You young pilgrims can look ahead to the future stretching out before you, so rich in promise. The Gospel parable of the sower and the seed reminds you of the great opportunity you have to embrace your vocation and produce an abundant harvest, a hundredfold crop.

Matthew, Mark, and Luke all place this story of the sower at the beginning of their collection of Jesus' parables. It explains some fundamental truths about the challenges of Christian discipleship and lists the alternatives to a fruitful Christian life. Fidelity is not automatic or inevitable. One detail makes the parable more plausible, because it seems the Jews in Our Lord's time threw the seed on the ground before they ploughed it, so explaining a little better the seed being in unlikely places rather than just in the furrows.

Are we among those whose faith has already been snatched away by the devil, as Our Lord explained the image of the birds of the sky gobbling up the seed? No one at this Mass would be in that category. Some might be like the seed on rocky ground that could not put down roots. Those here in this second category are likely to be striving to start again in the spiritual life, or at least examining the possibility of doing so. But most of us are in the third and fourth categories, where the seed has fallen on good soil and is growing and flourishing; or we are in danger of being choked off by the worries of life. All of us, including those who are no longer young, have to pray for wisdom and perseverance.

I have no problem in believing that Our Lord spelled out the meaning of this parable to His closest followers and that He would have been asked by them regularly to do so. But the disciples' enquiries provoked a disconcerting response, when Our Lord divided His listeners into two groups: those to whom the mysteries of the Kingdom are revealed and the rest for whom the parables remain only parables. This second group is described in words from the prophet Isaiah as those who "may see but not perceive, listen but not understand". Probably the background to this is the amazement of Our Lord's disciples at the large number who did not accept His teaching.

Why is this still so? What must we do to be among those for whom the mysteries of the Kingdom are revealed?

The call of the one true God remains mysterious, especially today when many good people find it hard to believe. Even in the time of the prophets, many of their hearers remained spiritually deaf and blind, while any number over the ages have admired the beauty of Jesus' teaching, but have never been moved to answer His call.

Our task is to be open to the power of the Spirit, to allow the God of surprises to act through us. Human motivation is complex and mysterious, because sometimes very strong Catholics, and other strong Christians, can be prayerful and regularly good but also very determined not to take even one further step. On the other hand, some followers of Christ can be much less zealous and faithful but open to development, to change for the better, because they realize their unworthiness and their ignorance. Where do you stand?

Whatever our situation, we must pray for an openness of heart, for a willingness to take the next step, even if we are fearful of venturing too much farther. If we take God's hand, He will do the rest. Trust is the key. God will not fail us.

How can we work to avoid slipping from the last and best category of the fruit bearers into those "who are choked by the worries and riches and pleasures of life" and so do not produce much fruit at all? The second reading from Paul's Letter to the Galatians points us in the correct direction, reminding us all that each person must declare himself in the age-old struggle between good and evil, between what Paul calls the flesh and the Spirit. *It is not good enough to be only a passenger, to try to live in "no-man's land" between the warring parties. Life forces us to choose, eventually destroys any possibility of neutrality.*

We will bring forth good fruit by learning the language of the Cross and inscribing it on our hearts. The language of the Cross brings us the fruits of the Spirit that Paul lists, enables us to experience peace and joy, to be regularly kind and generous to others. Following Christ is not cost free, not always easy, because it requires struggling against what Saint Paul calls "the flesh", our fat relentless egos, old-fashioned selfishness. It is always a battle, even for old people like me!

Commitment, Not Options

Do not spend your life sitting on the fence, keeping your options open, because only commitments bring fulfillment. Happiness comes from meeting our obligations, doing our duty, especially in small matters and regularly, so we can rise to meet the harder challenges. Many have found their life's calling at World Youth Days.

To be a disciple of Jesus requires discipline, especially self-discipline; what Paul calls self-control. The practice of self-control will not make you perfect (it has not with me), but self-control is necessary to develop and protect the love in our hearts and prevent others, especially our family and friends, from being hurt by our lapses into nastiness or laziness. I pray that through the power of the Spirit, all of you will join that immense army of saints, healed and reborn, that was revealed to Ezekiel, that has enriched human history for countless generations, and that is rewarded in the afterlife of heaven.

Let me conclude by adapting one of the most powerful sermons of Saint Augustine, the finest theologian of the first millennium and a bishop in the small North African town of Hippo around sixteen hundred years ago. I expect that in the next five days of prayer and celebration that your spirits will rise, as mine always do, in the excitement of this World Youth Day. Please God we shall all be glad that we participated, despite the cost, hassles, and distances traveled. During this week, we have every right to rejoice and celebrate the liberation of our repentance, the rejuvenation of our faith. We are called to open our hearts to the power of the Spirit. And to the young ones I give a gentle reminder that in your enthusiasm and excitement you do not forget to listen and pray!

Many of you have traveled such a long way that you may believe that

you have arrived, indeed, at the ends of earth! If so, that's good, for
Our Lord told his first apostles that they would be His witnesses in
Jerusalem and to the ends of the earth. That prophecy has been fulfilled
in the witness of many missionaries to this vast southern continent, and
it is fulfilled yet again in your presence here. But these days will pass
too quickly, and next week we shall return to earth. For a time, some
of you will find the real world of home and parish, work or study,
flat and disappointing.

Soon, too soon, you will all be going away. Briefly we are now
here in Sydney at the center of the Catholic world, but next week the
Holy Father will return to Rome, we Sydneysiders will return to our
parishes, while you, now visiting pilgrims, will go back to your homes
in places near and far. But when we part after these happy days, let us
never part from our loving God and his Son Jesus Christ. And may
Mary, Mother of God, whom we invoke in this World Youth Day as
Our Lady of the Southern Cross, strengthen us in this resolution.

And so I pray. Come, come O Breath of God, from the four winds,
from all the nations and peoples of the earth, and bless our Great South
Land of the Holy Spirit. Empower us also to be another great and immense army of humble servants and faithful witnesses. And we make
this prayer to God our Father in the name of Christ His Son. Amen.

Tuesday, July 15, 2008
World Youth Day Opening Mass
Barangaroo, Sydney

INDEX